Praise for

Differentiation for Gifted Learners

"*Differentiation for Gifted Learners* takes the reader on a journey that is both conceptual and practical at the same time. It offers direction and sophisticated solutions for issues faced by advanced and progressive schools."
—**Antarina S. F. Amir,** founder and CEO of HighScope Institute Indonesia

"Heacox and Cash clearly understand the landscape of schools and what is needed to make programming work. The many user-friendly lists and suggestions for classroom strategies make this book an excellent reference for daily use."
—**Felicia A. Dixon, Ph.D.,** author of *Programs and Services for Gifted Secondary Students* and editor of *The Handbook of Secondary Gifted Education*

"Richard and Diane have hit a home run with this book! It provides exactly what teachers, coaches, gifted specialists, coordinators, and administrators need to help high-ability students develop a growth mindset, reverse underachievement, develop autonomy, and direct their own learning."
—**Lora McHugh,** gifted and talented education program coordinator, Clark County School District

"*Differentiation for Gifted Learners* is an excellent resource . . . Filled with practical definitions and explanations, the book offers a straightforward understanding of what it means to be gifted and talented, and the components of a strong gifted program."
—**Susie Strasser,** high school English teacher, San Diego Public Schools

"At last, a comprehensive, up-to-date book that explicitly describes how to differentiate for gifted and talented learners. The authors include a variety of instructional strategies that educators can use immediately with their identified students. If you are looking for practical information on the topic of differentiation for gifted students, look no further."
—**Patti Drapeau,** gifted education consultant at the Maine Department of Education, adjunct faculty at the University of Southern Maine, and author of *Differentiated Instruction: Making It Work*

"Heacox and Cash have each made significant contributions to the field of gifted education. Together they more than double their impact in this thoughtful, easy-to-read book. They use current research to address timely issues like differentiating the Common Core State Standards for high ability students, co-teaching as a collaborative effort, and focusing on assessment as a critical element of the instructional process. They tackle topics not previously discussed like working with immigrant students and designing challenging honors courses for secondary students. This book is full of prac suggestions for classroom teachers, gifted education specialists, and principals. It is a must-have fc those eager to go 'Beyond the Basics.'"
—**Chrystyna V. Mursky,** director of professional learning at Smarter Balanced Assessment Conso: and educational consultant at the Wisconsin Department of Public Instruction

Differentiation for Gifted Learners

Going Beyond the Basics

DIANE HEACOX, Ed.D. | RICHARD M. CASH, Ed.D.

Foreword by Marcia Gentry, Ph.D.

free spirit
PUBLISHING®

Library of Congress Cataloging-in-Publication Data

Heacox, Diane.
  Differentiation for gifted learners : going beyond the basics / Diane Heacox, Ed.D., and Richard M. Cash, Ed.D.
      pages cm
  Includes bibliographical references and index.
  ISBN-13: 978-1-57542-440-8
  ISBN-10: 1-57542-440-1
1. Gifted children—Education. 2. Individualized instruction. I. Title.
  LC3993.H37 2014
  371.95—dc23

                                                            2013030278

Edited by Meg Bratsch and Cathy Broberg
Cover and interior design by Tasha Kenyon

10 9 8 7 6 5 4 3 2
Printed in the United States of America

Free Spirit Publishing Inc.
Minneapolis, MN
(612) 338-2068
help4kids@freespirit.com
www.freespirit.com

 **Printed on recycled paper** including 30% post-consumer waste

As a member of the Green Press Initiative, Free Spirit Publishing is committed to the three Rs: Reduce, Reuse, Recycle. Whenever possible, we print our books on recycled paper containing a minimum of 30% post-consumer waste. At Free Spirit it's our goal to nurture not only children, but nature too!

Free Spirit offers competitive pricing.
Contact edsales@freespirit.com for pricing information on multiple quantity purchases.

Dedication

To the educators whose classrooms and schools we have visited, as well as those we have yet to visit; it is our intent that this book strengthens and extends your instructional practices for gifted learners. We also hope that it provides much needed encouragement and support in your advocacy for the unique needs of gifted learners.

Acknowledgments

To our Free Spirit friends and pets, especially to Judy Galbraith and Meg Bratsch. Your encouragement, support, and celebration of our work has been extraordinary. You make us better authors, educators, and advocates!

From Diane

Richard, I get inspiration from your brilliant, creative and inquisitive mind and you make me laugh when I need to! Yours is always the first email I open since I know it is going to make my day. Working together is complete joy!

To my brother, Greg, whose passion for his work, his family and life itself serves as a daily inspiration for me.

To Kylie, my marine biologist daughter, may your new career bring you the joy and satisfaction that mine has brought me.

To my husband, John, for your steadfast patience with a very busy woman.

From Richard

The process of writing this book with my good friend and colleague, Dr. Diane Heacox, was a true pleasure. Diane, your continual striving for quality and intellectual integrity are an inspiration for me. Also, I love that you laugh at my jokes. I know we will have many more years of laughing and learning together!

To Craig Feltmann, and the "Steno Pool" (Roxxy and Vellma), thank you for keeping me from going off the deep end and always supporting me. I love you!

To my siblings (Susan, JC, and Robert), their families, and my friends: thank you for believing in me and always encouraging me to persevere.

Contents

List of Figures

Denotes figures included in the digital download. See page ix for more information.

List of Reproducible Forms

Download these forms at **freespirit.com/dfgl-forms**.
Use the password **4gifted**.

Foreword

Marcia Gentry, Ph.D.

Diane Heacox and Richard Cash are professionals who continue to make important contributions to gifted child education by helping teachers better differentiate their curriculum and instruction, and not surprisingly, they deliver with *Differentiation for Gifted Learners: Beyond the Basics*. Additionally, each author is a bright spot in the field bringing energy, integrity, and knowledge as they connect across disciplines and with educators within and outside of gifted education. In this book, as scholar-practitioners they bring scholarship and methods to teachers in a friendly, accessible, and useable format. This book and the workshops they each contribute will continue to help thousands of teachers reach and teach their students. Differentiation is often recommended, but many teachers struggle to implement it. *Differentiation for Gifted Learners* will help guide teachers to confidently practice differentiation strategies and, in doing so, benefit students across the country and around the world.

There are many reasons for you to read this book, namely, it is well written, filled with practical strategies that will work with students, and offers sage advice from two well-respected experts in gifted child education. However, as my differentiation-expert graduate student Jason McIntosh pointed out after he read it, there are also several circumstances under which you should NOT read this book. In fact, in developing a list of these circumstances, he used one of the strategies from the book called *reverse brainstorming*. He is convinced that you should NOT read this book if:

1. You do not need to learn new ways to differentiate using the Common Core State Standards.
2. You have already been exposed to the newly created Cash-Heacox Teaching and Learning Continuum.

3. All of your colleagues are on board with differentiation for gifted students and you do not need any tips for engaging them.
4. The term "Candy Wrapper Lesson Design" makes perfect sense to you.
5. You do not desire to see dozens of example activities that enrich, enhance, or extend content for students.
6. You have all stars and no steps when it comes to differentiation (see page 142).
7. You are a master at asking higher-level critical thinking questions of your students. You understand perfectly how to ensure an honors class is rigorous enough.
8. You know how the Autonomous Learner Model, the Holistic Development Framework, and Response to Intervention can be combined to create the Progressive Program Model.
9. You routinely empower all of your students to develop confidence through accountability, collaboration, and initiative.

For everyone else I highly recommend reading *Differentiation for Gifted Learners*. You will discover numerous practical strategies, discussions about recent brain research, and new ways of tackling old problems. I encourage you to challenge yourself as an educator just as much as you strive to challenge your students to think and work at advanced levels. The authors have put forth a teacher-friendly resource that takes differentiation to the next level. I believe this book will become one of those on your desk with worn and creased pages because you will use it so frequently. I predict that you will recommend it to your colleagues, but you will not let them borrow it!

Marcia Gentry, Ph.D., *professor of education and executive director of the Gifted Education Resource Institute at Purdue University*

Introduction

We both have gotten the calls. The school needs someone to come and provide training to all teachers on differentiation. We ask: "What can you tell me about services for gifted students in your school?" Then comes the answer: "Well, actually we had to cut gifted. With all the new initiatives, we just don't have the budget to support it anymore. But we told the parents that we would have an expert come in and work with our teachers so that the needs of our gifted students can be handled in the inclusion classroom." What needs to be said next is that differentiation for all is not the same as differentiation for gifted learners. Their learning differences are unique, unlike those of other students in the classroom. Some schools recognize and address this reality, but in too many schools, there is an assumption that differentiating will automatically meet the specific needs of gifted learners. In other schools, differentiation for gifted students does not follow best practices and appears shallow and trivial. Certainly in these circumstances, differentiation does not respond to the distinctive learning characteristics and profiles of gifted students.

About This Book

The purpose of this book is to clearly define and describe how effective differentiation is different for gifted and advanced learners and to show you how to meet the needs of these students. While differentiation is often talked about today as it relates to standards-based education, the term has been used widely in gifted education for decades. Experts in the field of gifted education originally defined *differentiation* as "modifications in content, process, or products in response to the specific learning differences of gifted and/or talented learners."

Differentiation for Gifted Learners: Beyond the Basics focuses on the specific learning needs of and differences among gifted students and offers effective ways that teachers can plan for these differences. We provide strategies, formats, templates, and examples of differentiation for kindergarten through grade twelve classrooms and represent a variety of curricular applications across all core content areas. In addition, we offer guidance for the design of programs and services for gifted students that specifically respond to their learning needs that extend above and beyond the inclusion differentiated curriculum in the inclusion classroom.

Chapter 1 is a reference point for educators in defining giftedness and understanding the differences among gifted students that require specific differentiation practices. We present an overview of the federal definition of giftedness as well as explore the implications of distinctions between gifts and talents. We note the challenges of gifted students who are also English language learners, who have ADHD, or who face other learning or behavior challenges. We also discuss the similarities between students who are gifted and students with Asperger's syndrome. Various cultural and ethnic communities sometimes associate different attributes with giftedness; we'll explore this and offer recommendations for providing equal access to and equity in services for gifted learners.

Chapter 2 addresses the specifics of differentiation for gifted learners. Based on neurological studies, we explain why differentiating for gifted learners is much more than just adding activities—even those we consider differentiated—that the learner may perceive as "more of the same." We provide practical strategies that enable teachers to focus content on advanced concepts and complex ideas. We also suggest ways to engage all levels and types of gifted students in using the tools of the practicing professional to produce significant products that have value to others.

Chapter 3 considers the implications of the Common Core State Standards (CCSS) for the education of gifted students. We present ideas for applying and extending the standards in ways that enhance the education of gifted learners.

Chapter 4 provides guidance in developing, refining, or extending quality programs and services for gifted students from elementary school through high school. The educational support systems and structures for gifted learners are typically not mandated or reinforced by state/provincial or federal rule or law. Therefore, districts and states/provinces are left to their own resources to provide equitable services and programs for these students. This chapter outlines a spectrum of services that address the varying needs of gifted learners and provide significant differentiation of content, process, and product to help each of them reach her or his maximum potential. We suggest that services for gifted students are not limited to one type of program, but are wide ranging with a focus on talent, academic, and social/emotional development.

Chapter 5 considers the design of honors and advanced courses at the secondary level. As schools become more diverse and funds dwindle, exclusive programming for gifted learners has become more difficult to sustain. In addition, if specialized courses are offered too often, there is little distinction between "regular" and "advanced" sections of a course, and the teacher frequently lacks training in differentiation for gifted learners. This chapter helps teachers ensure that courses for gifted students are distinguished by *articulation, alignment,* and *accountability,* or the "Triple A" method. In addition, this chapter offers an outstanding curricular framework that infuses the pedagogy of gifted education into secondary courses.

Chapter 6 discusses the changing roles of educators in the differentiated classroom. This chapter provides critical information on the specific educational and social/emotional needs of gifted learners that must be addressed in the general education setting. We also explore how the roles of teacher and students change within the differentiated classroom, and we present our model—the Teaching and Learning Continuum (TLC)—which outlines how to develop greater student responsibility, self-regulation, and learning autonomy in your classroom.

Chapter 7 describes co-teaching as a collaborative approach to differentiation for gifted learners. In many schools, classroom teachers have primary responsibility for meeting the needs of gifted students in their classrooms without the assistance or support of gifted education specialists. Such "inclusion" classrooms demand teachers who have specialized training in differentiation for gifted learners. However, when schools have gifted education specialists available to support the needs of gifted learners, co-teaching can be effectively used by these specialists and classroom teachers. This chapter details the co-teaching model and introduces six effective co-teaching strategies in differentiation for gifted learners. We also offer specific suggestions for building and maintaining effective collaboration between gifted education specialists and classroom teachers.

Chapter 8 provides valuable guidance for teachers who are challenged by gifted students who may underachieve and produce selectively or not at all. In this chapter, we discuss potential underlying issues related to these learners. We suggest potential causes for lack of school performance and offer strategies to break the cycle of underachievement. We also provide coaching tips for teachers that can be used to support school success and curtail a gifted student's slide into low production.

Chapter 9 addresses assessment for learning and its critical relationship to differentiation for gifted students. We suggest the ways in which preassessment and formative assessment specifically inform our planning for gifted learners. Informal assessment strategies are provided that minimize planning and preparation time for teachers. Because critical and creative thinking are foundational to differentiation for gifted learners, specific assessment strategies for assessing creative and critical thinking skills are detailed. In addition, we discuss the connections between descriptive feedback and student achievement, and provide guidelines and strategies to optimize the results of this feedback.

Chapter 10 contains ideas for how the gifted education specialist can provide leadership in embedding the strategies of differentiation for gifted learners in classroom practice. Most educators of the gifted are not school administrators but are on a teachers' contract as specialists, facilitators, directors, or teachers on special assignment. However, they are often expected to take on leadership roles in the school. This chapter discusses the challenges of "quasi-administrators" and suggests appropriate roles and typical responsibilities for these specialists, such as instructional coaching. We describe specific coaching strategies along with processes, procedures, and routines that gifted education specialists often find effective. Finally, we present a collaborative approach to supporting professional development and professional learning communities called *lesson study*. We offer direction for establishing lesson study as well as templates for quickly implementing the process in your school.

Chapter 11 provides some go-to resources for your practice. We present an easy-to-use reference to guide your planning of differentiated learning experiences. This collection of strategies enables you to consider content, process, and product differentiation across readiness, interest, and learning profile differences among gifted students. We also include a handy summary of what distinguishes differentiation for gifted learners, which will be a helpful resource in conversations on this topic with colleagues, parents, students, and other stakeholders.

All of the reproducible forms in this book are available as digital files. See page ix for information on how and where to download them.

If you wish to use this book in a professional learning community or book study group, a PLC Guide with chapter-by-chapter discussion questions and teaching suggestions is available. You may download the free guide at freespirit.com.

How to Use This Book

Differentiation for Gifted Learners extends the work of Diane's previous books, *Differentiating Instruction in the Regular Classroom* and *Making Differentiation a Habit*. And it expands principles and practices initially presented in Richard's book, *Advancing Differentiation*, to the specific needs of gifted learners. This resource builds on the strong foundations of differentiation presented in our previous three books, and it provides clear direction and guidance in effective differentiation for gifted learners.

Our intent is to inform the practices and support the work of classroom teachers and gifted education specialists, as well as school leaders such as curriculum specialists, building principals, teacher leaders, and professional development trainers. We also encourage college and university faculty to use the book with preservice teachers and graduate students to deepen their understandings of the learning differences of gifted students and to better differentiate instruction for them within inclusion classrooms.

You may wish to read through the book chapter by chapter, or you may want to go directly to a particular topic that is of immediate interest to you. For example, as your school works with the Common Core State Standards, you will want to read and review our thoughts and ideas on its best applications for gifted learners in Chapter 3. If you are involved in establishing, revising, or refining high school courses, consider going directly to Chapter 5.

This book will not only help you apply best practices for gifted learners in your classroom, but will also enable you to assertively and with great detail outline and defend the ways that differentiation for gifted learners differs from the practices used with other students. As advocates for the gifted, we need to step up and claim these differences and clarify others' understandings of them.

Finally, we want to strengthen your gifted programs and services, extend the strategies of differentiation you are already using, and provide new ideas, tactics, formats, and templates to make appropriate differentiation for your gifted learners both practical and doable.

Come with us as we go *beyond* the basics of differentiation to practices that address the unique learning needs of gifted students!

Chapter 1

Giftedness Defined in Diverse Groups

Definition of Gifts and Talents

Our definitions of gifted and talented learners have evolved over the years. Beginning with the 1972 Marland Report, the first national report on gifted education, the United States Office of Education worked to define what it means to be gifted and talented. This initial definition was broad and included academic and intellectual talent, leadership ability, visual and performing arts, creative and productive thinking, and psychomotor ability.[1] Psychomotor ability was removed from later versions of the federal definition, which was revised in 1978, 1988, and 1993. Here's how the 1988 definition read: "The term 'gifted and talented students' means children and youth who give evidence of high performance capability in areas such as intellectual, creative, artistic (visual and performing), or leadership capacity, or in specific academic fields, and who require services or activities not ordinarily provided by the school in order to fully develop such capabilities."[2] It should be noted that, although many schools currently provide some level of services to students with intellectual gifts or high academic abilities, the federal definition provided direction for much broader services.

Figure 1.1 on page 5 summarizes the characteristics of gifted students.

In 1993, the Office of Education revised its definition once again to define gifted and talented students as "Children and youth of outstanding talent who perform or show the potential for performing at remarkably high levels of accomplishment when compared with others of their age, experience, or environment."[3] Unfortunately, this definition suggests that gifted and talented students always perform at high levels. The reality is that some do not. Some gifted students are, in fact, academic underachievers. Yet they still need gifted services—especially academic interventions and services designed to break their cycle of underachievement. More information on underachieving and unmotivated gifted learners is provided in Chapter 8.

The 1993 definition also noted "Outstanding talents are present in children and youth from all cultural groups, across all economic strata, and in all areas of human endeavor."[4] The issues that stem from this notation in the federal definition have historically been and continue to be a challenge for schools. Today, culturally diverse students continue to be underrepresented in gifted education programs and services.

> **Gifts** are superior *innate* aptitudes; **talents** are outstanding *learned* capabilities.

For purposes of clarity, it is critical that we use a common definition for gifted and/or talented learners. The view of gifts and talents that we'll use in this book best reflects the work of Françoys Gagné[5] along with a general synthesis of other leaders and researchers in the field of

---

[1] Marland, 1972.
[2] Jacob K. Javits Gifted and Talented Students Education Act, 1988.
[3] U.S. Department of Education, 1993.
[4] Ibid.
[5] Gagné, 1985, 2005.

Figure 1.1: Educational Characteristics and Behaviors of Gifted Students* *(also included in the digital download)*

Visual/Performing Arts

Outstanding sense of spatial relationships	Good motor coordination
Unusual ability for self-expression through art, dance, drama, music, etc.	Keenly observes others who have artistic skill
	Demonstrates talent for extended periods of time
Desire for producing original product	Picks up skills in arts with little or no instruction
Practices talent regularly without being told	High sensory sensitivity
Strives to improve artistic skills	Sees minute details in art products or performances

General Intellectual Ability

Comprehends and formulates abstract ideas	Chooses challenging tasks
Processes information in complex ways	Makes quick and valid generalizations
Observant	Enjoys difficult problems
Excited about new ideas	Reasons things out
Uses a large vocabulary	Grasps relationships
Inquisitive	Solves difficult and unique problems
Learns rapidly	Generates sophisticated ideas and solutions
Self-starter	

Creative Thinking

Independent thinker	Improvises often
Exhibits original thinking in oral and written expression	Does not mind being different
	Creates innovative ideas or products
Comes up with several solutions to a given problem	Chooses original methods
Strong sense of humor	Engages in or indicates interest in creative activities
Challenged by creative tasks	Uses divergent thinking

Specific Academic Ability

High academic success in a special interest area	Widely read in special interest area
Pursues special interest with enthusiasm and vigor	Knows the correct answers
Good memorization ability	Corrects his or her errors
Advanced comprehension	Recognized by peers and other teachers as having high intellectual ability
Acquires basic skill knowledge quickly	Self-aware of academic aptitude
Self-directed and motivated	

Leadership

Likes structure	Assumes responsibility
Well-liked by peers	Fluent, concise self-expression
Considered a leader among peers	
Self-confident	Foresees consequences of decisions
Good judgment in decision making	Works well in groups
High expectations for self and others	Actively participates in group decision making

* Adapted from a model developed by Eastern Connecticut State University and from the work of Marcia Gentry, 1999.

gifted education. We will define gifts and talents in this way:

- **Gifts** are superior *innate* aptitudes in intellectual, creative, social, and perceptual mental domains and muscular and motor physical domains. Gifts are born-with superior (top ten percent) aptitudes. They are the "promise" of giftedness, which may or may not develop into talents over time.

- **Talents** are outstanding *learned* capabilities and skills and abilities developed over time through training, learning, and practice.

Talents reflect superior (top ten percent) performance in fields such as academics, science and technology, arts, social service, administration, business, games, or athletics.

Related to Gagné's model, gifts over time have the potential to become talents in particular fields. However, with gifted students, we are unable to initially predict what specific talents will emerge or even if talents will be developed. Gifted students hold the promise for talent development, but gifts do not always result in talents.

Gagné's Model

Gagne's model of giftedness (**Figure 1.2**) specifies two categories of catalysts, environmental and intrapersonal, that influence when and if talents are developed. Environmental catalysts include milieu: the physical, cultural, social, and familial contexts. Other environmental catalysts include significant individuals in the student's life as well as available educational provisions for developing gifts into talents. Intrapersonal catalysts reflect the student's physical and mental traits as well as goal management capabilities. Catalysts either facilitate or inhibit the development of talent.

The developmental process is influenced by both environmental and intrapersonal catalysts. In addition, the kinds of activities students engage in, their learning progress, and their investment

of time and energy all influence talent development. If gifted students do not or cannot put time and effort into the development of their talents, those talents will not emerge. Regardless of how gifted a student is, if the student does not spend time training, learning, and practicing, one cannot expect specific talents to emerge.

Intrapersonal catalysts also influence talent development and include physical qualities like health status; motivation, including the student's needs, interests, and values; volition, including willpower, effort, and persistence; self-management skills, reflecting persistence, work habits, and effort; and, finally, personality factors, including temperament, self-awareness, self-esteem, and flexibility. In considering intrapersonal catalysts, students who are highly

Figure 1.2: The Differentiated Model of Giftedness and Talent* *(also included in the digital download)*

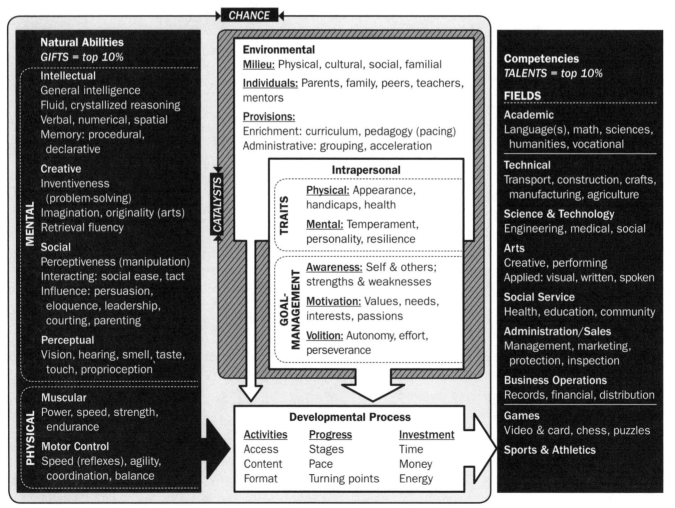

* Gagné, 2009.

interested in a particular subject or topic are more likely to put time into training, learning, and practice and, therefore, develop their talents in this field. Likewise, gifted students disinterested in a subject may not develop talents in this field because they are simply less motivated to put time into training, learning, and practice.

Environmental catalysts include the student's milieu (surroundings), reflecting family, social, and cultural settings; significant people in the student's life, including teachers, mentors, coaches, parents, and peers; provisions or opportunities to develop talents, such as gifted education services, school programs, or activities; and important events, such as awards, adventures, experiences, or encounters. Let's consider the potential effects of environmental catalysts using the example of a creatively gifted student who attends a school that does not provide music education. Such a student may not develop his or her innate musical talent because of a lack of opportunity for training, learning, and practice in this field. Conversely, a student given an opportunity to attend a summer STEM (science, technology, engineering, and math) camp may develop both a passion for engineering design and talent in the field of engineering.

According to Gagné's model, a student with outstanding talents in a particular field is also likely to be gifted. This is because superior talents often require a solid foundation in related aptitudes. However, a gifted student will not necessarily develop talents if particular catalysts are not in place. Thus, we may have students who are gifted intellectually but not talented academically. This is the case with academically underachieving gifted learners.

It should be noted that Gagné suggests that talents continue to emerge in gifted individuals over time, even into adulthood. There is a strong relationship between innate ability (gifts) and the ease and speed of developing new talents. Many gifted adults may indeed have "hidden talents" that are discovered, given the opportunity for training, learning, and practice.

If we were to apply Gagné's concepts to the federal definition of giftedness, intellectual ability and creativity would be considered gifts. Specific academic abilities, leadership, and visual and performing arts would be considered talents.

Gifted vs. talented . . .

For clarity and consistency, we will use the term *gifted* throughout this book.

Please keep in mind that we are thus referring to students who have innate superior aptitudes and who, over time and with the right catalysts and support for their gifts, develop into talented learners.

Identifying Giftedness Across Cultural, Linguistic, and Socioeconomic Communities

Gifted students are found in all communities, including those that are culturally, linguistically, and economically diverse (sometimes known by the acronym CLED). Keep in mind, however, that *smart* may be defined differently across these communities or eclipsed by the financial hardships of a child's family. As such, educators need to view the characteristics of gifted learners through the lens of the communities' values, practices, beliefs, and economic circumstances.

Cultural Concepts of Giftedness

Cognitive psychologist Robert Sternberg, a leading expert in giftedness, believes that how we identify gifted learners—and even the language we use when discussing giftedness—directly relates to our cultural values and concepts of giftedness. He suggests that the same children viewed as gifted in one culture may be seen as ordinary in another. For example, Sternberg's research found that Asian Americans tend to emphasize cognitive competence in their conception of giftedness, while Latino Americans tend to emphasize socioemotional competence. Thus, he suggests that Asian

Americans may be socialized in a way that promotes the development of cognitive competencies while Latino American children may be socialized to develop socioemotional competencies.[6]

> Children viewed as gifted in one culture may be seen as ordinary in another.

Sternberg's concerns over this cultural bias lie in the reality that so many countries, including the United States, are fast becoming multicultural. Student performance is a function of the culture in which they are raised. However, students from nondominant cultures are often enrolled in schools where the teachers and the leadership, including in gifted education, operates according to a dominant culture model. Thus, many current conceptions of giftedness are limited when we consider the breadth of our cultural communities. By ignoring a different culture's perception of giftedness, we may fail to identify students who are in fact gifted.

Sternberg argues that schools must understand cultural concepts of "gifted" in order to determine how particular students may compare to the norms of their specific community.[7] It can be extremely helpful to have conversations in a culturally sensitive manner with representatives of your school's various cultural/ethnic communities, generally asking the question, "How would you describe a student who is exceptional?" The various answers you receive to this question may lead you to reconsider students of particular cultures for gifted programs who you might otherwise overlook.

Following are some general characteristics associated with being gifted. Consider how these characteristics might be expressed in various cultural/ethnic groups with different values, practices, and beliefs[8]:

- a strong desire to learn
- intense, sometimes unusual interests

- uncommon ability to communicate with words, numbers, and symbols
- effective and often inventive strategies for identifying and solving problems
- exceptional ability to retain and retrieve information, resulting in deep knowledge of particular topics or subjects
- extensive and unusual questions, experiments, and explorations
- quick understanding of new concepts; deeper understanding
- ability to make connections: "This is like this … because … "
- logical approaches to finding solutions
- ability to produce unique, original ideas
- keen, unusual sense of humor

Identifying Gifted English Language Learners (ELL)

Much has been written about the difficulties in identifying ELL students who are gifted. We just provided some ideas on how different cultures may define *gifted;* however, with ELL students, we also need to carefully examine the methods we use to locate such gifted learners.

Many of the assessments used in gifted education services depend on language—a student's oral and written language skills. Yet with ELL students, advanced thinking and problem-solving abilities may be masked by limited use of the English language. This disadvantage also affects some students in rural settings, students in poverty, or those whose cultural or linguistic background differs from the native-speaking middle-class population for which such assessments were generally designed.

When considering which students, especially ELL students, might need gifted education services, it's best to use multiple criteria and draw information from as many sources as possible. This approach evaluates students from a variety of perspectives and, therefore, provides a more in-depth examination of their particular learning abilities and needs.

---

[6] Okagaki and Sternberg, 1993.
[7] Sternberg, 2007.
[8] Gosfield, ed., 2008.

How do we assess students without relying on language? Nonverbal standardized measures assess problem-solving skills using graphic representations with no language limitations. The Culture Fair Intelligence Tests, Naglieri Nonverbal Ability Tests, and Raven's Progressive Matrices are examples of nonverbal assessments used in many schools. Studies have found advantages and disadvantages of using each assessment, and particular assessments may be more effective with particular groups of ELL students. Schools have also sought to assess students in their native language.[9]

In addition to standardized measures, schools may set criteria that reflect exceptional ability in their particular ELL populations. Identifying such culturally based characteristics of giftedness may be particularly helpful to teachers who are learning how culture may disguise talents. These criteria will guide teachers as they observe students in their classroom. They may also be used as part of a behavioral checklist or inventory.

With more and more English language learners in our schools and classrooms, we need to carefully consider the ways in which we identify gifted learners in various populations. Understanding the cultural, linguistic, and cognitive skills of ELL students is an important first step in developing culturally based definitions of gifts and talents.

Socioeconomic Inequities
Results from the 1991 National Education Longitudinal Study of eighth-grade programs for gifted learners stands as an example of the economic inequities that have been present in gifted programs and services.[10] The data indicated that students whose families with incomes in the top quarter of the population were five times more likely to be in gifted programs than students from the bottom quarter.

Still today, gifted education continues to underserve poor children and serve more middle- and upper-middle-class children. To rectify this inequity, schools must evaluate the degree to which students involved in gifted programs reflect the realities of their school populations. For example, are students on free and reduced lunch represented in your gifted population? If not, what are the obstacles or barriers to their involvement? In what ways are your school's cultural values and views of giftedness limiting access for students who are living in poverty?

Gifted education has long struggled with issues related to access and equity. Moving forward, we need to continue to critically examine the ways that our belief systems and cultural practices may shape how we identify and serve students. Access to excellence, through appropriate gifted services, should be assured for students from all cultural and linguistic communities and socioeconomic groups.

Serving Recent Immigrant Children
As with ELL students, children whose families have recently immigrated represent a wide range of cultures and economic realities, and educators often face similar challenges in identifying and serving children from these groups who are gifted. A number of factors—including cultural and linguistic background, financial challenges, attitudes, conflicting peer expectations, cross-cultural stress, and even intergenerational family conflicts—increase the complexity of working with these families. Some students have had little, sporadic, or no formal education prior to immigration. In addition, hidden factors such as illegal immigration status, limited knowledge about how to access social and healthcare services, and physical and psychological problems resulting from political tensions in their country of origin may impact the students' educational progress and success. In some instances, immigrant children with English language learning status may not even be considered for gifted education services. Following are some suggestions for making gifted education services more accessible to children who have recently immigrated.[11]

Communication
- Explain the purposes for gifted services to parents in their native language.

[9] Lewis, 2001.
[10] U.S. Department of Education, 1991.
[11] Partially based on the work of Harris, 1993.

- Consider what aspects of your program would be valued by the student's culture, and communicate that to parents.

Identification

- Make an effort to learn about culturally based characteristics of giftedness related to immigrant children so you can better reflect on student learning behavior that occurs in the classroom.
- Assume nothing about the economic status or educational background of the families (for example, recent immigrants are sometimes assumed to have little money or education, which is certainly not always the case, depending on their reasons for immigrating).
- Interpret behavior in the context of the child's experiences.
- Consider using exploratory enrichment activities to observe how the immigrant student responds to new ideas and materials.
- Use referrals from peers inside or outside of the immigrant student's cultural group.

Services

- Prepare to work with immigrant students by gathering information about the immigrant group's culture, country of origin, religion, history, values, and expectations.
- Provide services that are culturally sensitive, relevant, and responsive to the context of the immigrant group.
- Identify ways that gifted services may conflict with the student's culture, and work to remedy those conflicts.
- Consider the immigrant group's aspirations, and plan curriculum that responds to these goals.
- Use references and resources in the student's native language.
- Create opportunities for immigrant students to develop relationships with gifted peers outside their cultural community.
- Periodically meet with the student's other teachers to discuss their attitudes and

possible biases. Hold informal sessions to identify problems and exchange ideas.

To provide both equity and access to gifted services for children who are recent immigrants, we need to consider communication, identification, and services within the context of the immigrant group's culture, history, values, and aspirations.

See pages 200–205 for specific resources on serving gifted students who are culturally, linguistically, or economically diverse.

Twice-Exceptional Learners: Gifted Students with Learning or Behavior Challenges

The gifts and talents of some students may be masked by other learning or behavior challenges. Referred to as "twice exceptional," these students may have cognitive difficulties, such as attention deficit hyperactivity disorder (ADHD) or Asperger's syndrome, as well as hidden gifts and talents that need to be acknowledged and nurtured.

> The gifts and talents of some students may be masked by learning or behavior challenges.

It has been suggested that between 5 and 10 percent of a school's gifted population may also have learning difficulties.[12] Although specific characteristics of giftedness for students with learning difficulties may vary, research does reveal some common elements.

Gifted Learners and ADHD

Some gifted students are identified as having attention deficit hyperactivity disorder. This disorder must be diagnosed by a trained mental health professional or physician. It may be especially difficult to accurately diagnose ADHD in gifted learners, since some of the characteristics

---

[12] Dix and Schafer, 2005.

◎ Characteristics of Gifted Students and Gifted Students with Learning Difficulties

General Characteristics of Intellectually Gifted Students*	Characteristics of Gifted Students with Learning Difficulties
Accelerated pace of learning; retain information with less repetition	May struggle with basic skills and reading due to processing deficits; may need compensatory strategies to ease learning
High verbal ability	High verbal ability but problems with written language; may use language inappropriately
Keen powers of observation	Strong observational skills; however, may have deficits in memory skills
Strong critical thinking, problem-solving, and decision-making skills	Strong critical thinking, problem-solving, and decision-making skills; excel in solving "real world" problems
Long attention spans, persistent, and intense ability to concentrate	Frequently have problems with concentration but in areas of interest are able to focus for long periods of time
Innovative; creative in generating thoughts, ideas, and actions	Unusual imagination; extremely divergent in thinking; generate original but sometimes "bizarre" ideas
Take risks	Often unwilling to take academic risks; take risks in non-school-related areas sometimes without considering consequences
May mature at different rates than same-age peers	Sometimes appear immature due to use of anger, withdrawal, and/or crying in dealing with difficulties
Independent	Require teacher support and feedback in deficit areas; can be more independent in interest areas; may appear stubborn and inflexible
Sensitive	Sensitive toward own deficits; can be critical of self and others; may engage in antisocial behaviors, though generally sensitive to the feelings of others
May have problems with friendships; may be isolated due to lack of intellectual peers or students with similar interests	May have problems with friends due to poor social skills; may appear to be loners since they do not represent a typical model of giftedness
Exhibit leadership abilities	May emerge as a leader among less traditional students; demonstrate "street smarts"; deficits may impact leadership abilities
Wide range of interests	Wide interests but deficits may hinder ability to follow them
Passion for particular topics	Passion for particular topics to the exclusion of others; interests often not school related

* Nielsen, E. M., et al. *Characteristics of Intellectually Gifted Students and Gifted Students with Learning Difficulties.* In an unpublished manuscript. Albuquerque Public Schools, 2000.

of ADHD are similar to the general characteristics of gifted learners. For example, both students who have ADHD and gifted students are creative, have high energy and abilities, and may be less inhibited and more likely to take risks.[13] Both may also create their own rules and become reluctant to disengage from a task they find fascinating. Their curiosity along with their need for stimulation may result in taking risks with little consideration of the consequences. Although these behaviors may "look" like ADHD, the students may simply be displaying the general characteristics of gifted learners.

In addition, psychologist Kazimierz Dabrowski suggested that a trait he referred to as *overexcitability* is unique to some highly gifted learners.[14] Overexcitability refers to having an unusual intensity and sensitivity. Dabrowski identified five interrelated areas of overexcitability. For those with this trait, high levels of activity are noted in all five areas:

1. **Psychomotor.** Students exhibit excessive energy, enthusiasm, drive, and restlessness; they are likely to talk rapidly and compulsively; they may act impulsively, have nervous habits, and can become "workaholics."

2. **Intellectual.** Students have high levels of curiosity and ask many probing questions. They carefully analyze ideas and are motivated to learn all there is about a topic. They may become preoccupied with problems in specific areas of interest. Also, they examine issues related to morality and ethics, and demonstrate high levels of moral thinking.

3. **Imaginational.** These highly creative students are both excitable and sensitive. Capable of creating strong visual imagery, they may easily engage in metaphorical thinking such as poetry. Their imaginations are quite active and, therefore, they may combine truth with fiction.

4. **Sensual.** These students exhibit pleasure in the senses: seeing, tasting, smelling, touching, and hearing.

5. **Emotional.** Students display both intense positive and negative feelings, resulting in emotional highs and lows. Highs result in positive energy; lows can bring both physical and psychological symptoms, including tenseness and anxiety, self-criticism, and feeling of inadequacy and inferiority. Such students are best described as being on an emotional roller coaster.[15]

Characteristics of overexcitability are similar to the poor attention, impulsiveness, and hyperactivity associated with ADHD. Therefore, it is critical that we accurately differentiate the high activity levels and unusual intensity of gifted students from the characteristics of individuals with ADHD. This takes the diagnostic skills of a trained mental health professional or physician who also thoroughly understands typical behaviors in gifted learners.

Gifted Learners and Asperger's Syndrome

Asperger's syndrome includes high-functioning autism. Students with Asperger's typically are linear and sequential thinkers who prefer order and predictability. Asperger's does not affect one's intellectual abilities; students with Asperger's typically fall in the normal to above average intellectual range.

Behaviors that are typical with Asperger's include[16]:

- introversion, social awkwardness, and aloofness
- attention problems
- overexcitability
- obsessive interests in limited topics
- hypersensitivity to such things as bright lights or loud noises
- motor clumsiness
- repetitive patterns of interests, activities, and play
- resistance to change
- an inability to interpret social cues; poor awareness of how others view them

---

[13] Baum and Reis, 2004.
[14] Dabrowski, 1967.

[15] Davis, 2006.
[16] Adapted from Davis, 2006.

■ excessive run-on talking and question asking

■ concerns with fairness

■ quirky sense of humor

Individuals with Asperger's do not typically remain aloof and withdrawn their entire lives; most show greater interest in others as they grow older. Many become well adapted but may still appear to be egocentric and idiosyncratic in their behaviors. People with Asperger's are sometimes described as "quirky."

Similar to the issues related to ADHD and the overexcitability of some gifted learners, the typical behaviors of Asperger's may also be common among students who are gifted. This raises two questions: Are introverted gifted students being misdiagnosed with Asperger's syndrome? Are we determining which gifted students also have Asperger's?[17]

> Typical behaviors of Asperger's may also be common among students who are gifted.

Researcher James Webb and colleagues provide guidance in identifying students who may not truly have Asperger's but are simply exhibiting the behaviors of gifted learners. According to Webb, the following "disqualifies" students from Asperger's diagnoses but indicate giftedness.

■ Students have normal friendships with others who have common interests.

■ They can read interpersonal situations and the emotions of others.

■ Their emotions are appropriate to the situation or issue.

■ They appropriately display sympathy and empathy.

■ They are aware of others' perceptions of them.

■ They have little or no motor clumsiness.

■ They tolerate abrupt changes in routines.

■ Both their speech and their sense of humor are more adult-like.

■ They understand both metaphors and idioms.[18]

Although it is certainly possible for students to have Asperger's syndrome and be gifted, we need to avoid making assumptions and to carefully consider both possibilities when these characteristics are present.

Chapter Summary

Definitions of gifted have evolved since the 1972 Marland Report as have the distinctions between gifts and talents. Poverty and differing cultural concepts of giftedness are critical issues in gifted education as they relate to equity and access for students in gifted services. The field continues to face challenges in providing services and properly identifying gifted students who are also English language learners, recent immigrants, or twice-exceptional students. Educators must take care to avoid mislabeling students who may be gifted but whose behaviors may mask characteristics or be misinterpreted.

---

[17] Davis, 2006.

[18] Webb, et al., 2005.

Chapter 2

Using Brain Research to Improve Differentiation

Differentiation for gifted students does not mean simply giving them more activities to do that the learner may see as more of the same (what we call "MOTS"). Instead, the content focuses on advanced concepts and complex ideas, and learners use strategies (step-by-step tasks) and thinking skills with greater degrees of sophistication. Indeed, these students should be using the tools of a practicing professional—a disciplinarian—to produce authentic products that have value to a real-world audience. This all takes place in an environment that builds students' intrinsic motivation to take on more responsibility for their own learning; that is, they become autonomous learners.

Let's examine what this might look like. In a typical seventh-grade social studies class studying World War II, most students will be learning about the causes and effects of the war, with additional scaffolding or challenge as needed. Gifted students, on the other hand, whether they are in a general or honors level class, will be working as journalists, social scientists, theologians, or economists (to name a few disciplines), looking through their lens at what led to so many nations becoming involved in the war. In these ways, their learning becomes quickly immersive and increasingly complex.

Why is this different approach important? In recent years, neuroscientists have concluded that gifted students have more neural connectors in their prefrontal cortex than do typical learners.[19] This generally means they are able to process information at a more rapid pace. Students with more neural connectors are also more likely to be capable of making abstract connections between ideas and thoughts. This information about the brain helps us understand that our most advanced learners should spend a large portion of their classroom time developing and using more complex ways of thinking. We also know that gifted students are quick to amass large amounts of factual information. This means that we need to provide them with greater degrees of depth in the curriculum, which will require that they use more of their brain to sort, categorize, and generalize abstract information.

Other research on gifted, talented, and creative individuals reveals additional characteristics that further bolster the rationale for providing these learners with differentiated educational programs, services, and curriculum. This chapter will examine how we can use the findings from brain studies to develop more appropriate differentiating instructional practices and curricular designs to address the learning needs of gifted students.

Brain Research and Giftedness

Results from any neurological study need to be interpreted before we can sufficiently bridge the research findings to the implementation. Regarding neurological studies on giftedness and classroom applications, best practices are still subject to criticism. Therefore the following information is intended to inform practice, not dictate it.

---

[19] Geake, 2008.

Before we delve into the specifics of brain research on giftedness, it is important to understand the basics of the brain. The human brain can be divided into three general domains: hindbrain, midbrain, and cerebral cortex. Each of these areas performs functions that are interrelated to the other areas of the brain.

Figure 2.1: The Brain's Domains

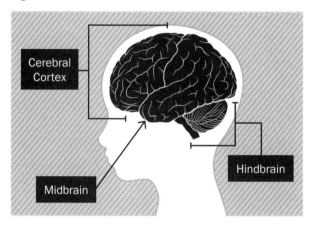

The Hindbrain: Rapid Recall and Skill Development

In the simplest of terms, the hindbrain performs those basic functions that keep us alive. The hindbrain controls, monitors, and adjusts all the autonomic systems in our body (such as the circulatory, digestive, respiratory, and nervous systems).

Also located in the hindbrain is the cerebellum, a word which means "old brain." The cerebellum controls our body's movement, balance, and coordination. Particular to the cerebellum is its capacity to hold on to both procedural and rote-level knowledge.

Procedural knowledge refers to those routines we perform so often that we no longer need to think about them, such as brushing our teeth, walking and talking at the same time, or driving our cars.

Rote memory (also called declarative knowledge) is the easy recall of facts—information that can be verified from other sources. The alphabet, multiplication/addition/subtraction/division facts, important dates, state or province capitals,

or our telephone number or home address are all examples of factual information. It takes little brainpower to quickly recall this information, leaving enough energy for the upper areas of the brain to process high-level thoughts and actions. This quick recall is due to what is called "neural efficiency." When neural pathways have been refined, either through practice or because of advanced brain development, the person learns information and is able to recall it significantly faster than others.

Again, for many gifted learners their brains develop greater neural efficiency more rapidly, thus allowing them to retrieve declarative or factual knowledge more quickly than the average person. Additionally, their neural efficiency may allow them to learn procedures (strategies and skills) more rapidly than others.

When it comes to routines and rote memory, the more we practice them, the more automatic they become. Such automaticity means we can perform some tasks without conscious thought, which frees up the higher evolved level of our brains to process more sophisticated thoughts. Consider, for example, what happens when you drive your car. Before this task becomes automatic, you needed to put in many years of practice—driving in all kinds of weather conditions and in different kinds of cars. Such authentic practice creates efficient neural pathways between your nervous, skeletal, and muscular systems and, as a result, you no longer have to "think" about the practice: automaticity occurs. This type of graduated practice is called "increasing levels of complexity."

> Gifted learners' brains develop greater neural efficiency more rapidly.

We can use this same type of graduated practice in the classroom with our gifted students. As you read in Chapter 1 about the typical characteristics of gifted learners, these students build rote and procedural memory very quickly. Therefore, to differentiate for them, teachers should offer increasing levels of complexity in the rote and procedural learning activities. This means students will spend less time on learning the facts and more time on putting them into context and deciphering why the facts are important to know.

See pages 17–19 for more information and examples of increasing complexity at this level.

The Midbrain: Emotions and Responses to Stimuli

The next level of the brain is the midbrain region. This area is where we process our emotions (the chemical response to external stimuli) and long-term memory. Through chemical reactions, the midbrain region unconsciously responds to stimuli from the environment and perceptions of the larger world. The chemical reactions signal the upper regions of the brain, primarily the prefrontal cortex, to adjust our outward responses, such as to make us feel happy or sad. Like everyone else, gifted students who do not feel safe or welcomed within a certain environment will "downshift" into more instinctual, impulsive, or ritualistic behavior. Research suggests that gifted students are more emotionally sensitive than many other children.[20] Indeed, gifted students may have a certain level of *asynchronous*, or uneven, development at play when it comes to midbrain responses. This means that their cognition (from the upper levels of the brain) is more advanced than their emotional development. As a result, their perceptions of fairness, inequities, and suffering may produce emotional responses that may seem inappropriate. Or we may view their emotional responses as beneath their cognitive development. Their over-the-top responses may also stem from their inability to see how their personal efforts can affect larger world or social issues.

We can differentiate activities for gifted students to help them learn how to tone down or adjust their responses to midbrain stimuli. Activities should focus on ways to respond to the feelings of powerlessness associated with large social or world issues. For example, we can structure activities that help gifted learners plan local, doable actions connected to larger global issues. Such activities can include service learning projects, volunteerism, or peer teaching. Chapter 4 offers ideas on integrating the social and personal development dimensions into your gifted program model.

As to what adults perceive as asynchronous behaviors, we can remind ourselves that first and foremost, gifted children are children. They will develop emotionally at a rate similar to other children. This means that they need guidance and support from caring adults as they learn about social behaviors, develop appropriate coping strategies, and practice techniques for reducing stress.

> Gifted children are children. They develop emotionally at a rate similar to other children.

The Cerebral Cortex: Sophisticated Thinking

The most advanced part of our brain is in the cerebral cortex. The cerebral cortex is divided into four lobes with different functions:

- *Occipital lobe:* sight
- *Temporal lobe:* smell, sound, processing facial and scene recognition
- *Parietal lobe:* integrating sensory information from our senses, the ability to manipulate objects, and visual-spatial processing
- *Frontal lobe:* conscious thoughts, advanced levels of thinking, and mood modulation

Research suggests that gifted learners have better coordination and integration between and within the regions of their brains because of their more advanced development in the frontal cortical areas. This enables them to think in more sophisticated ways at higher levels and to better manipulate abstract information in their working memory. Studies also show that when students have superior cognitive abilities, it is due to a combination of an efficient brain processing system and general knowledge and domain-specific competencies.[21] This suggests that being gifted is about hard work and how efficient the brain

---

[20] Daniels and Piechowski, 2008; Neihart, et al., 2002; Lehman and Erdwins, 2004.

[21] Grabner, et al., 2006.

processes information. Together these findings tell us that the closer the cognitive demand matches the brain processing efficiency, the more the learner will develop greater neural efficiency and capacity.

Putting the Research to Practice

This advanced cognitive development is why we need to differentiate for gifted students. Again, differentiating for such students is not about adding more activities. It is about increasing the pace of instruction, adding greater complexity in thinking, and providing avenues to depths within the discipline. Let's take a closer look at each aspect of such differentiation.

Pace

Pace is related to rate of instruction and management in the classroom. It is about moving more rapidly through the exposition and review and then on to the new learning so students can spend more time developing the new ideas. An increased pace does not mean talking fast or moving through core content more quickly in order to cover more material. Rather, it's about spending less time on background knowledge, offering fewer examples on how to do particular tasks, and giving less teacher-led practice. An accelerated pace gives students the opportunity to become independent sooner than in the inclusion classroom. Gifted students thrive when they are cognitively engaged in rigorous thoughts and experiences versus the sometimes mundane task of breaking apart skills and definitions. Additionally, discipline problems rarely occur when students are actively engrossed in challenges that are on target for their learning needs. See the **Ten Strategies to Differentiate Pace** on page 18.

Complexity

Complexity is defined as the levels of thinking used when students combine their content knowledge, domain skills, and personal attitudes to complete authentic (real-world) tasks. In most cases, complexity refers to the breadth of thinking and doing within a discipline of study. When activities are complex, the student must rely on substantial background knowledge and skills, and use greater self-regulating strategies (planning, organizing, persistence, and patience) to solve problems. On a neural level, students will be using more brain energy and efficiency to process information. Activities for gifted students should be designed to encourage multilayered levels of higher order thinking (analysis, evaluation, and synthesis), creative thinking, critical reasoning, decision making, and problem solving. These kinds of activities are called complex learning tasks. See **Figure 2.2** for examples.

In complex learning, students integrate their knowledge, skills, and attitudes; coordinate qualitatively different thinking skills; and often transfer what was learned in school to daily life and work.[22] Complex learning involves working through authentic tasks that encourage the use of technology to solve problems. Real-world problems should center around controversial issues and the tools of the twenty-first century to increase the degrees of abstraction and ambiguity. These situations encourage divergent thinking, which allows for more than one way to solve the problem and more than one correct answer. In complex learning tasks, students use more sophisticated levels of thinking and acting. High levels of learning occur in this rich social context, where interactions, negotiation, articulation, and collaboration are vital.

Peers play a significant role in the development of complex learning. When working with gifted students, be sure to allow them to share their expertise with one another. Many gifted students have passions and exceptional prior learning experiences that have helped them develop a certain level of expertise in various areas, like a particular subject or process. Another way to increase the level of complexity is to group gifted learners together.

The idea of forming like-peer groups of gifted students induces fear in some people. They claim that such like-peer groupings can lead to problems

---

[22] van Merriënboer and Kirschner, 2007.

◎Ten Strategies to Differentiate Pace

An accelerated pace is an essential part of differentiating for gifted students. Pace refers to the rate of instruction and management in the classroom. Following are ten proven strategies for differentiating the pace with gifted students:

1. Create the course syllabus with clear objectives, including what students will know, understand, and be able to do after each lesson, so that they know what to expect and focus on in the lesson.

2. Have students do review as homework or through online material (often called a "flipped" classroom). Class time should be used primarily to zero in on new learning points.

3. Make students responsible for noting homework in daily planners, or post the homework for each day on a website. Don't spend class time disseminating homework.

4. Implement a "study buddy" program. Partner each student with at least one other student in the class. The study buddies are responsible for keeping each other posted on work, assignments, and notes missed when they are absent. The study buddies also answer each other's questions about the material, whenever possible. This frees up teacher time to instruct. Of course, if neither student can answer the question, they pose it to the teacher. Every pair will also need a backup, in case both partners are absent on the same day.

5. Use the "anticipatory set" idea wisely. Begin lessons with a short activity that focuses the learner on the material to be covered or the new skill/strategy to be developed. This activity should last no more than two to five minutes and should be highly charged, engaging, and pique interest.

6. Along with or instead of the anticipatory set, use brain warm-up activities at the beginning of the class to set the stage for the lesson. Warm-ups can be brainteasers, questions about controversial issues, logic problems, or creative situations seeking a solution that are done for two to five minutes as students arrive. Students can post their answers to a website, email them to the teacher, or write them in their personal journal. At the next class meeting, quickly review the answers for no more than two minutes.

7. Have all the resources for the unit readily available to students prior to starting the unit. This will encourage gifted students to consider their own prior knowledge or investigate the topic before the unit begins. Or, prior to the unit, offer students a list of websites that can introduce the topic or extend the material.

8. Be prepared for every class session before the students arrive. Have all the lesson materials arranged and ready, or designate students to prepare the materials. Keep in mind that students will mirror the attitudes and behaviors you display at the beginning of class. The more focused on the learning you are, the more focused the students will be.

9. Design, teach, and practice classroom protocol for an efficiently run classroom. Avoid letting interruptions take you off task, and prepare the students for interruptions that are inevitable (such as fire drills, office announcements, and latecomers/early departures). Teach students how to quickly refocus on the task after the interruption.

10. During lessons, offer one or two examples or models and then move forward. Gifted students don't need as much practice as the general population. Move on to new learning as quickly as possible. Spend most of your time investigating and wrestling with controversial issues, complex problems, and in-depth conversation. This is where gifted learners blossom!

From *Differentiation for Gifted Learners: Going Beyond the Basics* by Diane Heacox, Ed.D., and Richard M. Cash, Ed.D., copyright © 2014. Free Spirit Publishing Inc., Minneapolis, MN; 800-735-7323; www.freespirit.com. This page may be reproduced for use within an individual school or district. For all other uses, contact www.freespirit.com/company/permissions.cfm.

in the classroom, such as the underperformance of other groups or a sense of elitism by the gifted. Karen B. Rogers, a well-known expert in gifted education, has extensively analyzed the research on grouping practices for the gifted. Her studies support the practice of like-peer grouping for these students, showing it leads to higher levels of achievement, engagement, and complexity of tasks.[23] When like-peers are grouped together, they encourage, support, and critique each other to justify views and opinions, and offer suggestions for deeper explanations. More on grouping practices is discussed in Chapter 4.

See **Ten Tips for Creating Complex Learning Tasks** on page 20 for more ideas. See **Reverse Problem Brainstorming** on page 21.

---

[23] Rogers, 1993, 2001, 2004.

Depth

Depth refers to the degree to which a student explores the content and understands the discipline. The efficiency of gifted learners' prefrontal cortex allows them to tackle abstract ideas and supports their need for deeper content. The content must be framed around greater abstractions of the concepts and interdisciplinary connections. In this way, gifted students learn and use the principles (rules) and theories of the discipline in more authentic situations than the general population of students.

Figure 2.2: Examples of Differentiating Complexity

Following are sample ways that complexity can be increased for gifted learners:

FACTS/ROTE MEMORY

Multiplication Table
Gifted education student: Once math facts have been memorized, students can synthesize how knowing math facts automatically can ensure greater efficiency in your daily life.

Periodic Table
Gifted education student: When students have successfully memorized the elements, they should synthesize why the elements are grouped in this order. Identify when knowing the element groups or families will increase the efficiency and effectiveness of lab experiences.

Spelling
Gifted education student: Using the words from the learned spelling list, create analogies, metaphors, or similes for each word.
or
Research the origins of the word, breaking it down into its sublinguistic categories/parts.

State/Provincial Capitals
Gifted education student: Choose one of the following tasks, using at least four different states or provinces to represent your answer:

- Justify why the capital is important to the state/province.
- Determine why the particular city was designated as the capital.
- Provide rationale for the location of the capital.

- Determine the significance of the capital beyond governmental purposes.
- Suggest alternative locations of the capital for the state/province and justify the location.
- Collect and analyze data regarding capitals that were moved to new locations and cite a common rationale for the move.

PROCEDURAL/PRACTICE MEMORY

Multiplication
Gifted education student: (When proficient with the strategy taught) use more complex numbers, such as negatives or fractions. Reflect on which strategies were used and how the results compare to simple numbers.

Experimentation
Gifted education student: (After an experiment) review the steps to determine how they can be improved or how the effect of the experiment can be lessened/decreased or weakened.

Descriptive Writing
Gifted education student: Using the descriptive method, create an easy-to-understand technical manual on how consumers can reduce their carbon footprint.

Research
Gifted education student: Using qualitative research methods, frame a question related to stress and then gather "life stories" from several senior citizens who have lived through dramatic/traumatic events (such as the depression, WWII, or civil wars). From this qualitative data, draw a conclusion to answer your question.

◎Ten Tips for Creating Complex Learning Tasks

1. Ensure all students are fully aware of the learning goals and objectives. For students to work within a complex task, they need to thoroughly understand the expectations and outcomes of the learning task.

2. Make all resources and materials readily available to students, or ensure that they can gather the resources and materials themselves.

3. Prepare activities that are authentic (real-world) and involve ambiguous and somewhat abstract problems.

4. Develop tasks that allow for trial and error so students will eventually automatize the skills. Automization occurs when students repeatedly practice using strategies successfully.

5. Use "reverse problem finding" to help students develop problem-finding and divergent thinking skills. Reverse problem finding is a brainstorming process that first explores what causes a problem rather than beginning with how to solve it.

6. Ensure that tasks will use both affective (emotional) and content knowledge strategies and skills. This is called the "Whole Task Method" of learning. Within a holistic scenario, students must consider not only how to create a solution, but also how the solution may affect people, the environment, animals, and so on.

7. Design tasks that encourage students to develop unique products or reinterpret old ideas or sophisticated methods of designs that involve creative thought.

8. Urge students to seek advice from experts in the field or to gather multiple perspectives on the problem before them.

9. Design, teach, and practice classroom protocol for an efficiently run classroom. Avoid letting interruptions take you off task, and prepare the students for interruptions that are inevitable (such as fire drills, office announcements, and latecomers/early departures). Teach students how to quickly refocus on the task after the interruption.

10. Set up problems that require students to cross disciplines as they solve the problem. For example, when researching the effect of inexpensive sewer systems on third world slums, students will use the principles of civil and environmental engineering, economics, chemistry, biology, and anthropology.

◎Reverse Problem Brainstorming

This technique combines brainstorming and problem solving in a reverse order. To brainstorm in this way, you start with the question "What could cause this problem?" rather than "How do I solve this problem?" This method works by looking for the opposite effect and in the process uncovers unique solutions.

Steps to Reverse Problem Brainstorming:

1. Clarify the problem.
2. Reverse the problem by asking:
   a. How could this problem occur?
   b. How can we achieve the opposite effect?
3. Brainstorm multiple reverse solutions or ideas. During the brainstorming process:
   a. Work quickly.
   b. Generate many ideas.
   c. Piggyback onto others' ideas (listening to others is essential).
   d. Defer judgment.
4. Apply one of the proposed reverse solutions or ideas to the original problem.
5. Evaluate the solutions. Can the solutions be adjusted or modified to potentially solve the original problem?

EXAMPLE

Original Problem:

The school newspaper must increase distribution by 25 percent within three months to cover escalating printing and distribution costs. What can the team do to increase the distribution of the school newspaper by 25 percent?

Reverse Problem:

What can the team do to decrease the newspaper's distribution by 25 percent?

Reverse Solutions or Ideas:

- Publish poorly written articles.
- Be late with the publication or publish irregularly.
- Use ink that rubs off on clothing.
- Put the publications in obscure locations.
- Publish stories that students don't care about.

When the brainstorming runs its course, look at how each of the reverse solutions could be viewed as a solution for the original problem.

Reverse problem brainstorming is an excellent creative thinking and critical reasoning technique that can lead to fun, robust conversations and unique solutions.

Reverse Solution	Solution to Original Problem
Publish poorly written articles.	Ensure that the writing of the articles is top notch.
Be late with the publication or publish irregularly.	Ensure the publication is distributed on a routine/expected date.
Use ink that rubs off on clothing.	Publish the paper online.
Put the publication in obscure locations.	Create an "app" for students' smartphones or tablets so the news is easily accessible.
Publish stories that students don't care about.	Publish stories that are relevant to the student population, are of high interest, and/or include articles about students in the school

You can increase the lesson depth by using concepts that call for students to combine the facts and their skills, spending substantial time investigating fewer topics within a discipline and working as a disciplinarian to solve authentic problems. In this model, students uncover the big ideas (conceptual knowledge) by asking questions and solving problems rather than receiving discrete didactic instruction of facts and skills. The main intent of this kind of curriculum and instructional practice is to promote the transfer of learning to authentic application and then through student self-assessment in the use and development of the knowledge.

> For gifted students, their brains' efficiency allows them time to go more deeply into an area of study.

Often the idea of curriculum depth seems to oppose that of breadth, due to time constraints. Breadth is the philosophy of exposing students to as many topics as possible within a subject area. This "coverage of subjects" may stem from the overwhelming push toward standardized assessments that don't often seek a depth of understanding. Yet for gifted students, their brains are much more efficient in learning facts and strategies with less repetition and practice than their same-age peers, and this efficiency allows them time to go more deeply into an area of study. Through the practice of curriculum compacting (see **Essential Steps in Curriculum Compacting** on page 25), teachers can eliminate the repetition and frequency of practice so that gifted students have time to work in depth on either a topic of interest or one that is not covered through the general curriculum. When curriculum is compacted, students exchange substantial instructional time, assignments, and unit projects for in-class time to work on a long-term independent learning project of their choice. These longer blocks of work time are available since the student does not need to participate in lessons, assignments, and activities related to goals already accomplished. Independent learning projects may extend or deepen that student's experiences related to a unit topic or theme, or they may be based on the student's interests outside the grade-level curriculum. Whatever the topic, it is important that the student is involved in the design of the learning experience. If students are not directly involved in the planning, they may lack motivation to do the work. Also, remember that with compacting the student's work needs to be *instead of, not in addition to,* the general tasks assigned to other students during the unit. Students who have compacted out may be included in unit tasks with other classmates when the student would benefit from the collaborative activity or from engagement in tasks focusing on critical or creative thinking, problem solving, or decision making. It's often helpful to develop an agreement for the compacting project, so all involved are clear about expectations, steps involved, and project delivery. See **Figure 2.3** on page 23 and **Compacting Form and Project Description** on page 24.

Figure 2.3: Example—Compacting Form and Project Description

◎Compacting Form and Project Description

Name of student: _ DeShawn Grade 5 _____

Signature of student: _____

Signature of teacher: _____

Signature of parent/guardian: _____

Curriculum Area(s)	Speed Up/Test-Out/Eliminate	Project Description
Mathematics: Compact Grade 5 Geometry Common Core Accelerated Experience Grade 6 Statistics and Data Common Core	Test-out/Eliminate Mastered Concepts Grade 5 Common Core: Graph points on the coordinate plane to solve real-world and mathematical problems. 1. Use a pair of perpendicular number lines, called axes, to define a coordinate system, with the intersection of the lines (the origin) arranged to coincide with the 0 on each line and a given point in the plane located by using an ordered pair of numbers, called the coordinates.	Design, conduct, analyze, & present survey research. Summarize numerical data sets by: a. Describing the nature of the attribute under investigation, including how it was measured and its units of measurement. b. Giving quantitative measures of center (median and/or mean) (grade 6 Common Core)

Resources needed:

Online modules on conducting survey research, analyzing data, and presenting results

Digital graphics software

Steps in the project:

1. Pre-test, eliminate daily instruction and work on grade 5 geometry concepts that have been previously mastered. Loop DeShawn into class activities as appropriate.
2. Complete online modules on survey research.
3. Determine research questions, develop survey.
4. Conduct research, analyze data, plan presentation using digital graphics.

Criteria for quality work:

Rubrics will be provided for the research design, analysis of data, and presentation to the class.

Due date: _ End of second trimester. _____

Adapted from *The Compactor* by Joseph S. Renzulli and Linda H. Smith (Mansfield Center, CT: Creative Learning Press, 1978). Used with permission.

◎ Compacting Form and Project Description

Name of student: _____

Signature of student: _____

Signature of teacher: _____

Signature of parent/guardian: _____

Curriculum Area(s)	Speed Up/Test-Out/Eliminate	Project Description

Resources needed:

Steps in the project:

Criteria for quality work:

Due date: _____

Adapted from The Compactor *by Joseph S. Renzulli and Linda H. Smith (Mansfield Center, CT: Creative Learning Press, 1978). Used with permission.*

◎ Essential Steps in Curriculum Compacting

Curriculum compacting enables teachers to streamline the regular curriculum, ensure students' mastery of basic skills, and provide time for challenging and interesting enrichment and/or acceleration activities.*

Curriculum compacting should:

- eliminate repetition of mastered content and/or skills
- increase the challenge level of the regular curriculum
- provide time for students to investigate topics beyond the scope of the regular curriculum or topics of interest**

STEPS TO CURRICULUM COMPACTING

1. Identify the key content standards all students must know, understand, and be able to do within the context of the unit.
2. Assess students' current understanding of the content standards.
3. When students demonstrate mastery of all the objectives, allow them to participate in enriched/enhanced/extended (E3) or acceleration activities.
4. When students demonstrate mastery of some but not all of the objectives, provide small group or mini-lessons on objectives not mastered so they, too, can move on to E3 or acceleration activities.
5. Create a contract with students that describes the E3 or acceleration activities, due dates, norms of self-study or small group work, and expectations and rubrics for final projects.

Compacting options for gifted students:

- E3 activities
- accelerated content (moving forward a year)
- interest or learning centers
- self-directed learning units
- passion projects
- online course work
- service learning projects
- working with mentors or experts in the field

Benefits of curriculum compacting for gifted students:

Compacting helps ensure that gifted students who have mastered the required content:

- continuously learn new information
- attain higher level of cognitive stimulation
- achieve a greater sense of self-efficacy
- develop self-regulation skills
- become more motivated to learn
- demonstrate persistence
- become more independent
- become willing to learn in small groups or through self-instruction
- learn to dig deeper into content areas

---

* Renzulli, J. S., and S. M. Reis. *Enriching Curriculum for All Students.* Thousand Oaks, CA: Corwin, 2008.

** Heacox, D. *Differentiating Instruction in the Regular Classroom.* Minneapolis, MN: Free Spirit Publishing, 2012.

◎ Designing Depth Projects

All students have the right to think at high levels and in depth. Gifted students should spend more of their learning time at more sophisticated levels of higher order thinking and in greater depth of content.

Ten Tips for Designing Depth Projects

1. Use relevant topics (from student interests) to frame the project.

2. Provide sufficient time for investigation by using the anchor activity model for ongoing projects. Anchor activities are ongoing assignments that encourage students to work at their own pace, independently and with self-direction throughout the course of a unit, semester, or school year

3. Use situations that are authentic (real-world) and meaningful (worth solving) for the student.

4. Give students the tools to manage the in-depth project (teach them organization, planning, monitoring, and evaluation strategies).

5. Connect the project to self, society, culture, technology, other disciplines, or community development.

6. Ensure that projects lead to a final product that has value to others.

7. Ensure students have access to the appropriate resources (both human and material) to accomplish the learning.

8. Use assessments that focus on what was learned and not on how it was presented.

9. Be sure that all projects include a student reflection and consideration for future study.

10. Encourage an authentic audience to evaluate the project for quality of presentation, information, and unique knowledge gained.

Most packaged curriculum or textbooks can be considered "encyclopedia" curriculum; that is, they cover numerous topics at a very shallow level. To achieve depth in learning, teachers will need to create opportunities for gifted students to investigate authentic problems that require them to apply, analyze, evaluate, and create new ideas and solutions. See **Designing Depth Projects** for more ideas (page 26). See also Chapter 5 for more ideas and examples on accelerated pace, complex thinking, and depth of content.

Although all students should be provided with complexity and depth in their learning, gifted students require higher levels of both. **Figure 2.4** illustrates how gifted students are able to focus on complexity and depth, and how this differs from the focus of other students.

Chapter Summary

Based on what neuroscience tells us about their brain functions, differentiating for gifted learners requires teachers to accelerate the instructional pace, build activities that require sophisticated levels of complex thinking, and encourage students to go in depth into the discipline. The gifted student's capacity to process information efficiently requires this type of differentiation.

Figure 2.4: Complexity and Depth

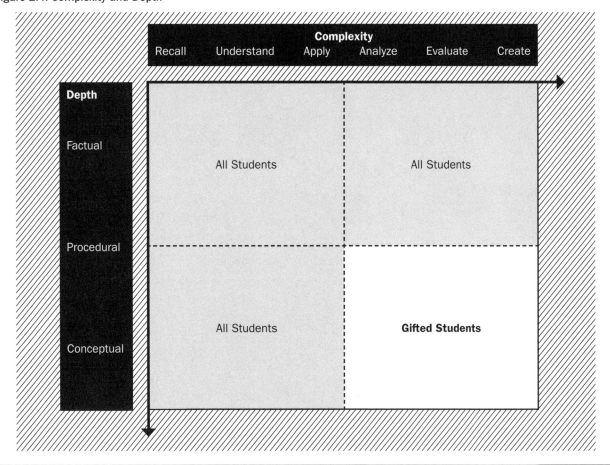

Chapter 3

The Common Core State Standards and Gifted Education

In the United States, the Common Core State Standards (CCSS) are framing the direction for curriculum in most states. Canada has a similar provincial framework that schools follow as they plan learning experiences for students. Before the CCSS were released in 2010, all U.S. states had established standards for students' learning, but there was limited uniformity across states. In addition, states held significantly different expectations regarding the level of rigor demanded of students. Learning progressions of skills and processes across grade levels were not defined, thus creating a hodgepodge of isolated, standalone skills and processes with little direction for defining the next step in learning should students reach grade-level goals early. This chapter will discuss the implications of the Common Core State Standards on planning instruction and programs for gifted learners.

How Common Core State Standards Affect Gifted Students

The Common Core State Standards are more general and broader in application than many states' previous academic standards. Advocates of the CCSS claim that these standards will potentially lead to higher level thinking compared with the former state standards, which were focused more on lower level, "test prep" student responses. The

CCSS focus on major concepts, ideas, and skills rather than on simply mastering set content. Students are directed to use curriculum content to examine questions, consider multiple perspectives, and solve problems as directed by the CCSS.

What do the Common Core State Standards mean when it comes to teaching gifted students? Misconceptions abound. To find out whether your own ideas about the CCSS are accurate, take the following quiz. Answers will be provided in the text that follows discussing the impact of CCSS on gifted students and services. (*Hint:* They're also printed at the bottom of page 29.)

Misconception or Not? Quiz

Mark the following statements "M" for misconception or "T" for true statement.

1. Some gifted programs focus on less robust and relevant content than in the general classroom curriculum.

2. Because of the challenging nature of the CCSS, the needs of gifted students can be addressed in the inclusion classroom and coursework.

3. Considering the grade-by-grade sequence of each Common Core standard enables educators to accurately determine where the gifted student is on a continuum of learning.

4. Since there is enough challenge in the CCSS, we no longer need to be concerned about differentiation for gifted learners in the inclusion classroom/coursework.

5. Advanced content will need to be considered because some gifted learners will reach grade-level standards early.

6. Gifted education services should not be involved in CCSS, and instead should focus on thinking skills and alternative curriculum topics.

7. Considering the grade-by-grade sequence of CCSS informs acceleration practices for gifted learners.*

Gifted students need multiple pathways to meet the CCSS. That's why it is important for those who work in gifted education services or in general classrooms that include gifted learners to be concerned about these standards. In particular, we need to remember:

- The majority of gifted learners are taught for most of their day in the inclusion classroom with a CCSS-based curriculum designed for typical learners. Not all gifted learners are proficient in all standards set for their grade level. Gifted learners represent a broad range of academic talent. They are often not equally talented in all academic areas. Thus, we need to avoid making generalizations about where gifted learners may be on a particular learning continuum of standards.

- Since not all students will progress through the standards at the same pace, preassessment and formative assessment are critical. These strategies inform teachers' planning related to where students are on the learning continuum as well as what's next for those who achieve goals early.

- Some gifted programs in the past have not provided robust curriculum experiences. Some intentionally chose curriculum topics outside those addressed in the inclusion classroom, thereby causing critics to question their relevancy. By building on or extending the CCSS, curriculum for the gifted is better able to provide relevant and substantiative content that goes above and beyond what would be appropriate for all learners.

_____
* Answers: 1, 3, 5, 7 are true; the rest are misconceptions.

- In times of school budget cuts, gifted services must demonstrate viability and relevance. To survive, gifted services must integrate and collaborate with general education.

The Common Core State Standards should be the point of departure for gifted curriculum.

CCSS and Characteristics of Gifted Learners

Again, not all programs and services for gifted learners have provided rich, significant, robust learning experiences for their students (see Chapter 4 on effective services for gifted learners). However, most have attempted to go beyond what the regular curriculum has offered in either content or processes.

Although much has been said about rigor and relevance of the Common Core State Standards for all students, CCSS should be the point of departure for all gifted curriculum, as well. We need to always be mindful of the learning differences of gifted students when we consider any new educational initiative. Remember the following general learning characteristics of gifted students that distinguish them from others:

Accelerated pace of learning. No more than two or three repetitions are needed for mastery (if they didn't know the material already!).

Intellectual curiosity. Students want to know more and know more deeply.

Drive to master in areas of high interest. Students have advanced and deeper knowledge of topics that may lie outside the grade-level curriculum.

Lack of alignment with grade-level curriculum in their area of interest or talent. Prior learning and/or accelerated pace of learning puts gifted learners ahead of their grade-level peers and curriculum.

Eagerness to engage in learning reflecting both depth and complexity. Students can readily see how what they are learning relates to content or concepts from other fields.

When considering new school initiatives, including the CCSS, educators need to think about whether the initiative supports, ignores, or undermines these general learning characteristics of gifted students. Is the curriculum differentiated in ways that reflect the learning differences of the gifted?

> Differentiation within the standards must be rigorous in every subject area.

The CCSS are aligned with expectations for success in college and the workplace; therefore, they are designed to stress rigor, depth, complexity, and coherence—all characteristic of appropriate learning experiences for gifted students. However, when working with the standards in your school and planning for the needs of gifted learners, keep the following considerations in mind. Differentiation within the standards must be rigorous in every subject area.

✓ There should be multiple pathways for gifted learners to attain the CCSS on an accelerated schedule.

✓ Teachers must be prepared to provide advanced content, skills, and processes for students who reach the CCSS early or who have attained them through prior learning.

✓ Assessments should be performance-based, which encourages more rigorous learning experiences than traditional paper/pencil assessments.

Responding to the Common Core

We recommend adhering to the following guidelines as you consider ways to adapt the standards for gifted learners:

1. Accelerate and streamline the standards to address the students' advanced pace of learning.

2. Combine less complex standards to create a more complex standard.

3. Add complexity and depth, and incorporate opportunities to create and innovate.

4. Use cross-disciplinary content and integrate standards from two or more disciplines. For example, CCSS English Language Arts (ELA) emphasize informational text. These standards can be incorporated into the nonfiction reading students are doing to build knowledge or understanding in any curriculum area.

Accelerate

Avoid holding back gifted students while you provide other students with the time, instruction, and support they need to meet a particular standard. Instead, enable gifted students to move on once they have met grade-level standards, or use the next grade-level standards as a guide when accelerating their learning.

Use preassessment to pace the sequence of CCSS. Because gifted students may have prior knowledge and can learn at a faster pace, it is even more critical that we rely on preassessments and formative assessments when planning instruction for these students. Preassessment helps us determine whether learners should be within the mainstream curriculum for some or all of the time.

If particular students demonstrate mastery of some but not all of the standards in a curriculum unit, consider whether the student should "loop out" of particular lessons. Unlike compacting, which replaces longer periods of instructional time with personalized learning experiences, looping is used over the short term, with instructional decisions being made on a day-to-day basis. Using looping as an instructional management strategy, students are with the teacher for whole-group instruction that involves content, processes, or skills they have not mastered. On days when the lesson focuses on content, skills, or processes that, based on the preassessment, they have already mastered, these students "loop out" of the lesson and day's assignment. During this time, the students either engage in a more complex application of the material or in enrichment, extension, or more in-depth tasks. Second, on days that gifted students engage in looping activities, they need to understand that the alternative activities they are doing are their primary work for the class period; it is not busywork. They are accountable for focused engagement with the tasks, and high-quality work is expected.

Tips for Looping Activities
The tasks should:

- replace direct instruction and the daily work or assignment
- provide next-level instruction, not more of the same
- reflect more in-depth or complex learning experiences
- be engaging and interesting
- be written specifically enough so students can proceed independently
- offer some short tasks that can be done in a class period as well as tasks that may require a couple of class periods to complete
- allow for quick reviews by the teacher

To find looping activities, review enrichment or extension materials or activities provided by your textbook publishers or found online or in teacher resource materials. For example, if a pre-assessment indicates that a student had strong prior knowledge of the fundamentals of geometry, first consider enrichment ideas or resources offered by the textbook publisher. Be sure to carefully examine the complexity of such tasks so the student is not simply doing more of an already mastered application.

Games focusing on next-level learning goals are always a popular looping choice for gifted students. If computers or tablets are available, consider using "cyber stations" with bookmarked Web pages, apps, or gaming software. Webquests are great online learning experiences (webquest.org) that could be used as tasks for students who have looped out of a lesson. Always consider meaningful activities that provide next-level learning. Looping tasks should never be busywork or worksheet packets.

If a student tests out of a significant number of learning goals in a unit, it may be more appropriate to offer the student a compacting contract. While looping moves students in and out of instruction on a day-by-day basis and alternative/replacement tasks are typically completed in a day, compacting provides a continuous block of independent work time. (Please refer to Chapter 2 for the specifics of compacting.)

Use formative assessment to determine student learning progress on a standard. The CCSS are written as learning progressions across the grades. They note how the skill or process appears in the current grade's application. However, teachers can also refer back to previous grades' applications as well as look forward to consider how the skill or process is used in subsequent grades. This provides guidance in acceleration. Keep in mind that gifted learners need fewer repetitions with the subject matter to master the learning. Plan for what to do when they are there early and other students need more time, instruction, or practice for mastery. Consider whether you will accelerate those students on to the next grade level's application of the standard. (Refer to Chapter 9 for more specifics on assessment.)

Use the Common Core State Standards to guide acceleration for gifted learners. Consider the following ELA CCSS:

Kindergarten
CCSS.ELA–Literacy RI.K.9
With prompting and support, identify the basic similarities in and differences between two texts on the same topic (e.g., in illustrations, descriptions, or procedures).

Grade One
CCSS.ELA–Literacy RI.1.9
Identify basic similarities in and differences between two texts on the same topic (e.g., in illustrations, descriptions, or procedures).

Grade Two
CCSS.ELA–Literacy RI.2.9
Compare and contrast the most important points presented by two texts on the same topic.

Reading across the three grade-level standards, teachers can clearly see what would be the next level of learning. If a kindergartner has accomplished the grade-level standard by identifying similarities and differences in text, the acceleration pathway becomes clear by examining the CCSS for grades one and two. Likewise, the pathway for accelerating informational text is laid out by reading across grades three, four, and five.

Grade Three
CCSS.ELA–Literacy.RL.3.6
Distinguish their own point of view from that of the narrator or those of the characters.

Grade Four
CCSS.ELA–Literacy.RL.4.6
Compare and contrast the point of view from which different stories are narrated, including the differences between first- and third-person narrations.

Grade Five
CCSS.ELA–Literacy.RL.5.6
Describe how a narrator's or speaker's point of view influences how events are described.

The CCSS provide clear direction related to next steps for students who would benefit from acceleration or who reach goals earlier than their grade-level peers. Using the example of informational text standards, the pathway from grade three (distinguish point of view) to grade five (describe how point of view influences how events are described) is clearly laid out. CCSS guide the teacher to meaningful next-level experiences, thereby ensuring that students are truly being challenged and accelerated rather than working on additional goals disconnected from the learning progressions established by the CCSS.

Combine

Combine less complex standards to create a more complex standard for gifted learners. In this way you telescope the CCSS, allowing students to move through the material at a pace that matches their individual needs. For example, combine the following CCSS on informational text:

CCSS.ELA–Literacy.RI.6.9
Compare and contrast one author's presentation of events with that of another (e.g., a memoir written by and a biography on the same person).

CCSS.ELA–Literacy.RI.7.9
Analyze how two or more authors writing about the same topic shape their presentations of key information by emphasizing different evidence or advancing different interpretations of facts.

When you combine these standards, you create a more complex standard: *Compare and contrast the presentation of events of two or more authors, considering differences in key information or evidence and how emphasis may result in different interpretations of facts.* Consider the ways in which telescoping several standards into a more complex and rigorous standard would provide acceleration for gifted learners.

Add Depth and Complexity

Consider the standard; then design more depth and complexity into student tasks. Gifted education expert and professor Sandra Kaplan designed a foundational model for increasing depth and complexity in learning for gifted students.[24] This model encourages students to actively engage with the content by acting as disciplinarians who work through issues and generate new thinking. Complexity engages students in critical thinking by deeply examining key concepts and multiple variables as well as synthesizing ideas within or across disciplines. You can use the following planning menus to incorporate more depth and complexity into tasks for gifted students as they work on the CCSS. (They are also included in the digital download. See page ix for more information.)

Use the CCSS to Increase Depth by . . .
- ✓ developing the specialized vocabulary of a field beyond simple academic terms
- ✓ determining essential attributes
- ✓ identifying factors or variables
- ✓ forming hypotheses
- ✓ proving or defending through evidence

---

[24] Kaplan, 1994.

✓ identifying recurring events, activities, or actions

✓ generating predictions

✓ establishing courses of action

✓ determining political or ethical effects

✓ judging influences

✓ examining differing ideas, viewpoints, or perspectives

✓ creating innovations based on data

✓ determining evidence to support ideas

✓ examining unanswered questions

✓ creating structures, hierarchies, or orders

✓ determining stated or unstated assumptions

✓ resolving dilemmas or controversies

✓ determining effects or consequences of actions

✓ developing theories or principles

✓ creating connections or establishing interrelationships

Example: If we apply this strategy to CCSS.ELA–Literacy.RL.4.2 "Determine a theme of a story, drama, or poem from details in the text; summarize the text" and use the depth menu item of "proving or defending through evidence," a student task becomes "Provide evidence to support the theme of good and evil in *Snow White* or *Sleeping Beauty.*"

Use the CCSS to Increase Complexity by . . .

✓ examining past, present, and future

✓ determining multiple variables

✓ examining change over time

✓ evaluating different perspectives, viewpoints, or positions

✓ critically examining opposing viewpoints

✓ engaging in more abstract applications

✓ connecting ideas to another field or discipline

Example: To increase the complexity of CCSS.ELA–Literacy.RL.4.3 "Describe in depth a character, setting, or event in a story or drama, drawing

on specific details in the text (e.g., a character's thoughts, words, or actions)," using the complexity menu item "examining change over time," the student task becomes "Consider the ways in which Snow White changed over time. Use specific details from the text (e.g., the character's thoughts, words, or actions) to describe how she changed from the beginning to the end of the story."

Integrate

Use cross-disciplinary content and integrate standards from two or more disciplines. For example, students in seventh-grade CCSS math studying ratios and proportional relationships are asked to "identify the constant of proportionality (unit rate) in tables, graphs, equations, diagrams, and verbal descriptions of proportional relationships" (CCSS.Math.Content.7.RP.A.2b). In grade seven science standards in Minnesota, students "determine and use appropriate safety procedures, tools, measurements, graphs and mathematical analyses to describe and investigate natural and designed systems in a life science context." (7.1.3.4.2). If we integrate this math standard with this state science standard, then students will use online data sets to analyze, compare, and contrast wildlife populations in different regions of Minnesota and produce graphs, diagrams, or equations to share their conclusions.

Considerations in Reframing Curriculum for Gifted Students

In what ways might the Common Core State Standards impact curriculum for gifted learners?

As we develop specialized curriculum for send-out programs, specialized courses, or schools for gifted learners, we need to critically examine the CCSS and build from these standards. Following are suggested steps in integrating CCSS into curriculum for gifted students:

1. Start with the CCSS standards.

2. Consider the grade-by-grade sequence of CCSS standards as it informs acceleration practices.

3. Combine or redesign standards to reflect greater complexity and/or depth.

4. Develop differentiated tasks or products to work on each standard.

5. Develop performance assessments that reflect authentic applications of CCSS.

The Common Core State Standards and Gifted Education Services

The CCSS also have implications for the services we offer gifted learners. Following are recommendations for addressing the CCSS within gifted education services.

In the Inclusion Classroom or Section of a Course

Do not limit learning to the foundational expectations established by the CCSS, which are too limited for gifted students. Instead, be sure to:

✓ Use preassessment to plan for differentiation.

✓ Consider acceleration as appropriate to the students' needs and guided by the CCSS grade-by-grade sequence.

✓ Use formative assessment to adjust the pace of instruction.

✓ Use flexible grouping to address readiness differences.

✓ Match students to materials and resources based on their readiness needs.

✓ Engage students in progressively more complex learning.

✓ Commit to each student's continual learning progress.

In Cluster Classrooms

Adhere to the inclusion classroom elements outlined above, and:

✓ Regularly group and regroup gifted students in a variety of ways so they can interact with intellectual peers as well as those with similar talents, interests, and readiness needs.

In Send-Out Programs

In programs that pull students out of the inclusion classroom, be sure to:

✓ Consider how your program may extend and advance learning experiences in CCSS.

✓ Offer CCSS experiences that will take students into greater depth and complexity as well as engage them in both critical and creative thinking.

In Self-Contained Gifted Classrooms or Specialized Courses

Here you will have greater flexibility to:

✓ Use preassessment and formative assessment to carefully monitor the students' progress in the CCSS.

✓ Adjust the pace of instruction based on assessment results.

✓ Consider acceleration guided by the grade-by-grade sequence provided by the CCSS.

✓ Consider standards beyond students' grade level.

✓ Provide a qualitatively different experience with the CCSS than would occur in an inclusion classroom or section of a course.

As educators of the gifted, we need to consider how to best use the Common Core State Standards or provincial standards in serving the unique needs of gifted students. We must not lose sight of the distinct learning differences of the gifted but rather use these differences as a lens to critically examine how the standards are being implemented in our schools. It's also important that we become involved in developing our school's implementation plan for CCSS or provincial standards so we can advocate for the needs of gifted students. We need to use critical elements of the CCSS, such as the grade-by-grade standards sequence, to promote practices such as acceleration for gifted learners. And, finally, through our programs and services, we need to ensure that gifted students are engaged in learning experiences that add depth and complexity to the CCSS or provincial standards.

Chapter Summary

In today's classrooms, the Common Core State Standards provide direction for the curriculum in most U.S. states, and Canada has a similar provincial framework for planning learning experiences for students. Teachers need to remember that CCSS are not suggesting that all students march through the standards in lock step, nor do they ignore that some students will master the standards at a different pace or in a different manner. Differentiating for gifted learners within the context of the CCSS requires teachers to accelerate the instructional pace, build activities that require students to use sophisticated levels of complex thinking, and encourage them to dig more deeply into curriculum topics. The gifted learner's capacity to process information efficiently requires this type of differentiation. Failing to provide this type of learning can result in underperforming, unmotivated, and disengaged students. Beyond the loss of student potential, we also lose human capital to further our knowledge into the twenty-first century.

It's important that we become involved in developing our school's implementation plan for CCSS so we can advocate for the needs of gifted students.

Chapter 4

Defensible Programs and Services

Quality educational programs take into account the varied degrees of learner differences and opportunities. In most cases, school districts offer a wide range of services for students who need academic supports, as mandated by federal and state/provincial laws and regulations. In other cases, the educational support systems and structures for gifted students are not mandated or reinforced by state/provincial or federal rule or law. Therefore, districts and states/provinces must use their own resources to provide equitable services and programs for these students and to provide differentiation that addresses their diverse needs.

> All students require a spectrum of services that address their varying needs and provide significant differentiation.

What is best for gifted students is what is best for all students: a spectrum of services that address their varying needs and provide significant differentiation of content, process, and product in response to their diverse needs. The National Association for Gifted Children's Gifted Education Programming Standards recommends "students with gifts and talents participate in a variety of evidence-based programming options that enhance performance in cognitive and affective areas."[25] This chapter will outline how school systems can provide services, programs, and options for all gifted students that can be differentiated to help learners reach their full potential at every grade level.

But first, it's important to understand the traits and needs of gifted children at different ages. While this chapter is not intended to develop an identification protocol, identification procedures and measures must mirror the program design, and the program design must recognize the various ways that giftedness, talent, and creativity are represented in students.

General Characteristics of Gifted Elementary Students

Developmentally, students at this age are learning about themselves and their world. According to Jean Piaget's theory of cognitive development, elementary students are developing and using language to think about things and events in past, present, and future terms—processes associated with the more sophisticated development of the prefrontal cortex.[26] They are learning to understand and contextualize abstract ideas, make rational judgments, ask questions, and explain their thought process.

Research suggests that the following characteristics are common among primary gifted children:[27]

- use and understanding of elaborate language
- drawing recognizable pictures
- development of early writing skills
- reading fluently by age four
- independence in learning new things

---

[25] NAGC, 2011.

[26] Piaget, 1937/1954.
[27] Sternberg and Zhang, 1995; Jackson, 2000; PerLath, et al., 2000.

- numeracy (understanding number relationships)
- a sense of task completion

Keep in mind that the general characteristics of giftedness (page 39) also apply to primary gifted children. Additionally, these characteristics should be significantly stronger in gifted children than their same-age peers.

When identifying primary-grade gifted students from culturally, linguistically, and economically diverse backgrounds, a broader range of identifiers should be used. Some CLED (culturally, linguistically, or economically diverse) students may not have had enriching experiences prior to coming to school. Consider using more qualitative characteristics as a way to expand the number of students from underrepresented populations into your gifted programs.

The Social Emotional Needs of Gifted Elementary Children

There have been conflicting views on the general social and emotional adjustments of gifted children. Some suggest that gifted students are at greater risk for depression, suicide, or feelings of "not fitting in." Others argue that little research supports that gifted children are socially and emotionally maladjusted.[28] Whether or not this is an issue, what can promote the positive social and emotional development of gifted children? Family, community, and educational environments that support the child's need for rigorous and complex learning experiences as well as social learning. Social learning refers to how children learn socially appropriate behaviors from those around them. In other words, we learn how to get along with others by observing how the people around us get along.

In the case of gifted elementary children, they may be the only ones who think as they do in their early learning experiences. As a result, they may either self-isolate from their classmates or be shunned by their peers because they think, act, and talk differently. This is one of the reasons young gifted children prefer to spend time with

adults or older children. Yet when gifted children do not interact with their same-age peers, they may fail to develop healthy social skills or may develop socially in asynchronous ways that are not age-appropriate (for example, they may use sophisticated humor or sarcasm that other children may find hurtful).

As for the emotional development of gifted children, again, research offers little evidence to suggest they are less well-adjusted than their same-age peers. However, it is widely accepted that gifted children may have asynchronous or uneven development here as well, having difficulty managing complex emotions based on their worldviews. In some cases, elementary children with advanced intellectual development may want to solve complex world issues (such as world hunger) but not have the emotional maturity to understand their limitations.

Many school districts do not identify gifted children prior to third grade. In situations where districts are unable to provide gifted services for primary children, we strongly recommend that students who demonstrate above average or superior intellectual behaviors be grouped together at least part of their day. This allows the students with similar intellectual abilities to practice strategies for social learning and emotional development. Such a grouping process can be done either within the inclusion classroom or through a pull-out programming structure (described later in this chapter). During these times, students should be coached on how to develop healthy social relationships and appropriate emotional responses. Teachers should model social strategies and hold students accountable for using appropriate language and interactions to communicate effectively.

General Characteristics of Gifted Secondary Students

The adolescent years (grades six to twelve, ages eleven to eighteen) are a unique and sometimes confusing time for students who are gifted. Adolescence in general is considered the time of

---

[28] Neihart, 1999; Moon, 2004.

transition biologically, socially, and cognitively. Biologically, children are developing into adults by entering puberty. Tremendous physical and emotional changes are happening within their bodies. During this period children are trying to find their fit within a world that often doesn't seem to fit them. However, adolescence is a period in life that is essential to human development and success is based on learning how to make social adjustments.

Cognitively, the adolescent brain is also changing during this time. In a process called neural circuit refinement, the brain is pruning unused neural connections and strengthening more heavily used connections, predominantly in the prefrontal cortex (the brain region of executive functioning). As a result, the way that students approach learning evolves during this period and becomes more sophisticated. This evolution signals a shift in the way students like to learn and what they will pay attention to.

Middle School Years (Grades 6–9)

Typically, the middle school years are when students move from the holistic nature of an elementary program to separate classes with multiple teachers. These transitional years can be difficult on all students, not just the gifted child. Learning how to manage multiple projects, several homework assignments, different teaching styles, and diverse learning environments is critical during the middle school years. Because of the nature of the transitional years, the program designs we recommend place a greater emphasis on learning how to become more self-regulated, develop organizational strategies, and manage deadlines.

The High School Years (Grades 9–12)

The beginning of high school marks entry into another critical transitional period. In some cases, the middle school years are nurturing, helping students develop a sense of self, learn to work with others, and transition out of the holistic nature of elementary school. When students enter the high school setting, the complexity of managing classwork, teacher differences, and perhaps

a larger network of peers grows exponentially. In addition, the high school years set the tone for postsecondary schooling. Therefore, in the program design for high school we emphasize collaboration, postsecondary schooling, and career development as well as scholarly development.

The cognitive development and social awareness of adolescents who are gifted is seen as more sophisticated and intricate than that of their peers. In general, these learners have an easier time mastering complex operations, thinking dialectically (finding more than one right answer), and being open-minded.

Combine the natural awkwardness of adolescence with the complexity of giftedness, and you may find students who struggle during this period of life to a greater degree. The intensities of social mindfulness, cognitive needs, personal awareness, identity development, existential consciousness, and goal attainment profoundly affect their daily lives. Therefore, it is essential that any program for gifted adolescents include a strong personal and social component. Students who are able to succeed in the twenty-first century need to be willing and able to interact and work with others (generally known as soft skills), as well as be capable of critically analyzing information and creating new ideas. Since secondary students are preparing for their future beyond the K–12 setting, programming for gifted adolescents should include more sophisticated levels of the soft skills as well as deep levels of learning within content areas.

> It is essential that any program for gifted adolescents include a strong personal and social component.

Typically, elementary programs for gifted children focus on developing talents and learning techniques. Secondary programs for gifted teens focus on developing deep content knowledge, sophisticated learning techniques, and effective communication and collaboration skills.

◎ General Characteristics of Gifted Learners

"Typical" Characterisitics of Gifted Learners

- strong desire to learn
- interested in experimenting and doing things differently
- wide range of interests
- sense of wonder
- willingness to take intellectual risks
- thrive in problem situations; select more difficult tasks
- ability to retain a great deal of information
- ability to learn/acquire skills more quickly and with less practice
- self-initiating: pursue individual interests
- ask extensive or unusual questions
- unusually large vocabulary for age
- ability to read earlier than age mates
- greater comprehension of the subtleties of language
- keen powers of observation
- highly developed curiosity and limitless supply of questions
- longer attention span, persistence, and intense concentration
- tendency to put ideas or things together in ways that are unusual and not obvious
- generate alternatives or suggest several directions; exhibit flexible thinking
- visualize relationships between disparate data or concepts
- perceptually open to environment; employ all senses in new/unfamiliar settings
- show little patience for routine procedures and drills
- use imagination
- reveal originality in oral and other forms of expression (such as music, dance, drama, drawing, playing)
- elaborate well
- high degree of common sense
- may mature at different rates than age peers (asynchrony)
- leadership abilities
- sensitivity toward self and others
- unusual sense of humor

Negative Behaviors of Gifted Learners

- obstinacy
- disruptiveness
- inferior/careless work
- failure to follow directions
- underachievement/nonproductive
- disinterested in skills development
- lack effort skills
- antisocial demeanor
- impertinence
- emotional immaturity
- hide ability in order to "fit in"
- over-involvement
- lack of judgment
- lack of strategies to deal with failure
- poor study habits
- disorganized
- lack problem-solving skills
- egotistical
- arrogant
- impatient with others

What Happens When Needs Are Not Met

- lower total test scores
- inferior student performance
- impertinence
- disruptiveness
- underachievement/nonproductive
- parent pressures
- depression
- insecurity
- loss of social capital
- loss of academic confidence

Gifted Programming Models

Let's begin by defining what we mean by a "program"; this refers to the spectrum of services offered to students based on their academic and social/emotional needs. A spectrum of services is best defined as the specific options for students to enhance and expand their abilities and talents. Services for gifted students are not limited to one type, but offer a wide assortment of services, ranging from individual to whole group, with a focus on talent, academic, and social/emotional development. The elements most critical to a defensible, quality program for gifted students are (1) staff that is prepared to meet these students' needs; (2) sustainable financial resources to accomplish the program goals; and (3) political, administrative, parental, and community support to maintain the programs for all students even in hard/lean financial times. Programs for gifted students should not reside outside the models used in other parts of the school district.

To create a comprehensive design for a gifted program, we suggest using one or more of three agreeable and prominent programming models: the Response to Intervention Model (RtI), George Betts's Autonomous Learner Model (ALM), and Moon and Dixon's Holistic Development Framework (HDF). We also include our own model, the Progressive Program Model (PPM), which incorporates elements from the other three. It is important to remember that in program design for gifted students, we must not only address their academic development but also cultivate the healthy development and nurturing of their social and emotional characteristics. All of these models provide an effective structure for meeting the academic, social, and emotional needs of gifted students.

The Response to Intervention Model

One popular district-wide academic and behavioral support programming model is Response to Intervention/Instruction. Essentially, the RtI model is a systemic process that:

- uses scientific, research-based instruction and interventions
- is based on the continuous measuring and monitoring of student achievement
- involves collaborative decision making based on data

The RtI model is a three-tier progressive method of intervening when students need more intensive instruction and/or behavioral support, including:

1. Core curriculum and instruction for all students within the general classroom
2. Secondary supports for some students who have not shown proficiency in tier 1
3. Tertiary supports for students who require more intensive intervention or focused instruction beyond tier 2

While RtI was initially conceived as a model for addressing the needs of students in special education, some now view the model as a way to ensure *all* students' needs are being recognized and met—including the academic needs and behavioral difficulties of gifted learners.

We believe that by using the RtI model with gifted students, a school or district systemically implements and sustains efforts to monitor learning progress and behavioral needs, as well as provides access to effective differentiated curriculum and instructional practices. All students benefit when there is:

- early recognition of potential or talents
- universal guidance and protocol for delivering quality learning and behavioral interventions
- provisions for tiered supports or scaffolds to higher levels of learning
- dynamic ongoing assessments that inform instruction and curriculum implementation
- collaborative planning with educators and parents/caregivers to meet the needs of individual children

Ultimately, the focus of RtI is on *early intervention*—the early provision of services that build on students' strengths and address their learning needs.[29]

Adapting the RTI Framework for Gifted Services

Some gifted programs have begun to use the RtI structure for addressing different levels of gifted service for students. **Figure 4.1** summarizes how the RtI framework can be used in gifted education.

As in the original framework, services are focused on three tiers divided into two areas of intervention: academic and behavioral. Gifted students may be placed at any one of three tiers

[29] Coleman and Hughes, 2009.

of the academic or behavioral interventions. Classroom differentiation reflects tier 1 interventions. If issues are not resolved through classroom interventions, students may move to tier 2. Tier 2 strategies include using small groups and more intensive instruction that is reflective of flexible instructional groups and tiered assignments. If students do not adequately respond to the tier 2 interventions, the special education referral and due process procedures are initiated in tier 3. At this point specific individual modifications, accommodations, or adaptations may be recommended. (*Please note:* Services are cumulative at the elementary level; if students are at tier 3, they also are given tier 1 and 2 services.)

Figure 4.1: RTI Framework Adapted*

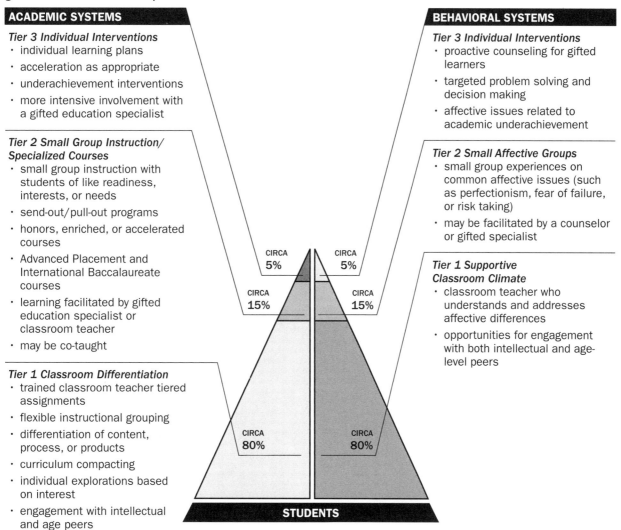

ACADEMIC SYSTEMS

Tier 3 Individual Interventions
- individual learning plans
- acceleration as appropriate
- underachievement interventions
- more intensive involvement with a gifted education specialist

Tier 2 Small Group Instruction/ Specialized Courses
- small group instruction with students of like readiness, interests, or needs
- send-out/pull-out programs
- honors, enriched, or accelerated courses
- Advanced Placement and International Baccalaureate courses
- learning facilitated by gifted education specialist or classroom teacher
- may be co-taught

Tier 1 Classroom Differentiation
- trained classroom teacher tiered assignments
- flexible instructional grouping
- differentiation of content, process, or products
- curriculum compacting
- individual explorations based on interest
- engagement with intellectual and age peers

BEHAVIORAL SYSTEMS

Tier 3 Individual Interventions
- proactive counseling for gifted learners
- targeted problem solving and decision making
- affective issues related to academic underachievement

Tier 2 Small Affective Groups
- small group experiences on common affective issues (such as perfectionism, fear of failure, or risk taking)
- may be facilitated by a counselor or gifted specialist

Tier 1 Supportive Classroom Climate
- classroom teacher who understands and addresses affective differences
- opportunities for engagement with both intellectual and age-level peers

CIRCA 5%   CIRCA 5%
CIRCA 15%   CIRCA 15%
CIRCA 80%   CIRCA 80%

STUDENTS

* National Association of State Directors of Special Education, 2004.

Following are specific recommendations for intervening at each of the three levels on both sides (academic and behavioral) of the RtI pyramid. Keep in mind that the RtI model defines the person responsible for providing the intervention rather than the suggested level of programming. Note that as the student progresses from tier 1 to tier 3, the responsibility shifts from the classroom teacher (tier 1) to a gifted education specialist.

Three Tiers of Academic Interventions

At tier 1 instruction, students' needs are addressed by a classroom teacher trained in differentiation for gifted learners. At this level, you should use tiered assignments and flexible instructional grouping as well as strategies like compacting curriculum and individual explorations of topics of interest, as necessary and appropriate. In addition, consider and differentiate content, process, or products as appropriate to students' needs. In this tier, ensure that students have opportunities to engage with both intellectual and same-age peers in the inclusion classroom setting. At both the elementary and secondary levels, it's appropriate to cluster gifted learners within the general classrooms at this tier.

Students who need more intensive interventions are offered tier 1 and tier 2 services. At this level, gifted learners engage in small group learning experiences with other gifted learners. Curriculum topics and instruction should reflect best practices in gifted education.

Specialized courses—including accelerated, enriched, or honors courses as well as Advanced Placement and International Baccalaureate curriculum—would also be considered tier 2 services. At the secondary level, when gifted students are placed in specialized courses, these tier 2 services take the place of a tier 1 inclusion classroom or course.

Tier 2 experiences may be facilitated by the classroom teacher or a gifted education specialist. Classroom teachers and gifted education specialists may also co-teach tier 2 services. (See Chapter 7 for more information about co-teaching.)

Finally at the third tier of instructional interventions, gifted students receive tier 1 (unless they are in advanced, accelerated, AP, or IB courses) and tier 2 services, and they engage in individual learning plans based on their distinct learning needs. Typically, a gifted education specialist works with the students, parents, and the classroom teacher in determining student needs and developing an appropriate learning plan. These plans may include acceleration.

In addition, gifted students who are academically underachieving engage in problem finding and targeted work on their underlying achievement issues. Plans are developed to break their school failure cycle through appropriate goal setting.

Three Tiers of Behavioral Interventions

The behavior side of the RtI triangle addresses affective differences of gifted learners. Here students are placed on a particular level of service based on their affective needs. Gifted students on tier 1 work with classroom teachers who understand their affective differences. They have opportunities to learn with both intellectual and same-age peers, a process which builds acceptance and understanding.

Placed at tier 2, students participate in small group sessions focusing on the affective issues of gifted learners. Topics for these sessions may include perfectionism, stress, isolation, and fear of failure. These sessions may be facilitated by a gifted specialist or a school counselor.

At tier 3, proactive counseling is offered. Individual interventions may include targeted problem solving and decision making related to issues the student encounters in school. Gifted students who are academically underachieving may work directly on the affective issues underlying their school performance.

The Autonomous Learner Model

The Autonomous Learner Model (ALM) emphasizes the cognitive, social, and physical development of the individual. The goal of the model is to "facilitate the growth of students as independent, self-directed learners, with the development of skills, concepts, and positive attitudes within the cognitive, emotional, social and physical

Figure 4.2: Autonomous Learner Model*

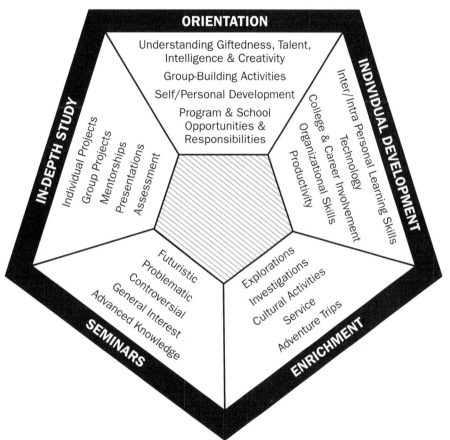

* Betts and Kercher, 1999. Reprinted with permission from George Betts.

domains."[30] The model works to develop autonomous learners from the very basics of identifying the self as a gifted learner to the more complex self-directed learning experiences. (See **Figure 4.2**.)

While the ALM was initially designed as a program for secondary classrooms, it was later revised to encompass grades K–12. The major strength of this model is that it helps all people who work with the gifted child to understand the unique characteristics of giftedness. Other positive characteristics of the ALM are that students:

- pursue in-depth opportunities in an area of interest
- work with mentors in multiple content areas
- learn to become self-directed in their learning
- develop a healthy sense of self

[30] Betts and Kercher, 1999.

The Holistic Development Framework

In the Holistic Development Framework (HDF), programming is framed around the needs of the whole child, as well as the needs of the gifted learner. The HDF is a balanced approach that addresses the needs of gifted students through the cognitive, personal, and social dimensions (see **Figure 4.3** on page 44).

The cognitive dimension of the HDF directs learning toward specific areas of giftedness. In most cases, during the elementary years students are said to be more "globally" gifted. Gifted students' strengths are typically in the areas of reading and arithmetic, the main content areas of the elementary school years. As gifted children transition into adolescence, their specific aptitudes become more apparent and may predict differences in future schooling pathways and career options. More sophisticated methods of instruction are now required along with more

Figure 4.3: Holistic Development Framework*

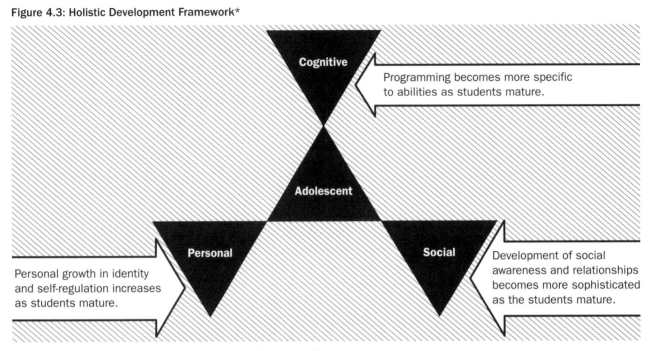

* Moon and Dixon, eds., 2006. Reprinted with permission from Prufrock Press.

complex material and challenging coursework. At this point, students will require more freedom in choosing learning topics as well as more authentic experiences, tasks, problems, and ultimately products. The HDF model also takes into account the ways students like to learn information and perform.

Life choices and decisions for gifted students may be more complex than that of the general population. Therefore, when it comes to personal development, it's important that gifted students learn skills in self-regulation, self-efficacy, and healthy well-being. Instruction on the personal dimension should also focus on accepting oneself as gifted and on growing as a person.

Moving out from the personal dimension is the social dimension. As Sidney Moon and Felicia Dixon suggest, the child's ability to build and maintain strong social relationships may facilitate or inhibit the development of talent, especially during adolescence. Gifted students who learn to negotiate complex social situations "enjoy higher levels of well-being and success in school than their peers who experience social alienation or hide their talents in order to be accepted and popular."[31] Through the social

dimension students learn social skills, including how to develop supportive friendships, work on a team, collaborate, and communicate effectively. Strong social skills are essential for success in the twenty-first century.

The Progressive Program Model

The Progressive Program Model (PPM) is our own model. Its foundations come from both the ALM and HDF, and it also incorporates the RtI three-tiered approach. Please keep in mind that while the RtI approach signifies who does the intervention at each level, the PPM defines the intensity of service at each level. In the PPM (see **Figure 4.4**), the three dimensions of *cognitive*, *personal/emotional*, and *social* are differentiated into three tiers of *all, some,* and *few*. The all/some/few method relates to the numbers of students served at each tier. In the transformation from the bottom of the pyramid to the top, note how the tiers of the cognitive dimension are differentiated from simple infused programming to individualized sophisticated specialty programming. In the personal dimension, the methodology moves from group orientation to individual focus. The social dimension shifts from broad social awareness

---

[31] Moon and Dixon, eds., 2006.

Figure 4.4: Progressive Program Model

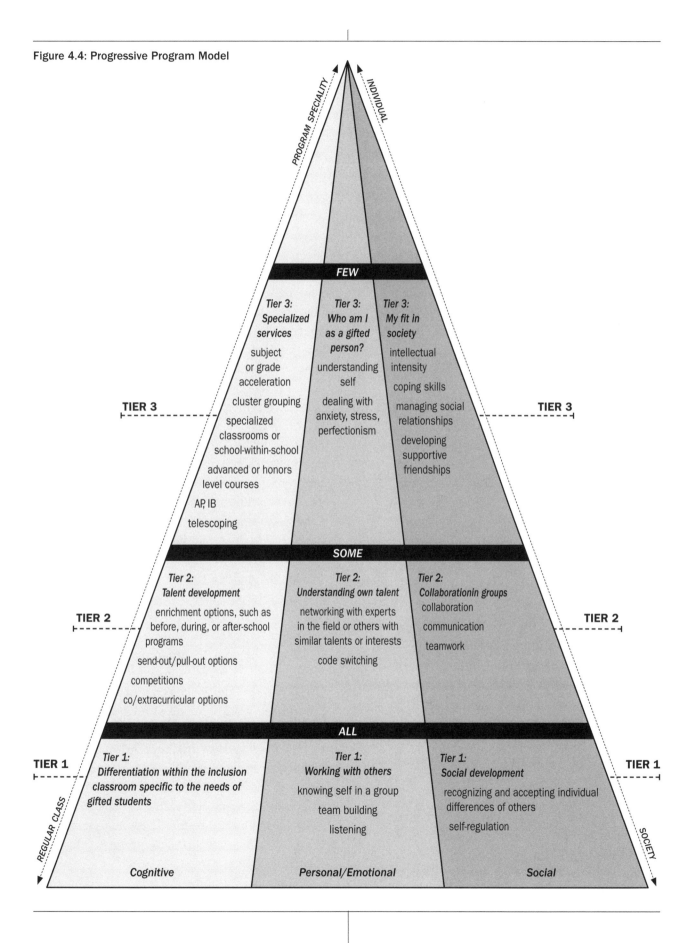

FEW

SOME

ALL

PROGRAM SPECIALITY

INDIVIDUAL

REGULAR CLASS

SOCIETY

TIER 3

TIER 3

Tier 3:
Specialized
services

subject
or grade
acceleration

cluster grouping

specialized
classrooms or
school-within-school

advanced or honors
level courses

AP, IB

telescoping

Tier 3:
Who am I
as a gifted
person?

understanding
self

dealing with
anxiety, stress,
perfectionism

Tier 3:
My fit in
society

intellectual
intensity

coping skills

managing social
relationships

developing
supportive
friendships

TIER 2

TIER 2

Tier 2:
Talent development

enrichment options, such as
before, during, or after-school
programs

send-out/pull-out options

competitions

co/extracurricular options

Tier 2:
Understanding own talent

networking with experts
in the field or others with
similar talents or interests

code switching

Tier 2:
Collaborationin groups
collaboration

communication

teamwork

TIER 1

TIER 1

Tier 1:
Differentiation within the inclusion
classroom specific to the needs of
gifted students

Tier 1:
Working with others

knowing self in a group

team building

listening

Tier 1:
Social development

recognizing and accepting individual
differences of others

self-regulation

Cognitive

Personal/Emotional

Social

to explicit character development of the gifted learner.

At the **elementary level** it, the PPM should include three main objectives:

1. Support and advance identified gifted learners.
2. Discover and uncover the gifts and talents of students underrepresented in gifted programs, specifically culturally, linguistically, and economically diverse (CLED) students.
3. Develop the talents and creativity of all learners.

The program model at the **secondary level** should coordinate with the elementary program by including similar main objectives:

1. Support and advance identified gifted learners into postsecondary educational options and career opportunities.
2. Discover and uncover the gifts and talents of all students, especially those underrepresented in gifted programs, such as CLED students and twice-exceptional students (2E).
3. Develop the talents and creativity of all learners.

> In this program design, the tiers of services are designed to uncover/discover latent talent.

The PPM is differentiated from the most inclusive to the most complex levels of services. Based on the model's three objectives, all students should have access to and be involved in experiences that help them develop their talents. Teachers, administrators, and district leaders should be continually looking for students from traditionally underrepresented populations, such as students from diverse backgrounds and those who live in poverty, to include in gifted services, as appropriate. In this program design, the tiers of services are designed to uncover/discover latent talent. When we address students' talent areas, we encourage and nurture students into more advanced classes in upper-elementary school and beyond.

To align with both elementary and secondary programs, use the same all/some/few structure. The focus of the program will differ slightly at each level, from elementary to secondary. For example, the elementary tiers focus on recognizing students' potential, exposing them to numerous talent areas, and building an awareness of giftedness; the secondary level program focuses on developing more specific talents and career pathways along with personal development as social beings and scholars.

The PPM: Cognitive Dimension

The highest tier of the model's cognitive dimension (see the left face of the pyramid, **Figure 4.4**) addresses the specific needs of gifted students. The services provided for these students increase the pace, depth, and complexity of instruction and content, requiring the student to develop independent learning skills.

Most models of academic services for gifted students address the needs of elementary students. In our model, we address elementary programs as well as spell out specific options at the secondary level. Research on secondary level programs for gifted students is relatively nonexistent. In most middle schools and high schools across the United States, Pre-Advanced Placement and Advanced Placement (AP) programs, International Baccalaureate (IB), and advanced/honors level courses are considered programs for gifted students.

While AP and IB programs are exceptional programs that have consistency around the United States—and in the case of IB consistency around the world—for all students, they do not sufficiently address the broad exceptionalities of gifted high school students. Advanced/honors level courses are not based on a consistent curriculum design or instructional pedagogy, thus calling to question the validity of such courses in meeting the needs of gifted secondary students. More on honors level programming is offered in the next chapter.

The Association for Middle Level Education (AMLE), in its essential attributes of educating young adolescents,[32] strongly recommends that curriculum, instruction, and assessment for general middle years education be challenging, engaging, relevant, and meaningful. For gifted learners and in identifying/nurturing talent, this aspect of education during the middle years can be differentiated through PPM.

As with the program models used in the elementary and middle school years, AP, IB, and advanced/honors level courses are a part of the spectrum of services offered to students at the secondary level. Keep in mind that AP, IB, and many advanced/honors level courses may be open to all students. Open-enrollment courses can be considered at tier 2 on the spectrum of service. To be considered for the third tier of service, courses must have specific content and process differentiation to fit within the range of courses for gifted students.

Services offered to gifted students at the third tier of service must:

- employ sophisticated levels of complex thinking
- provide deep content that explores unique world issues
- offer acceleration of content and materials
- promote interdisciplinary study
- infuse metacognitive reflections (promoting awareness of one's thinking process)
- explore topics of study outside of traditional school subjects
- offer mentorships or access to experts in the field
- require the completion of self-selected or self-study options

The PPM: Personal/Emotional and Social Dimensions

Any program model that is to serve gifted students effectively must include an academic dimension as well as personal/emotional and social dimensions. It's essential that gifted students develop their own personal identity, build emotional strength, and learn how to negotiate the social landscape. Therefore, programs that aim

to nurture and help develop gifted students must include a scaffolding of the personal/emotional and social domains. Alongside the academic dimension of the PPM are the personal dimension (see the center face of the pyramid, **Figure 4.4**) and the social dimension (see the right face).

In some cases, personal/emotional and social development is appropriate for all students. Similar to the academic dimension, there is a progression from general to specific requirements necessary for meeting the needs of gifted students. Also as with the academic services, the personal and social service options are differentiated to include personal identity development as well as social competence from general group dynamics to the specific needs of gifted students.

> Any program model that is to serve gifted students must include a personal/emotional and social dimension.

Personal identity development should include efforts to help students increase:

- a sense of personal worth and traits
- a sense of personal freedom
- skills for dealing with nervous symptoms, such as:
  - bad dreams
  - nail biting
  - stress
  - cutting
  - suicidal ideation
  - depression
- knowledge of social skills versus antisocial behaviors
- school relations:
  - appropriate classroom/school behaviors
  - strategies for avoiding or curtailing underachievement
  - strategies for building effective relationships with parents and significant adults
  - career pathways and guidance

---

[32] AMLE, 2010.

Social competency includes:

- skills for relationship building
- strategies for dealing with peer pressure
- strong self-regulation skills to deal with more complex work levels, schedules, and personal management
- strong self-efficacy skills to understand strengths/weaknesses, resist sociocultural stereotyping, and develop resilience in adversity
- awareness of personal traits and skills for communicating and collaborating with others

PPM Cognitive Dimension, Tier 1 (ALL): Developing the Talents of Every Student

The least complex tier of services includes the options that are the most inclusive and appropriate for all students. Services are addressed in the inclusion classroom by differentiating the content, process, and product. The options incorporate student interests, respect the diversity of learning profiles, and pay attention to readiness for more advanced levels of materials and actions.

As in the elementary level of the program, middle school and high school general education classrooms should allow for enrichment, extension, and enhancements (E3) of the curriculum. Another way to address the needs of all students in talent development is by offering exploratory or elective classes, such as career and technical education; family and consumer sciences; science, technology, engineering, and math (STEM)/ (STEAM—including art, music, theater); physical education; and world languages. Use these general exploration or elective courses to expose students to the vast array of career opportunities within each discipline as well as to introduce them to new information and ways of learning.

Classroom Enrichments: Focus the Topic

Enrichment means focusing on a specific component of a topic. When studying the solar system, for example, students involved in an enrichment activity would concentrate on a specific planet or

items within the solar system, such as meteors or meteorites. See the list of E3 ideas, pages 49–51.

Classroom Extensions: Broaden the Topic

While enrichment activities involve narrowing in on a topic, extension activities take the topic and expand it to the larger discipline. In this case, students studying the solar system would extend the topic to the discipline of astronomy. Students might investigate famous astronomers or study what astronomers do. By broadening the topic in this way, the learning extends beyond the unit of study to the discipline or career options. Students would then report their findings throughout the unit of study to continually incorporate the extension with the class time. See the list of E3 ideas, pages 49–51.

> While enrichment activities involve narrowing in on a topic, extension activities take the topic and expand it to the larger discipline.

Classroom Enhancements: Interrelate the Topic

Enhancements take the concept embedded within the unit of study and expand it. For instance, the solar system unit is focused on the concept of systems. This unit could be enhanced by interconnecting the idea of systems. Students would look for other systems and then compare and contrast those systems to the solar system. See the list of E3 ideas, pages 49–51.

Other general options within the classroom for differentiating learning experiences for gifted students:

- tiered assignments
- open-ended questioning
- expert guest speakers
- academic contests and competitions
- compacting
- contracts
- anchor activities
- small group activities

Figure 4.5: E3 Examples

Subject	Unit	Enrichment	Extension	Enhancement
ELA	Mythology	Determine the influence the Titans had on humans in ancient Greek period.	Identify a common influence of mythology in art through the ages.	Myths vs. theories. In what ways might theories be glorified myths?
ELA	"The Raven"	Compare the events in the poem with the author's life.	Study how gothic literature reveals psychological disorders among creative people.	Analyze how people interpret psychological issues over time.
ELA	Novel study: *Freak the Mighty*	Investigate patterns of the use of the death penalty and prison sentences across the United States.	How might parole be truly viable? Justify the ethical use of the death penalty.	List reasons why prisoners hurt the economy more while in prison or after release.
ELA	Mythology	Research Greek gods and the myths associated with the gods.	Interpret how the Greek culture impacted the development of Greek mythology.	Analyze Greek linguistics and show its connection to the English language.
ELA	*A Lesson Before Dying*	Study the Jim Crow–era laws in your state or other forms of racial discrimination in your province.	Define how racial issues have influenced government actions.	Create a campaign that seeks to right injustice.
ELA	Figurative language	Study metaphors and similes.	Study how the poem "La Muralla" by Nicolas Guillen tells us about Cuban social injustice.	How does poetry reflect the life and times of a poet?
ELA	Fairy tales	Cite several examples of Cinderella across cultures.	Compare and contrast how fairy tales are used in different cultures.	Using a current event, create a fairy tale that has purpose and meaning.
ELA	Heroes	Select two specific heroes and compare and contrast their characteristics.	How are heroes/antiheroes used in literature?	What effect do heroes and anti-heroes have on society?
Math	Division	Suggest multiple ways to solve problems using division.	Define the relationship between multiplication and division.	Log division's impact on our daily life over the period of one week.
Math	Percentages	Describe how percentages, decimals, and fractions are used in sports.	Describe how statisticians use percentages, decimals. and fractions.	Which is more effective to use and when: percentages, decimals and fractions, and why?
Math	Fractions	Show how fractions are applied in music.	Demonstrate how fractions can change the mood or the genre of the music.	Describe situations where fractions were used to change opinions.
Math	Transformation (geometry)	Show how transformation is used in real life.	Demonstrate how transformation is used by musicians.	How is mathematical transformation similar/different to making a movie?
Math	Money	Compare money from various countries. Define how they are similar/different.	Examine coins for symbols and determine the meanings in the context of the nation of origin.	Analyze the countries that either accepted or declined the use of the Euro and how that decision affected the country's economy. →

Figure 4.5: E3 Examples (continued)

Subject	Unit	Enrichment	Extension	Enhancement
Science	Magnets	Research things that are magnetic.	Study inventions/tools that use magnets.	Hypothesize a world without magnets.
Science	Water cycle	Investigate tools to measure weather-related data.	Investigate careers in meteorology.	Determine how climate and weather are interrelated.
Science	Energy	Study at least three alternate sources of fuel.	Compare/contrast various country's consumption and use of alternate fuels.	Write an opinion on the importance of developing alternate fuel sources.
Science	Weather	Study the general nature of hurricanes.	What general lessons can be learned about the effect of a major weather event (such as the effect on the economy, people's behavior, or community responses)?	Investigate two famous U.S. or Canadian natural disasters and show their effect on the general economy. Define the similarities and differences.
Science	Energy	Discuss various types of energy.	Relate how the various types of energy coexist with each other.	How has the harnessing of energy changed society?
Science	Water	Define water's effect on the local economy.	Investigate professionals who specialize in water quality and cite their importance to the local community.	Study how water is used to control or manipulate communities.
Science	Seasons	Define how the weather changes between seasons.	Interpret how the rotation of Earth affects weather and climate.	Define how cycles affect our daily life.
Science	Electricity	How is alternating current/ direct current used within a school building?	Describe how electric cars work.	What was made possible in our nation due to the discovery of electricity (both positive and negative).
Science	Geology	Study the important periods of the geological time scale.	Study significant geologists.	Define the role geology plays in geotechnical engineering.
Science	Geology	Define how the Gold Rush changed the United States.	Study how mineral rights are used across the United States and Canada.	Consider a current controversy dealing with mineral rights (such as fracking) and write an opinion to the local paper.
Science	Relative density	Define how surface tension works.	Show how surface tension is used in sports.	Demonstrate how cohesion and adhesion are used to improve our daily lives. Or create a new product that makes use of cohesion/ adhesion.
Science	Astrophysics	Study the life of Carl Sagan.	Define how you can make what you are learning transcendental to others.	Modify a current product to improve human life.
Science	Gravity	Define the various forces of gravity.	Show how engineers use gravity to build bridges or keep planes in the air.	Discuss how gravity is used to improve our daily lives. →

Figure 4.5: E3 Examples (continued)

Subject	Unit	Enrichment	Extension	Enhancement
Social Studies	Native Americans	Study the various groups of natives of Minnesota or another state/province.	In what ways has our society been shaped and changed by the native populations in each region?	What are the lasting and significant contributions of the native cultures on the United States or Canada?
Social Studies	Colonization	Compare the efforts of Spain, France, Britain, and the United States to colonize the new world.	Compare the motives of colonizing groups, relating them to the success or failure of the colony.	Compare the effects of successful and failed colonization globally.
Social Studies	Geography	Describe the economy of one state or province.	Compare/contrast the economies of different regions of the United States or Canada.	Study unemployment across regions and connect it to the regions' economic foundation.
Social Studies	Discovery of the Americas	Journal the journey of Columbus to the "New World."	Describe the effects the "discovery" had on the Spanish, indigenous peoples, and Africans.	Discuss why humans explore the unknown.
Social Studies	The U.S. Constitution	Interpret the 2nd amendment to make sense in the 21st century.	Study famous/controversial weapons advocates or arms dealers.	Study how new technological innovations, such as weapons in WWI, have changed how war is fought.
Social Studies	U.S. or Canadian history	Study primary sources of a significant slave (such as journals or letters).	What are the significant contributions ex-slaves have had on the development of the United States or Canada?	Create a campaign that seeks to end slavery today.
Social Studies	Disabilities	How did Helen Keller, Franklin D. Roosevelt, or returning war vets overcome disability, or how did their disability shape their character?	Describe various careers that support people with disabilities.	Define how disabilities have been viewed over time and what are the significant shifts in thinking?

PPM Cognitive Dimension, Tier 2 (SOME): Uncovering and Discovering the Talents of CLED Students

As we discussed in Chapter 1, students from culturally, linguistically, and ethnically diverse (CLED) populations, including those from poverty and recent immigrants, are severely underrepresented in gifted programs. Their limited presence in gifted programs is related to various factors, including:

- limitations of the traditional measures of academic achievement
- insufficient programming and identification efforts by school districts
- lack of enriching experiences prior to kindergarten
- families' historical mistrust/distrust of the educational system
- limited awareness by parents of the educational system

To expand the participation of CLED students in gifted programs, schools and districts must make a concerted effort to provide programming and measures to identify students who would benefit from expanded educational options. Implementing services during the early years can significantly increase the numbers of diverse students in later years' programming.

Options at this tier within the total program should be tailored to the needs of CLED students, taking into account any possible limitations. All offerings within this level must include support or scaffolding systems to help ensure the students are successful.

The support or scaffolding systems should include:

- direct instruction focused on student strengths to compensate for weaknesses
- direct instruction of self-regulation strategies of goal setting, planning, organizing, monitoring, and metacognition (thinking about one's own thinking)
- use of techniques that scaffold the learner to higher levels by using a graphic organizer designed in a step-by-step fashion to support their progress
- resources for dealing with stress
- mentors or tutors
- home/school connections
- the school's connection to community and local culture
- psychological support for students and parents/guardians

Structural designs that can be considered include:

- multiage classrooms (partnering younger CLED students with older students)
- cluster classrooms (clustering CLED students into the gifted or advanced cluster classroom)
- resource room send-out program (to address specific gaps in achievement or for social/emotional support)
- introductory advanced-level lessons/assignments (students work with advanced content supported more directly by the teacher)

Options that address the CLED students' interests, readiness levels, and learning profiles:

- E3 activities (see pages 49–51)
- before, during, and after-school contests or competitions
- Saturday programs
- summer programs
- individual or small group investigations
- field trips (both virtual and real)
- mentorships with experts

Though all students can benefit from talent development (as described above), secondary level students who have specific, more articulated talents should be nurtured through supplementary programming. This type of programming can be held before, during, or after school. Similar to the design used at the elementary level, the program design for the middle and high school years also incorporates competitions, extracurricular activities, and clubs. Students with specific talent areas are directed toward these program options either through district or building-wide assessments or self-selections. Some of these experiences can also occur through summer programming or vacation-type schools, camps, or programs on university campuses. Keep in mind that academic competitions, contests, extracurricular activities, and clubs are a part of a gifted program; they should not be considered the entirety of the gifted program.

When considering competitions to address the talent areas of students, be sure to include a variety of options that span from academic to social to artistic.

Suggested competitions include:

- National History Day
- Lego League
- Science or Math Olympiad
- Young Writers Competition
- Young Playwrights National Playwriting Competition
- Dance competitions
- Young Musicians

- National Economics Challenge
- Federal Junior Duck Stamp Conservation and Design Program
- Intel Science Talent Search
- National Geographic Photo Contest
- Robotics

Schools should also consider offering an array of club or group options to students. Different from competitions, clubs focus on the special interests of the learner and in some cases may be used to advance students' social side.

Suggested clubs include:
- performance band, choir, and/or orchestra
- yearbook
- book club for boys
- book club for girls
- community service club
- theater

Co/extracurricular options are meant to nurture and develop aspects of the middle-level student that may not be directly addressed during the regular school day. In many cases, these options expand on the social/personal dimensions of talent development. It is essential to offer broad categories of co/extracurricular options.

Co/extracurricular activities include:
- athletics and outdoor education
- performing and visual arts activities
- service learning activities
- significant school leadership opportunities

Consider conducting an audit of school-sponsored and community-based experiences available to students within your school. See **Figure 4.6** on page 54 for an example of an audit form and page 55 for a blank Enrichment Activities Checklist. What talents and interests does each opportunity reflect? Determine what talent or interest areas are missing or served to a more limited degree. Next, carefully consider which opportunities require registration fees or

material costs. Ensure that school-sponsored or community-based experiences are readily available to families with limited incomes.

PPM Cognitive Dimension, Tier 3 (FEW): Supporting and Advancing Young Gifted Learners

When students who have been identified as gifted learners, whether through an IQ measure or standardized tests or a more thorough screening and evaluation process, they need advanced-level classes to address their intellectual needs. Our experience in the K–12 system strongly supports grouping or clustering these gifted students into advanced-level classes or courses for the majority of their school day. The nature of young gifted students intellectually and socially/emotionally makes it imperative that these students receive a distinctly differentiated curriculum and instruction.

Acceleration

Grade-level or subject acceleration is one of the most well-known options for gifted young students. As the authors of *A Nation Deceived* describe, "Acceleration is an intervention that moves students through an educational program at rates faster, or at younger ages, than typical. It means matching the level, complexity, and pace of the curriculum to the readiness and motivation of the student."[33] We have been accelerating gifted students in this way for a long time with substantial success.

Two types of acceleration are considered at this tier for young students:

Grade Acceleration

Some gifted students prefer older students as intellectual peers and friends due to their advanced cognitive development. With gifted K–2 students, we can admit them into kindergarten early or accelerate them to first or second grade. This option works best for meeting the academic and social needs of students who are developmentally mature.

---

[33] Colangelo, et al., 2004.

Figure 4.6: Enrichment Activities Checklist: Middle School Example

ACTIVITY	SCHOOL/GROUP	L/M	V/L	V/S	B/K	M/R	N/S
Language Arts							
Book Club	O/OG/VV		✓				
Enriched Book Club	O		✓				
Writing Club	OG		✓				
Spelling Bee	O/OG/VV		✓				
Promising Young Writers	OG		✓				
Mind Works	OG		✓				
School Yearbook	O/OG/VV		✓	✓			
TV Production	O		✓	✓	✓		
Social Studies							
Geography Bee	OG		✓	✓			✓
Stock Market Game	O/OG/VV	✓					
Student Council	O/VV	✓	✓	✓			
News Bowl	O	✓	✓				
Science							
Science Olympiad	O/OG/VV	✓		✓			
Recycling Club	O						✓
Peace Garden	O			✓	✓		✓
Math							
Math Counts	O	✓					
Math Team	O/OG	✓		✓			
Music							
School Musical	O/OG/VV		✓	✓	✓	✓	
Band/Choir/Orchestra	O/OG/VV					✓	
Physical							
Intramurals	O/OG			✓	✓		
Ski Club	O/OG			✓	✓		✓

O= Olson OG= Oak Grove VV= Valley View
L/M= Logical/Mathematical V/L= Verbal/Linguistic V/S= Visual/Spatial
B/K= Bodily/Kinesthetic M/R= Musical/Rhythmic N/S= Naturalist/Spiritual

◎Enrichment Activities Checklist

ACTIVITY	SCHOOL/GROUP	L/M	V/L	V/S	B/K	M/R	N/S

L/M= Logical/Mathematical V/L= Verbal/Linguistic V/S= Visual/Spatial
B/K= Bodily/Kinesthetic M/R= Musical/Rhythmic N/S= Naturalist/Spiritual

Subject-Specific Acceleration

Another option for accelerating students is by subjects. This option accelerates the student in one or two content areas of strength. In most cases, subject-specific acceleration is limited to reading and/or math. This option works best with students who are gifted in a subject area but who may be less developmentally mature.

The intervention of acceleration, while well documented and researched, has numerous critics in the school setting. Arguments against acceleration range from a question of equity to fears of social/emotional damage to the child. None of the arguments have been substantiated by research, but they nonetheless have a mythological hold on the educational system. To counteract distortions of the research, gifted and talented specialists and building administrators should become well versed in the research that supports appropriate acceleration.

In our experience, acceleration, when done well, has tremendous benefit for the child, the teacher, and the parents. The keys to appropriate acceleration are in the data collection, team process, and longitudinal practice.

> Acceleration, when done well, has tremendous benefit for the child, the teacher, and the parents.

When considering acceleration, it is imperative to collect quality data to support the needs of the child. The *Iowa Acceleration Scale* is a helpful tool that can be used by a child study team considering acceleration. Designed on a solid research base of students who have had successful accelerations, this guide offers a manageable format for an acceleration child study team to collect and discuss objective data, including the child's academic and social/emotional areas of strengths and needs for growth. (See www.acceleration institute.org for more information)

The acceleration child study team should consist of:

▮ the parents or guardians

▮ gifted and talented specialist

▮ building administrator

▮ school psychologist or social worker

▮ current classroom teacher

▮ teacher of the accelerated grade level

▮ district administrator for curriculum and instruction (optional)

▮ community member (optional)

Provide all team members with information about gifted students and their academic and social/emotional needs and the researched benefits of acceleration.

Once acceleration has been determined to be the appropriate intervention strategy, it's important to develop a longitudinal educational plan. This plan follows the student from grade to grade. Again, in our experience when acceleration fails, it is usually because some parties were not aware that the child was accelerated in earlier grades. When this happens, the child's natural progression of maturity may be mislabeled as obstinacy, asynchronous social skill development, or academic underperformance, to name a few possibilities. Additionally, subsequent teachers may resist the acceleration plan, thus denying the student continuous progress year after year.

Cluster Grouping

Another exceptional way to meet the needs of gifted young students is through cluster grouping. Cluster grouping is defined as "placing several high achieving, high ability, or gifted students in a regular classroom with other students and a teacher who has received training or has a desire to differentiate curriculum and instruction for these 'target' students."[34] For smaller school districts or schools where there may not be enough highly able students for a full-time classroom or advanced courses, cluster grouping presents a doable option. Clustering also works well for developing academic leaders among CLED students or students from poverty. Financially, clustering has benefits, as it requires less funding than many other program designs. However, it's essential to train cluster teachers in the learning differences of gifted students as well as strategies for differentiation. To be considered a component of

---

[34] Gentry, 1999.

gifted services, cluster classrooms need to include differentiation that is different from what occurs in other classrooms at the grade level.

Specialized Classroom/Schools within Schools

Another programming option for tier 3 is a specialized classroom or a school-within-a-school structure. Students in a specialized classroom are selected based on their advanced academic needs that are beyond the scope of the general grade-level curriculum. The teacher is trained and supported to meet gifted students' academic, personal/emotional, and social needs. The curriculum scope and sequence must be uniquely differentiated for the students' advanced levels of cognition and sophisticated levels of thinking. In most cases, students will meet or exceed state, national, or provincial standards at a much earlier grade level and may even accelerate through grade levels to reach high school graduation sooner.

A school-within-a-school (S-W-S) model is used when students from more than one grade level are involved with the same specialized classroom. In this case, the scope and sequence of the curriculum goes beyond one year and incorporates the multiple grade levels the students will progress through. The values of a S-W-S model is that no additional funds are needed to provide the supports for the classrooms (nurse, cafeteria, janitorial, and so on) and the general classroom teachers are exposed to and use the pedagogy of gifted education (the "spillover" effect).

In our experience, one area to remain vigilant about when using the S-W-S model concerns isolationism or elitism. Students in such a program may feel isolated from their grade-level peers if the general classrooms and the specialized classrooms do not interact or interact only rarely. To counter this, provide time for the classes to intermingle, such as during music, art, and physical education classes, or locate the specialty classroom in the same area/on the same hallway as the general classrooms. We also recommend identifying students by their grade level or teacher, not by the specialized classroom or S-W-S program name (for example, rather than calling the students "The Dimensions Academy class" they should be called "Mr. Vasquez's fourth graders").

PPM Cognitive Dimension, Tier 3 (FEW): Supporting Adolescent Gifted Learners through Postsecondary and Career Opportunities

Because adolescent gifted learners have unique thinking abilities and social development, they need uniquely differentiated class structures. Secondary school programs for identified gifted learners should include:

Advanced/Honors-Level Classes

Typically, advanced or honors level courses offer curriculum at an accelerated pace and in some cases provide greater depth and complexity. Successful honors level courses articulate the pace, depth, and complexity utilized within the curriculum and instructional practices. For more on pace, depth, and complexity, see Chapter 2. An honors level course moves at an accelerated pace, as well as includes greater degrees of performance within the discipline (depth) and infuses increased levels of thinking (complexity) throughout daily lessons and learning activities. See Chapter 5 for more on honors courses.

Telescoping of Programming

Telescoping is the act of shortening the time a student or group of students will need to complete several years of schooling or curriculum. For instance, typical middle school programs are grades six, seven, and eight covered in three years. A telescoped program for gifted students would include grades six, seven, and eight over two years. This programming option allows gifted students to move at an accelerated pace, cover essential curriculum, and then move on to high school and college sooner than their same-age peers. In international studies, students in accelerated classes outperformed students in non-accelerated classes, who were equivalent in age and intelligence.[35]

Specialized Secondary Schools-within-Schools

Similar to the elementary S-W-S model, the secondary school S-W-S model allows identified gifted students to move as a cohort through sophisticated levels of core courses (math,

[35] Rogers, 2002.

science, social studies, English/language arts) while interacting with general education students in other courses. This model can also be used for just some subject areas of learning such as:

- Humanities Model: ELA, social studies, art/music, and world language
- Science, Technology, Engineering, and Math (STEM) Model: math, science, principles of engineering, and family and consumer sciences
- Arts Model: art, music, and social studies
- Physical Education Model: physical education, health, science, and math

Another option within this model is to partner with colleges or universities to create an early college/university high school. Many gifted students are allowed to begin their postsecondary career in tandem with their high school coursework. The dual enrollment option allows students to earn both high school credit and college/university credit simultaneously, while taking more advanced levels of core curriculum. Most often this option is only available to high school juniors and seniors.

To extend this option, schools could consider a partnership with colleges/universities where high school freshmen and sophomores are allowed to participate in postsecondary coursework through a balanced approach based on the students' maturity level. Ninth- and tenth-grade students may not be developmentally ready for immersion into a college/university-level course with much older students. Therefore, it is best to offer the college/university course in the high school or in a select area of the college/university campus.

PPM Personal/Emotional Dimension, Tier 1: Working with Others

All students can benefit from developing collaboration skills. Indeed, learning to work in groups and with others is an essential tool for the twenty-first century. Students should be learning about themselves as individuals, about physical development, and about overall social competence. All students need coaching on developing as a person and a learner. In this level of the model, students should gain skills in working with others who have different intellectual needs, from low to high. School counselors often provide these services to all students, but when a school doesn't possess this resource, teachers will need to learn how to infuse the personal/emotional dimension into the general classroom and coursework.

Other skills that should be introduced and developed at this level include:

- team building
- leadership
- listening skills
- working with others effectively
- being flexible
- sharing responsibility
- goal setting for personal development

PPM Personal/Emotional Dimension, Tier 2: Understanding One's Talents

Since talent development is the focus of this level, teaching students how to build their potential should be the goal of the personal/emotional dimension. In small groups or in subjects specific to their talent area, students learn how talents develop, how they can be nurtured, and in what career fields their talents and/or interests may be best utilized.

CLED students need to learn how to maintain their talents in light of community, social, or peer pressures. Show them how to build support networks or provide mentors or same-age peer "buddies." Additionally, help them develop the art of "code switching," an essential tool to balancing the worlds of academia and community. Code switching is the ability to fluidly move back and forth between different languages or language varieties. For example, a code switcher can easily move between their home language, say Spanish, and the language of school, academic English. This also applies to dialects within a language, such as nonstandard English.

◎ Top Ten Rationale for Cluster Grouping

1. Widely researched, recommended, and often used strategy for meeting the needs of high-achieving/gifted/high-ability students in the inclusion classroom

2. Narrows the range of ability in each classroom

3. Allows for full-time services for gifted students

4. Other high-achieving students are allowed to emerge

5. All staff benefit from professional development and the pedagogy of gifted education

6. More efficient use of Title I and special education services

7. High expectations for all students

8. Gifted students are clustered with intellectual peers as well as age mates

9. Flexible instructional grouping in other academic areas is still recommended—allowing for those talented students to be challenged

10. Best practice for children

PPM Personal/Emotional Dimension, Tier 3: Understanding One's Gifts

Students at this level of giftedness need help learning how to recognize and appreciate themselves as gifted individuals. Gifted students may struggle with issues related to being different from most other students; therefore, they need to know how to deal with a sense of difference. Sessions should include:

- working with others who may not understand you
- dealing with personal perfectionism, intellectual arrogance, or elitism
- dealing with mediocrity when you are goal oriented
- working with others who may be more or less intelligent than you
- acknowledging that academic competence cannot compensate for personal interaction incompetence
- understanding that one person cannot change the entire world but can make changes in the world
- setting appropriate goals for self-development and academic achievement (some gifted students will choose goals that are far beneath their abilities and needs)

PPM Social Dimension, Tier 1: General Social Development

All students can benefit from social development activities. At this level, lessons on affective issues are not designed specifically for gifted students. Rather, activities at this level help all children recognize and accept their individual differences, including intellectual differences. Additionally, affective lessons should help students develop self-regulation strategies to focus attention, set goals, plan, and metacognate (think about their own thinking).

Following are strategies that all students can use as they develop the critical skills of self-regulation and learn relaxation techniques to reduce the effects of stress:

- deep breathing
- visualizing serene environments
- conscious awareness of all five senses—to assist students in understanding how all five senses are interrelated, it is important to know that when one or two senses become overly stimulated, it can cause our entire sensory system to become imbalanced. This is extremely important for those gifted students who have heightened sensory sensitivities or overexcitabilities.
- techniques of self-control, for example:
    - rewarding yourself for avoiding temptations or distractions
    - setting a goal to limit distractions during homework, such as only having soft music on while studying

Including affective lessons is a powerful way to approach the social/personal dimension for all students. Affective lessons are authentic experiences that teach students how to deal with day-to-day challenges in a rational, proactive manner.

PPM Social Dimension, Tier 2: Collaborating within a Group

Gifted students will need assistance in developing a sense of self as learners. Some CLED students may not have academic role models within their community, making it difficult to cultivate an internal drive for success in school. Social/emotional lessons should include coping strategies for:

- learning in advanced classes, such as study habits, goal setting, time management, monitoring, and organizational skills
- dealing with challenges from family, friends, and community
- dealing with feelings of anxiety, sadness, or depression that may accompany the stresses of advanced classes
- accepting differences (whether CLED or intellectually)
- addressing discrimination, stereotyping, and injustice

Also, be sure to provide families and communities of CLED students with supports for nurturing their children. In some cases, they may need clear information about giftedness, what advantages and disadvantages are associated with it, and how to best encourage their children through the struggles of school and society. Supporting parents of underrepresented children with positive parenting techniques, such as interacting with the child during play and learning, can have a profound effect on their child's academic achievement and personal growth.

PPM Social Dimension, Tier 3: Fitting into Society

Gifted students have social and emotional needs that are uniquely different from the general population. Their intensity as learners and their asynchronous emotional development are in contradiction to each other. Therefore, the social dimension for young gifted students should include sessions and lessons on:

- dealing with their own unique intellectual intensity
- coping and working with others who are not intellectually similar to them
- learning how to "turn off their brain" when not doing schoolwork
- learning now to relax and enjoy downtime
- managing social isolation
- strategies for overcoming underachievement or low performance
- strategies for self-advocacy
- developing appropriate emotional responses

The PPM is designed to provide schools and districts a comprehensive model for nurturing and developing the academic and affective dimensions of gifted students. From a sound theoretical base, the PPM offers suggestions on how to build a spectrum of services that can be effective in any school setting or district. Much of the PPM should not require extensive funding because many of the services may already exist. The model helps you define what services already exist and which need to be enhanced or added.

Effective Grouping Practices within Gifted Program Options

One of the main ideas in the PPM design is for students of like abilities and social/affective needs to be grouped together for at least a portion of their school day. Grouping gifted students together can have a profound positive effect on their learning and social development. What must be kept in mind, however, is that the grouping process is only as effective as the function and design of the groups.

> Keep in mind that the grouping process is only as effective as the function and design of the groups.

Common arguments heard in education revolve around grouping practices, especially when it comes to grouping the highest performing students together. While no grouping arrangement is inherently bad or wrong, the exclusive use of one type of grouping practice can lead to concerns over academic favoritism, instructional imbalance, and social inequity. We suggest using flexible grouping as one of the varied formats to meet the needs of gifted learners.

Grouping students is a practical and educationally sound method of teaching and applying the twenty-first century skills of:

- cooperation
- collaboration
- communication
- risk taking
- flexibility
- motivation
- engagement

The research strongly suggests that it is not only *how* you group students that improves achievement; it's also what you do with the students in the groups that can affect achievement, either positively or negatively.[36] However, in most grouping types when like-ability students are grouped together, there is a positive effect on achievement.[37]

While we support grouping gifted students together by ability for major academic learning experiences, we recommend using flexible grouping techniques for other classroom experiences, particularly those involving social and personal skill development. Flexible grouping is defined as grouping that is not static, where members of the group change. Groups are formed and change routinely depending on the learning outcomes and the needs of the students.

We define five types of grouping arrangements, ranging from grouping by likeness to grouping by differences: tracking, ability/aptitude grouping, performance grouping, cooperative grouping, and flexible instruction grouping.[38] See page 63, **Grouping Formats and Purposes.**

Tracking

Tracking is the most structured and least flexible of grouping arrangements. In this practice, students are placed in groups based on achievement test scores within a subject level; the groups are in place for an entire course and even from year to year. While many argue that tracking is an ineffective method of instruction, it is still used in many schools today. Tracking is commonly used in mathematics, especially in middle and high schools where schedules dictate student placement.

The basic tenants of tracking are:

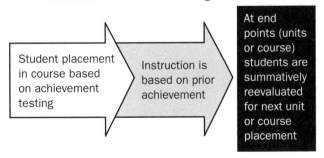

The main opposition to tracking relates to:

- inequities of instructional differentiation within the various tracks, specifically the lower level track
- inability for students to easily move both in and out of the track
- poor use of data analysis for placement of students within the tracks

Flexible Instructional Grouping

- When forming *flexible groups,* it is most effective to group students by their likeness, based on the students' readiness, interests, or learning profiles.

The tenets of flexible grouping are:

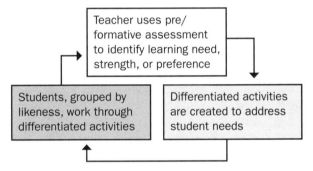

Ability/Aptitude Grouping

Student placement in *ability/aptitude groups* is based on formalized or standardized assessments that identify ability or achievement. These groups are less flexible mainly due to the timing of the assessments.

The basics of ability/aptitude grouping are:

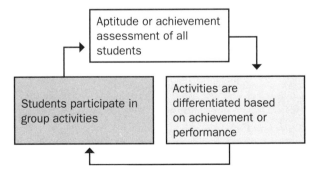

---

[36] Kulik and Kulik, 1989; Oaks, J., 1985; Reis, S., et al, 1993; Rogers, K., 2002; Slavin, R., 1993.

[37] Rogers, 2002.

[38] Heacox, 2012.

◎ Grouping Formats and Purposes

Tracking	Ability/Aptitude	Performance	Cooperative	Flexible Instructional
Determined by general learning abilities (e.g., 98% of intelligence or aptitude in total or composite score)	Determined largely by scores on standardized tests provincial assessments	Determined by grades, achievement, or statewide/provincial assessments	Determined by teacher assignment or student choice (random)	Prescribed by teacher based on student readiness, interest, or learning profile
Grouped by likeness related to general ability	Grouped by likeness related to ability or aptitude	Grouped by likeness related to achievement and/or classroom performance	Grouped by differences in readiness or work habits	Grouped by likeness in readiness, interest, or learning profile
Based on perceptions about general ability rather than specific academic talents	Based on aptitude for a specific subject area	Based on achievement and/or classroom performance in particular subject areas	Random as to student ability, readiness levels, learning profile	Based on specific readiness needs, strengths, limitations, interests, or learning profile
Rigid group membership across all subjects; students are together most, if not all, of the day	Rigid group membership but likely grouped by particular subject area strengths (e.g., accelerated math, enriched English)	Rigid or flexible membership in the classroom. Teachers may preassess unit by unit and then change members in groups as appropriate	Fluid group membership	Fluid group membership based on purposefully matching students to particular tasks
Groups tend to work on similar or identical tasks	Groups tend to work on similar tasks	Groups tend to work on similar tasks	Each group works on the same task or on one facet of the same task	Within assigned groups, students may work alone, with a partner, or in a small group as determined by the teacher; Tasks differ based on readiness, interest, or learning profile
Students may or may not be regrouped within the classroom	Students may or may not be regrouped within the classroom	Students may or may not be regrouped within the classroom	Students are purposefully mixed as to readiness, interests, and learning profile to provide peer instruction or leadership within the groups	Students are purposefully grouped and regrouped based on common instructional needs
Occurs daily	Occurs daily	Occurs daily	Frequency determined by the teacher	Occurs as necessary and appropriate to the learning needs of the students

From *Differentiation for Gifted Learners: Going Beyond the Basics* by Diane Heacox, Ed.D., and Richard M. Cash, Ed.D., copyright © 2014 Free Spirit Publishing Inc., Minneapolis, MN; 800-735-7323; www.freespirit.com. This page may be reproduced for use within an individual school or district. For all other uses, contact www.freespirit.com/company/permissions.cfm.

Cooperative Grouping

The main goal of *cooperative groups* is to develop students' abilities to work in teams. Cooperative groups have been found to be effective in developing collaborative and social skills.

The essentials of cooperative grouping are:

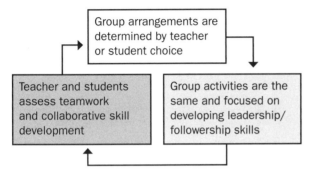

Grouping Using the Candy Wrapper Lesson Design

Another effective classroom group practice is called the "Candy Wrapper Lesson Design" (**Figure 4.7**). In this method, the lesson begins with the entire class listening to the teacher who sets the tone, introduces the lesson, and/or shares information that all students need to know. At this point, the teacher also communicates expectations for each of the group actions. In the next phase of the lesson, students break into groups to perform the specified action or activity. This is called the "Candy" or the "Sweet Spot" of the lesson. The actions or activities are differentiated to address the specific learning needs of the students in each group, whether it is based on readiness, interest, or learning profile. After the activity, the class comes back together to debrief (the other side of the wrapper). Here the teacher and students share what each group achieved, how the students worked together or separately, or what they thought of the learning process.

Figure 4.7: The Candy Wrapper Lesson Design

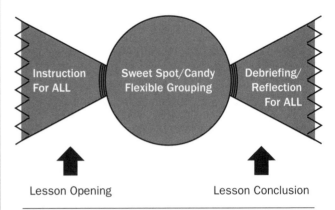

Grouping for Gifted Elementary Math Students

Many teachers struggle with meeting the needs of gifted students in mathematics at the elementary level. Gifted elementary math students often become frustrated by "waiting" for others to catch up to them. While subject acceleration is an effective way to meet the needs of these students, we recommend working to develop the gifted students' mathematical reasoning and problem-solving skills. Rather than racing students through the arithmetic of mathematics, have gifted math students spend more time on the comprehensive nature of mathematical thinking and reasoning. Page 65, **Effective Practice in Flexible Math Grouping,** offers suggestions on how to flexibly group students at a grade level without accelerating students into the next text.

Grouping Gifted Students within a Gifted Classroom

In all classroom settings, students have different readiness, learning profiles, and interests. This holds true within a classroom where all the students are identified as gifted. These students will still have varying degrees of abilities or preparedness, interests, and learner preference. Following are suggestions for addressing each of the three avenues for differentiation within a group of gifted students. Keep in mind that gifted students acquire knowledge more rapidly than other students, so the interventions or strategies may not need to be used as frequently as with the general population.

◎Effective Practice in Flexible Math Grouping

This practice requires that grade-level teachers team up during a common math period and differentiate both curriculum and instruction to meet the needs of students in each flexible group.

Steps:

1. Using the district pacing suggestions, meet as a team to discuss and collaboratively agree on the duration of the math unit.

2. Develop a comprehensive unit preassessment. You may consider using the end-of-chapter test or teacher/publisher-designed pretests.

3. On a predetermined date, have all students at the grade level take the preassessment. Assure students that the preassessment will help determine if they already know certain components/objectives of the unit. Tell them that all students will be provided enriched learning experiences throughout the unit of study. Do not allow students to struggle through the preassessment, as this may frustrate some students before the unit begins. (If students seem to be struggling or become frustrated, have those students stop the testing.)

4. Review the preassessments and rank order students based on their skill and knowledge of the unit. Based on the rank order, decide how to group the students for this unit. Remember, the flexible nature of this type of grouping can offer students focused instruction to meet their individual needs. Suggestion: The students with the greatest needs should be in the smallest group with more teacher interaction and hands-on activities.

5. Throughout the unit study, actively engage students in learning through manipulative work, games, and authentic experiences. Avoid having the gifted learners race ahead in the math units. Instead, guide these students in taking the math concepts to deeper, more complex levels. FOR ALL STUDENTS, remember: While rote memorization is an efficient tool for learning facts, elaborative rehearsal (putting the facts into context—using the facts in an authentic way) is much more effective for long-term learning.

6. On the predetermined date post-test all students.

7. Begin the cycle again.

Ten Tips for Productive Group Work

1. Be clear with students about the reasons for and benefits of group work.

2. Ensure that all group members clearly understand the rules, procedures, and norms of group work.

3. Assign tasks that match group types.

4. Create group in sizes that fit the function of the task (groups with three to five students usually work best).

5. Offer group members feedback about their performance and functioning.

6. Be flexible with the group membership; when the group is functioning below expectations, shift the membership to ensure productivity.

7. Ensure that all members feel a part of the group and have duties to fulfill.

8. Balance the group membership so students bring out the best in each other.

9. Allow the group leadership to be selected democratically, either by the teacher or by the students.

10. Practice with students the effective and efficient movement in and out of the group.

Readiness

Some gifted students may lack sufficient academic or learning skills and knowledge. Here are some strategies to bridge such gaps:

Before instruction:

- Provide students with both academic and content-specific vocabulary lists and descriptions of lessons or units of study.

- Offer previews of upcoming units to build or unearth prior knowledge; video files or websites can be highly effective for this purpose.

- Deliver mini-lessons (a quick one- to three-minute review or lesson) on specific strategies necessary for the day's lesson.

During instruction:

- Assign study buddies or helpmates to each student in the classroom. Be sure not to assign the highest-level student to the lowest. Coordinate the pairing so students are more alike in ability rather than different.

- Give students graphic organizers to guide or justify their thinking or link ideas. Gifted students often think more abstractly but may not have an efficient way to organize their thinking. Use graphic organizers such as the Frayer Model. (Note: When using general graphic organizers, consider ramping them up as shown in **Figure 4.8**.) Other suggested graphic organizers have been included on pages 69–72: Character Diary Plan, Inference—Justifying Your Thinking, Skill Understanding Graphic, and Visible Thinking for Understanding

- Focus students on the tools of learning. Offer specific learning strategies; however, don't overwhelm students with too many. In most cases, gifted students like to stick to one or two strategies they find useful.

Figure 4.8: Frayer Model Graphic Organizer: Ramped-Up Example

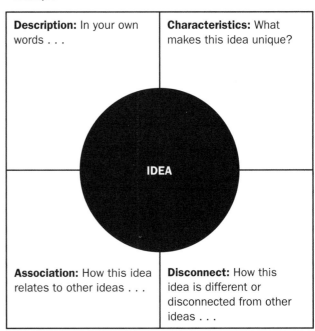

Description: In your own words . . .	**Characteristics:** What makes this idea unique?
IDEA	
Association: How this idea relates to other ideas . . .	**Disconnect:** How this idea is different or disconnected from other ideas . . .

After instruction:

- Provide students with second-glance options or sites. Second glances are meant to be short and not very in depth. They are quick refreshers of the materials that have been covered. This can be a Wiki, blog, or Moodle site. Or, offer hard-copy forms of second-glance material, perhaps having students collect the forms from stations around the room.

- Continue to link past content to future study or career options. When students find content to be meaningful and relevant to their lives, they are more likely to retain the information over the long term.

Interest

Gifted students often have wide and deep interests. Recognizing their interest base, we can group students in what are called "expert groups." Consider:

Before instruction:

- Form expert groups based on general interests to uncover topics that may not be covered in the unit or lessons. Example: For a unit on the body systems:

    - Expert groups interested in the medical field may choose to research the effect of HIV/AIDS on the various body systems.

    - Expert groups interested in sports may choose to research how athletic equipment is being designed to protect the body systems.

    - Expert groups interested in the arts may choose to research the effect of music on the neurological system.

During instruction:

- Have expert groups meet regularly to connect their topic to the general class topic.

- Encourage groups to routinely seek outside experts or resources to support the ongoing lessons in the class.

- Throughout the study, have expert groups present their topic research either in parts or in whole at the end of the unit.

After instruction:

- Encourage students to research related career possibilities or postsecondary learning options.

- Have students reflect on how their interests help them or distract them from focusing on the general topic.

Gifted students may need to discuss ideas throughout the learning process.

Learning Profiles

Like other students, gifted students have a wide range of learning preferences. What may be more prevalent among gifted students is the need to discuss ideas throughout the learning process. However, this does not mean that all gifted students are highly verbal. Some may actually be more introverted in their learning reflection, requiring more time for introspection. Here are ways you can design learning experiences that make the best use of gifted students' varied profiles:

Before instruction:

- Help gifted students recognize their learning preferences, whether a cognitive preference (such as from Howard Gardner's list of Multiple Intelligences) or a modality (auditory, visual, or kinesthetic).

- Teach students how to stretch their learning preferences or work outside their comfort zone through nonthreatening games or experiences.

During instruction:

- Offer various options for gathering and accumulating information from graphic organizers (visual) to recordings (auditory), from partner work (interdependent) to independent work (intradependent).

- Group students based on their like preferences to work as a team to gather materials or construct projects.

- Assess students using their preferred way of learning and doing for a clear understanding of what they learned.

After instruction:

- Have students reflect on how their preferred way of doing impacted their acquisition of knowledge, identifying the pros and cons of the preference.
- Ask students to consider career and postsecondary pathways where their preferred way of knowing and doing will be most advantageous.

Chapter Summary

As schools become more diverse and theirs funds limited, exclusive programming for gifted learners becomes more difficult to sustain. We highly recommend making rigorous curriculum and programs available to all students. While this is a worthy mission, we know that some students may be far beyond what the secondary school can or will provide. Meeting the needs of gifted students is essential to the operations of a school district of quality. It's important to consider the needs of gifted learners and to implement relevant programs in all district-wide initiatives.

◎ Graphic Organizer: Character Diary Plan

This graphic organizer requires the student to define unique qualities or characteristics of characters from text. They must cite specific text from the work that substantiates the characteristics they have chosen. The final box is for them to write a "journal entry" the character may have made that demonstrates that quality.

Unique Quality or Characteristic	Citation to Support Characteristic	Journal Entry

Adapted from McKnight, K. S., and M. Scruggs. *The Second City Guide to Improv in the Classroom: Using Improvisation to Teach Skills and Boost Learning.* New York: Wiley, 2008.

◎Graphic Organizer: Inference—Justifying Your Thinking

In the center of the Frayer Model, write text (this can be either a passage from a novel or a complete poem). Each quadrant offers students an opportunity to flesh out their thinking about the text. This graphic can be used several times over the course of studying a text or as a final justification of the student's ideas on the reading.

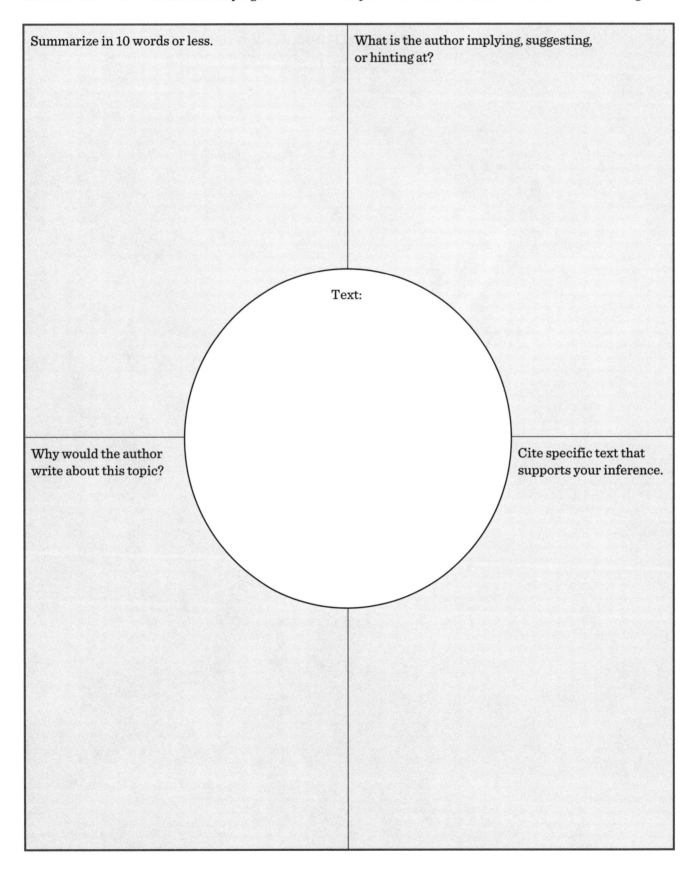

Summarize in 10 words or less.

What is the author implying, suggesting, or hinting at?

Text:

Why would the author write about this topic?

Cite specific text that supports your inference.

◎ Graphic Organizer: Skill Understanding Graphic

This model can be used when learning or trying to interpret a skill or strategy. It can be used to preassess knowledge about the skill/strategy, as a thought collection device throughout the learning of the skill/strategy, or as a final assessment to demonstrate full understanding of the skill/strategy.

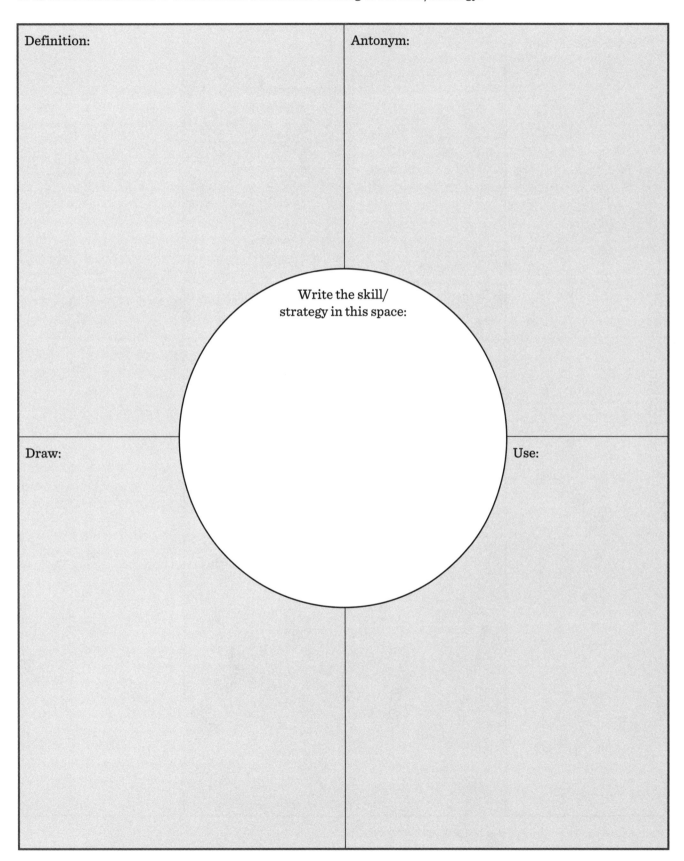

Definition:

Antonym:

Write the skill/ strategy in this space:

Draw:

Use:

◎ Graphic Organizer: Visible Thinking for Understanding

This graphic is a great way to have students gather information about what they are thinking either when reading text or in a classroom discussion. The center-column boxes are filled in during the reading or discussion while the outer left and right columns are used to extend the thinking.

Further questions . . .	Observe and describe:	Explain and interpret:	Dig deeper: Hypothesize, theorize, generalize . . .
	Reason with evidence:	Make connections:	
	Diverse perspectives:	Essence and conclusion:	

Based on Ritchhart, R., M. Church, and K. Morrison. *Making Thinking Visible: How to Promote Engagement, Understanding, and Independence for All Learners.* New York: Wiley, 2011.

Chapter 5

Creating Authentic Honors Courses

Honors or advanced-level courses are a common way to meet the needs of gifted students at the secondary level. As program directors, we have struggled with finding a consensus on a description of an honors/advanced-level course. There is no universal definition. Unlike Advanced Placement (AP) or International Baccalaureate (IB) programs, honors courses lack consistent curricular and instructional practices. Without consistency, these courses justly deserve scrutiny and continuous review. In some cases, university and college placement officers have been "un-honoring" courses on applicants' transcripts because of the perceived course inflation factor. In a U.S. educational system full of plans for better high schools, more and more courses have impressive labels, such as "honors," "advanced," "college prep," and "Advanced Placement." But many researchers and educators argue that the teaching often does not match the title.

"A company selling an orange-colored beverage under the label 'orange juice' can get in legal trouble if the beverage contains little or no actual juice," said a report from the National Center for Educational Accountability. "But there are no consequences for giving credit for Algebra 2 to students who have learned little algebra."[39]

As a result, to ensure fidelity and integrity of practice, we recommend that honors courses at the secondary level be continuously reviewed for consistency and merit. This chapter will define the "Triple A" method of honors course review: articulation, alignment, and accountability.

Articulation: Clearly Defining the Rigors of an Honors Course

Honors courses are designed to meet the differentiated academic needs of gifted secondary students. Defining the practice within the honors course means clearly articulating the differences between the honors level course and the regular level course. One of the greatest challenges in developing a well-articulated honors course definition is to limit the use of educational-ese that can be interpreted in many different ways. Words such as *rigor*, *depth*, and *complexity* are the most often used terms in honors course descriptions. But, what do those words really mean and how does the honors course reflect rigor, depth, and complexity? In Chapter 2, we defined these terms as they apply to gifted education. If you use these terms in describing honors courses, be sure to clarify specifically what is meant.

Before creating course descriptions, schools should develop a basic definition of honors courses. Following are four essential principles of what an honors course should entail:

1. Honors courses should be *enhanced and enriched learning experiences*. The classroom environment of an honors course is rich in substantive conversation. Substantive conversation requires[40]:

   a. considerable interaction between and among students and teacher

---

[39] *Washington Post*, 2009.

[40] Newmann, 1996.

b. deeper shared understanding of and encouragement for the development of new ideas

c. subject matter that encourages critical reasoning, idea generation, and the creation of additional questions

d. going beyond simple recalling of facts to more complex analysis of information, arguments, and thesis development

e. students to share the responsibility for generating, moving, and concluding dialogue

f. ongoing scaffolding from one lesson to the next

g. sustained effort throughout the course

2. The content in an honors course is *extended beyond the core curriculum*. Extending curriculum means adding topics that are current, relevant to the student, and provocative in nature as well as those that offer varying degrees of ambiguity. Sample topics range from:

a. abortion rights

b. affordable healthcare

c. bullying

d. censorship

e. civil rights

f. climate change

g. drug legalization

h. genetic engineering

i. gun control

j. homelessness

k. immigration

l. invasive species

m. marriage equality

n. organ donation

o. racism

p. state's/provincial rights vs. federal control

q. suicide

r. U.S. involvement in foreign political issues

s. welfare

t. other ethical issues

3. Honors courses place additional *emphasis on independence in learning, critical thinking, and advanced research skills*. Tasks in the honors classroom involve:

a. authentic/real-world problems with no clear answer

b. issues important to humanity

c. questions and answers that are meaningful and that matter to others

d. interdisciplinary skills, tools, and knowledge

e. extensive collaboration and communication between and among students

f. resources from a variety of sources and experts, including primary sources

g. authentic outcomes or productions for real audiences

4. Honors courses cultivate *habits of independent thinking, creativity, collaboration, leadership, and advanced intellectual skills*. Students work toward greater learning autonomy through:

a. developing sophisticated skills of self-regulation

b. building confidence through and/or expert teacher coaching and consultation

c. initiating learning through topics of interest

Using these four guiding principles, teachers should include concept-based teaching and learning in honors courses that pursue content at a much deeper level. Concept-based curriculum and instruction also allow for greater interdisciplinary study. When we use concept-based curriculum and instruction effectively, we challenge students to reflect on controversial issues and topics. And when students are encouraged to wrestle with ambiguity of issues, ideas, or topics, they learn to apply the content information in an authentic and meaningful way.

When students wrestle with ambiguity of issues, ideas, or topics, they learn to apply the content information in an authentic and meaningful way.

Sample Honors Course Description

Below is a sample honors course description. Note how the guiding principles have been used to clearly articulate what is included within the course.

> Honors courses are classes that provide academically talented students an **enhanced and enriched learning experience**. Curriculum in an honors course is **extended beyond the core topics** and places **additional emphasis on independence of learning, critical thinking, and advanced research skills**. Honors classes require students to cultivate **habits of independent thinking, creativity, collaboration, leadership, and advanced intellectual skills**. Most materials will be presented at a lexile above 1100L.[41]

The ability to clearly articulate what will be expected of students at this level is essential when developing an honors course description. The more specific and definitive detail you can provide, the more likely families and students will understand the rigorous nature of an honors course.

Differentiating an Honors Course

As stated in Chapter 2, curriculum and instruction for gifted learners is differentiated in three distinct ways:

- Pace: Accelerating the instructional practices
- Depth: Deepening the discipline knowledge and practices
- Complexity: Using sophisticated levels of advanced thinking

These three methods may be applied to honors courses by employing the following strategies.

Strategies to Accelerate Pace

Spend Less Time on Low Levels, More Time on High Levels

There are specific ways to accelerate the pace in honors courses. Based on the objectives of the unit, consider spending less time on the didactic (factual level and/or observable) information and more time on the advanced levels of questioning and deep discussion. The idea of substantive conversation was defined on pages 73–74. This methodology, where less time is spent on introduction and more time on discussing, allows the honors student to apply learned information in a meaningful way.

Begin Instruction with the Big Ideas

To initiate substantive conversation and thus increase the pace of instruction, begin with the practice called *essential question forming*. Here teachers guide students through the process of developing essential questions, or questions that are worth asking and answering and that facilitate learning. A tool for assisting students in creating such questions can be found on page 76, **Concept Development Steps in Creating Essential Questions**.

Use "Flipped" Instruction

Flipped instruction means swapping the usual order of classroom and home dynamics. Instead of students receiving instruction at school and then bringing work home to do, the "homework" is done at school and the instruction occurs at home. This has become possible with the increasing availability and advances in technology. Students can now access instructional videos and other forms of instruction on their home computers. Flipping the classroom is a time-shifting practice that allows more time for face-to-face interaction and conversation between students at school and application or extension of tasks related to the new information.

While the idea of students preparing for class discussion the night before is not necessarily new, the enhancements of technology and abundance and ease of access to information makes this methodology more effective for twenty-first

---

41 Adapted from Bloomington Public Schools, MN.

◎ Concept Development Steps in Creating Essential Questions

1. **Engaging Question:** Ask a thought-provoking question that requires students to use prior knowledge and uncover preconceptions about the topic.

   a. Example: (Concept: change) What is happening to this leaf? Why do you think it is happening?

2. **Generate Ideas:** Have students list examples and non-examples of the concept. Use whole or small group brainstorming, think-pair-share,* or other discussion techniques to create lists.

3. **Develop Generalizations:** Have students organize their lists into categories. Then, from these organized lists, have them formulate sentences/statements that can be "almost always or always true."

4. **Creating Essential Questions (EQs):** From the generalizations that have been developed, have students turn their statements into well-formed questions. Well-formed questions require multiple answers and are open-ended. EQs can be created by each student, in small groups, or as a class. EQs should be posted in the room to remind the students and teacher to work at answering the questions throughout the course of study.

5. **Gathering Sources:** Students should collect at least two outside resources that can assist them in answering the EQs. Possible sources include outside experts, websites, text or resource books, magazine or newspaper articles, videos/podcasts, or recordings.

6. **Unit of Study:** Throughout the unit of study, the teacher and students continually reflect on the EQ and write, at least weekly, ideas to formulate an answer. Activities during the lesson should add to the students' knowledge base and allow students to explore a broader range of ideas related to the concept.

7. **Conclusion:** Students should display their new knowledge and answer the EQs. This can be accomplished through tests, oral presentations, performances, or projects.

* Think-pair-share requires students to think individually about a question, pair and share ideas with a partner, and finally share with the larger group.

century learners. In an honors level class, students will not only prepare for in-class activities but will also do background investigation, pose questions for other class members, or acquire knowledge as part of their homework, leaving class time for discussion and group problem-solving endeavors.

> Flipping the classroom allows more time for face-to-face interaction and conversation between students at school.

Teachers can use the technology of the flipped classroom for such activities as:

- developing prerequisite knowledge for classroom discussions
- supporting or reviewing material from past classroom sessions
- allowing for self-pacing of the content, especially related to reading materials

You may also want to consider using the technology to create stations or learning centers for deeper investigations on topics within units of study. Students can then share their findings via Moodle or Blackboard, programs that are housed on internal networks or servers. Students can also create videos or websites on their topics of investigation, thereby creating new learning stations for other students or the public.

Use Technology in Advanced Ways

Consider using technology to help in accelerating the pace of classroom instruction. Send via email or through a blog site, Moodle, or Blackboard (on internal school district servers) questions that students should use as guides for studying, when collecting new information, or while preparing for class. These forms of communication can also be useful when students want to carry on classroom discussion, or as forums to wrestle with related questions that arise outside of the classroom.

Use Sophisticated Note-Taking Tools

The practice of note taking may be foreign to some gifted secondary students. This is mainly because they did not need to take notes in previous classes

where they were not challenged or when simple memorization was sufficient. In advanced classes, you may need to guide students through the practice of effective note taking. To do this, it can be helpful to provide students with a skeletal outline of the class session and then require them to fill in the notes through the class period.

You can also increase the sophistication of note taking in an honors class by requiring students to use technology. Products and applications (such as NoteLedge) offer students multiple ways of collecting notes and information in electronic files. Students can upload video clips, websites, blog interchanges, and old-fashion notes into an electronic file that can then be organized into categories or topics for future use and study.

Another useful technology tool for both note taking and idea gathering is a "discussion board." Discussion boards are an asynchronous online posting site that allows teacher and students to post questions, comments, ideas, or thoughts. Other students or the teacher can join the conversation by remarking or responding to the questions, ideas, and thoughts. Multiple "threads" (different conversations or topics) can be run on the same site, allowing for various conversations to occur at the same time and in the same place.

Offer Assistance When Necessary

Not all honors courses are intended for gifted students. Some schools may choose to develop honors level courses that offer a broader array of students the opportunity to be exposed to an advanced-level course in middle school or high school. In this case, it is essential to provide a parallel support structure for students who may be less prepared for such courses. Programs such as Advancement Via Individual Determination (AVID) have been shown to be highly successful in supporting and nurturing students in honors or advanced-level courses. The program, designed for elementary-age students and up, focuses on students in the "middle" who have the motivation and desire to advance into more challenging classes and college/university.

Teachers can also offer support through a "second-glance" method of information review.

To do this, create a website that provides information from the daily class sessions as well as Web links to more information on the topic. Using the second-glance site will help students develop self-regulation and study habits. Or, offer the services of tutors or mentors for assistance.

Be sure that students do not see offers of assistance as additional work or as requirements to be present before or after school. Students who are encouraged to pursue honors level courses but who may need additional support should receive that help during class sessions or in place of other courses—for example, one course per day or week could be eliminated to allow time for the support session. Or, use school-wide Response to Intervention (RtI) time, study hall, or homeroom/advisory sessions to embed the support practice into students' schedules.

Consider Self-Directed Learning Options

Some gifted students work best when they can pursue independent topics of study. This can also be a way to accelerate the pace of the class—by having students work independently to gather background knowledge required for the class, say over the summer break.

Self-directed learning can also be used as a jigsaw activity for acquiring basic information on the topic. In such an activity, small groups of students are responsible for gathering certain information and preparing the information for the larger group. Each small group either teaches the other students the information or prepares it in a format that the other students can access it, such as a WebQuest, handout, or posters/pamphlets.

Use Varied Instructional Methodologies

As in an inclusion classroom, it is important to keep in mind the varied instructional methodologies that can engage gifted students. Instruction should flow seamlessly from large group to small group to individual. Students should be flexibly grouped throughout the instructional periods based on their interests, learning profiles, or readiness for information.

Accelerating pace in the honors classroom requires that you:

- Proactively plan:
  - Decide which information can be learned in other ways than through lecture.
  - Decide which information should be required before the course begins.
  - Decide when the students will be responsible for the information gathering.
- Clearly define the objectives and outcomes:
  - Begin with the big ideas.
  - Assign the students responsibility for collecting background or prerequisite information.
  - Focus the objectives on the "doing" and "understanding" level.
  - Ensure that outcomes display what the students have learned, not what they know.
- Prepare materials ahead of time:
  - text
  - websites
  - experts
  - mentors
  - tutors
  - other resources
- Develop questions in advance of the class sessions:
  - Focus on the higher order strategies of analysis, evaluation, and synthesis.
  - Create questioning templates with
    - why . . .
    - how might . . .
    - where could . . .
    - when might . . .
    - in what ways . . .
- Use descriptive feedback. Ensure the feedback is:
  - relevant
  - useful
  - immediate
  - specific for improvement

- Prepare for re-teaching:
  - ▓ Have a variety of resources available for students who need support.
  - ▓ Offer second glances or second chances.
  - ▓ Provide time for students to catch on.
- Perfect classroom management techniques:
  - ▓ Have methods for moving students around the room.
  - ▓ Clearly define guidelines for independent or small group work.
  - ▓ Set high expectations and stick to them.

More on effective instructional practices in an honors course can be found in Chapter 6, Changing Roles for Educators of Gifted Students.

Strategies to Increase Depth

As was stated in Chapter 2, depth refers to the level of information needed to solve complex and abstract problems within and across disciplines. When students work in depth, they are expected to use the facts and procedures with *automaticity*. Automaticity means that students can quickly recall factual information and have developed and practiced numerous strategies for working at the skill level. They also think more abstractly by working within the conceptual level. When students are working in depth in a discipline, they are also incorporating and using advanced levels of self-regulation, such as planning, organizing, goal setting, monitoring, and reflection.

Work as a Disciplinarian

As the word suggests, acting as a *disciplinarian* requires a high level of personal or self-discipline from the student. In an honors course, for students to act as disciplinarians they will be required to:

- possess exceptional time management skills
- stay focused on the task at hand
- avoid distractions
- use appropriate classroom etiquette (such as listening, collaboration, effective communication, and negotiation)
- always be prepared for class and work

- accept feedback and critique as forms of personal and intellectual development
- take personal responsibility for workload, work readiness, and work completion
- be persistent and patient, and persevere to complete tasks

Working in depth in a subject requires students to research or study a specific branch of a broader subject area. Here are some examples of branches for different disciplines:

Arts and Humanities:
- archaeology
- art and design
- cinema and photography
- history
- journalism
- linguistics
- media communications
- religious studies

Health Sciences
- personal health/wellness or fitness
- exercise/sports science
- medicine
- dentistry
- social work or psychology
- veterinary medicine

Science, Technology, Engineering, and Math (STEM)
- biological ethics
- environmental science
- computer engineering
- geography or earth science

Social Sciences
- anthropology
- business management
- economics
- education
- hospitality, leisure, or tourism
- law
- marketing
- politics

Before working within specific areas as disciplinarians, students should have a broad base of knowledge within the subject area. Then and only then are they able to work in depth into the discipline. Dr. Sandra Kaplan, an eminent researcher and curriculum specialist in the field of gifted education, defines a *disciplinarian* as one who is an expert in a particular field of study; researches and publishes findings; performs specialized tasks rather than conducts basic operations; and collaborates across disciplines.[42] In some cases, professions or careers are directly linked to the discipline. For gifted students, working within the discipline can lead to career avenues, university options, or lifelong passions.

> A *disciplinarian* is an expert in a particular field of study, researches and publishes findings, performs specialized tasks, and collaborates across disciplines.

When students work as disciplinarians, they also develop the skills of a scholar. We encourage teachers of advanced secondary level courses to address their pupils as *scholars* rather than students. A scholar is one who learns and processes information with purpose and produces useful outcomes. A scholar also develops a scholarly disposition by being:

- open- and fair-minded
- inquisitive
- flexible in thinking and acting
- interested in seeking out reason
- immersed in acquiring more information
- respectful of and expecting diverse points of view

Use the "How People Learn" Approach

Another method for using the study of disciplines is to incorporate the process of how people learn. Based on work by the National Research Council, we have modified the four principles of a high-quality learning environment set forth in *How People Learn* (HPL) for the needs of gifted

learners in an honors class.[43] These principles provide the grounding for how students should study within an honors course.

- *Learner centered.* Keep in mind that gifted learners have varied and more rapid ways of learning information; often have more positive attitudes and are more motivated to acquire knowledge; possess more abundant prior knowledge and skills; and seek to move deeper into investigation of topics.
- *Knowledge centered.* Keep in mind that gifted learners should be working at the experience level to acquire information beyond the factual and process level. The goal is to master the conceptual knowledge and to transfer knowledge from one content area to another.
- *Assessment centered.* Keep in mind that gifted learners should monitor and adjust, as necessary, their own learning and achievement progress; critical descriptive feedback is essential to cognitive development and personal growth.
- *Community centered.* Keep in mind that gifted learners often feel isolated, different, or out of sync with their same-age peers; building learning communities where intellectual risk taking is accepted and expected, all learners have the shared goal and values of intellectual development and advancement.

Students begin learning about the content by questioning what disciplinarians know, how they know it, and why the information is important. In this way, students become familiar with the concepts, generalizations, principles, and theories of the subject. Students learn more about how the knowledge of the field is generated and justified. Finally, students are able to use their understandings to formulate new questions and develop new ideas.

To use the HPL approach effectively for gifted students, we recommend using a modified version of the Legacy Cycle[44] to challenge gifted students in an honors course (see **Figure 5.1**). This approach

[42] Kaplan, 2002.

[43] Bransford, Brown, and Cocking, 2000.
[44] Klein and Harris, 2007.

progresses through steps embedded within a unit of study. The steps include:

1. Framing the question
2. Generating ideas and multiple perspectives to answer the question
3. Researching to find a hypothesis
4. Analyzing the hypothesis
5. Presenting the conclusion

Figure 5.1: Legacy Cycle*

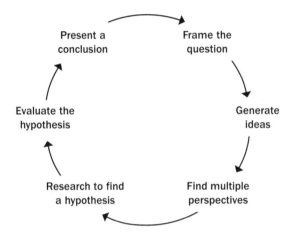

Using the Legacy Cycle in Advanced Courses

* Based on the work of Klein and Harris, 2007.

Framing the question: Example

In a U.S. History class studying the American Revolution, students choose a specific disciplinarian who would undertake this study, such as a historian, artist, theologian, politician, or journalist. Using the essential question framed by the curriculum as a consistent guide, students study the topic of the American Revolution through the lens of the disciplinarian they have chosen. To facilitate the development of essential questions, see the **Concept Development Steps in Creating Essential Questions**, page 76.

Let's say that the essential question is: In what ways are revolutions both positive and negative? The student who is studying the revolution from the angle of a historian may come up with different ideas or thoughts than the students studying through the lens of a theologian. Or, the students may gather together to study the American Revolution through the various lenses, stimulating a wide array of ideas that deepen the topic.

Generating ideas and multiple perspectives to answer the question: Example

Throughout the lessons, students would be gathering additional information from multiple perspectives to support or challenge their ideas. Students should select experts or resources outside the classroom from the discipline of their choice. For example, the historian will seek out expert historians to gather more ideas on how revolutions have affected history. The theologian will seek out expert theologians to question religious revolutions' positive and negative effects. The artist will seek out expert artists to investigate positive and negative effects revolutions have had on the art world.

Researching to find a hypothesis: Example

Students then begin to develop a hypothesis to answer the essential question from the perspective of their chosen disciplinarian. Following our example above, the historian may begin to answer the question about how revolutions have affected history in positive and negative ways and then offer suggestions on how to limit the negative effects. The theologian may begin to answer the same question by listing the positive and negative effects on the religious world or how religious revolutions have had positive and negative effects on society. The artist may begin to answer the question as it relates to art or answer how artistic revolutions have had both positive and negative effects on the art world.

Analyzing the hypothesis: Example

Students present their hypothesis to the entire class for analysis, critique, and review before formulating a final conclusion. Through this process, students learn to offer each other meaningful feedback or suggestions of ideas or solutions not considered. After the review of the hypothesis, students should be allowed time to revise or refine their final hypothesis statement.

Presenting the conclusion: Example

The concluding action in this method is for students to somehow display their product, which can range from an oral presentation to role playing or simulations to a final exam. The conclusion should be presented in a public forum or event. The assessment of the final product must be a fair appraisal of what the students have learned and not just what they know.

Strategies to Create Sophisticated Levels of Complexity

As defined in Chapter 2, complexity is the process the brain goes through to manage information. This includes thinking creatively, reasoning critically, problem finding and solving, the advanced levels of Bloom's Taxonomy (analyze, evaluate, and create), and self-regulation. All of these skills, as well as communication and collaboration, are considered essential for thinking and performing in the twenty-first century. In an honors class, all of the twenty-first century skills are taught and used at a more sophisticated level.

Sophisticated levels of thinking require:

- advanced levels of background or prior knowledge
- open-mindedness to critique personal bias/ opinions/misinformation
- disposition of a scholar (see page 80)

In an honors class, sophisticated thinking is directly taught as well as acted upon by infusing open-ended questioning and tasks, and through authentic problems that are ambiguous and/or controversial. Strategies to embed sophisticated levels of thinking into the course can include:

- the Socratic method: a method of discussion based on asking and answering questions that stimulate critical thinking and decision making.
- problem-based learning: in small groups, students investigate a problem to identify solutions. This model proves useful when developing self-directed learning.
- concept mapping or thinking mapping: a strategy for diagramming or mapping ideas.

This is a useful way for visualizing abstract connections between concepts.

- leveled questioning: see below.
- case methods: see page 83.

Leveled Questioning

Questioning is an essential part of learning. Not only should teachers use multiple layers of questions to challenge students, but students should also learn to ask good questions. Gifted students must learn how to ask various levels and types of questions as they seek deep understanding. Asking the "right" question can make a huge difference in effective problem solving.

A method to increase the sophistication in thinking, which is a must in your honors classes, is through leveled questioning.

There are four levels to questions that can be asked:

1. **Factual questions:** questions that seek factual answers that are either right or wrong. These questions are verifiable through text and form the foundation in a content area.

2. **Convergent questions:** questions that ask for lists of verifiable information and are often closed-ended. The information needed to answer these types of questions can also be found in the text, but reaching a conclusion will require a level of interpretation, inference, and evaluation.

3. **Divergent questions:** questions that open up differing lines of thought, seek creative and imaginative solutions, and may have multiple answers. When forming answers based on this level, students must have a solid knowledge base of information, which allows them to project, use intuition, and draw on their imagination to come up with new ideas or solutions.

4. **Analytical questions:** questions that require more thought than is required for simple answers and involves deeper logic and interpretation. As the name states, these questions are analytical in nature and seek to connect content areas, consider various

possibilities and effects, and are open-ended. (See **Figure 5.2.** Also in the digital download.)

Additionally, there are various typologies of questions that can be asked in the classroom. **Figure 5.3** (on page 84 and in the digital download) gives examples of the different types of questions that gifted students should be asking and answering. Be sure to vary the types of questions students use and respond to; doing so will help them think more flexibly and learn to ask the right questions to seek the right answers.

The Case Method

You can also advance sophisticated thinking by using the "case method." This method, which is similar to the "case study method," uses inductive pedagogy; students are given an authentic

> With the case method, students learn how to form good questions that can help them in analyzing the root causes of the problem and guide them toward solutions.

problem in condensed form (a "case") and are required to take on the roles of decision makers. In the process, students learn how to form good questions that can help them in analyzing the root causes of the problem and guide them toward solutions. Students take the lead in identifying issues, recognizing the need for greater information, and learning healthy emotional and intellectual ways to negotiate solutions. The case method can be a useful tool when you are differentiating content, process, and product.

Figure 5.2: Four Levels of Questions *(also included in the digital download)*

Factual	Convergent
Verifiable, found on the page, tests foundational knowledge in the content, one right answer	Verifiable, found within the text, tests comprehension/interpretation/inference/evaluation of material, often closed-ended
Examples:	*Examples:*
• Who was in love with Hamlet?	• What were the reasons Ophelia went mad?
• What are the common elements of alkali metals?	• In what ways do alkali metals differ from other metals?
• Which country has the highest gross domestic product for 2010?	• Why do some countries continue to have high gross domestic products every year?
• What is the sum of 320 x 46?	• What are some other ways to solve the equation . . . ?

4 LEVELS OF QUESTIONS

Divergent	Analytical
Validity is based on probability or possibility, found through the text, knowledgeable logical projections, intuition, creation or imagination (synthesis), open-ended	Connects the texts to other content areas, takes the learner beyond the text, uses sophisticated levels of thinking, may involve multiple logical or affective thinking processes, open-ended answers require perspective for interpretation
Examples:	*Examples:*
• What might have become of Hamlet and Ophelia's relationship had Hamlet not been so obsessed with revenge?	• What are the similarities and differences between the deaths of Ophelia and Juliet?
• How might alkali metals be used more effectively to improve the human situation?	• In what ways are alkali metals some of the most dangerous chemicals?
• How might newly industrialized countries increase their gross domestic product?	• What are the political actions of countries with high gross domestic products related to their steady growth?
• Create a unique way to explain the solving of this equation (such as through the use of metaphor).	• How is data used to persuade opinion?

Figure 5.3: Questioning Typology *(also included in the digital download)*

Type	Question Examples
Defining the issue	What is the situation? What is it all about? What are the various issues involved? Who is involved in the case? What are we expected to find out?
Fact vs. opinion	What do we know? What don't we know? What opinions do we have? How do the facts support/oppose our opinions?
Prediction and inference	What is at stake? What may happen if the situation is not resolved? What is a possible outcome if the situation is resolved? Why did the people involved act the way they did? How do the people involved feel? Why might the people involved not want a solution? How would the people involved benefit from a solution?
Inquiry	What questions do we have? What other information do we need? Where can we find data? How can we find the data? What are you taking for granted? What else needs to be considered?
Seeking point of view	What is your point of view? What does every member believe? Do we believe the people involved see it the way we do? What are the key issues you are focused on? Is your point of view reasonable? Which point of view makes the most sense given the situation? What evidence do you have to support your point of view?
Cause and effect	What effect will each option have? What are the values or limitations of the options? What implications will each option have on the people involved? Why are these options effective ideas? What are the consequences if no decision is made?
Criteria forming	What criteria will we use to select an option? How do we consider all members' opinions? Why do you believe the criteria to be sound? What information do you need to form sound criteria? What other experiences have you had that can help you form a sound decision?
Shifting point of view	What have you heard from others? Does that help or change your point of view? What conclusions can you come to after hearing others' point of view? How might each point of view be helpful in creating a decision?
Considering all sides	How might your opinion or view be seen differently? In what ways do other points of view support/oppose your point of view? How can other points of view be adjusted to support/oppose your point of view? In what ways do others interpret your point of view?
Looking backward	What might the people involved have done differently to alleviate or avoid the situation? How might this situation been different if any one person/event were eliminated? How did each event/person assist in creating the situation? How might the situation have been different? →

Urging follow-up	Tell me more. What do you mean by that statement? What else needs to be considered? Could you clarify your thinking for us? Provide examples to support your claim. Tell me how you got to that conclusion.
Guiding to collaboration	Why you think she has that idea? What are the various viewpoints so far? Why do we have differing opinions/viewpoints? In what ways can you support each other in this process? What are the strengths of each member and how can they help create a workable solution?

How the Case Method Supports Common Core and Other Initiatives

With the advances of the Common Core State Standards (CCSS) in the United States and the provincial framework in Canada, the case method offers a platform for critical thinking and reasoning. Students must make a claim, collect evidence to support their claim, reason through the material, define counterarguments, and then consider the audience to which they will appeal their case. All these strategies and techniques are central tenets of the CCSS.

Another pivotal tool of the twenty-first century is technological literacy. The case method requires students to research current events and issues by gathering data from multiple sources to make their claim, developing arguments, and fleshing out counterarguments. Using the Internet to collect valid information from credible sources will be essential. Also, presenting the information in a pleasing and effective way will require students to use technology beyond PowerPoint.

The case method helps students develop the skills necessary for sophisticated levels of thinking. Students are also encouraged to think in creative and divergent ways to work out solutions. And this method allows them to practice collaborating, develop communication skills, and build their skills in problem finding and solving and decision making.

Finally, the case method requires students to develop and use more sophisticated levels of self-regulation. Students must monitor and adjust their thoughts, feeling, and behaviors to successfully complete the process.

You can incorporate the case method into the general course cycle, but be sure to allow enough time for students to take the information they learned from the course and apply it to the solution of the case. Students will need time for discussion and active investigation to resolve the case. Remember, cases should be authentic and involve real problems that are complicated and messy. There will not be one right answer. Cases are also large issues that will require students to be prepared for class discussions, will necessitate multiple steps to developing a solution, and will involve a variety of intellectual skills. Students will need to communicate and collaborate in large and small groups to find a workable solution.

Creating a Good Case

Here are some tips on creating a good case for gifted students:

1. Provide key information but keep it as limited as possible. The less information you give students, the more likely they are to grasp the ideas and develop a solution. Too much information can clutter the process. However, too little information will not provide enough background or nuances for students to find a workable solution. The magic is in creating a case that has just the right amount of information.

2. Include evidence in the case information that is both relevant and irrelevant, and present it in a range of forms—from narrative to quotations to tables/graphs and charts to news articles. The key is in the balance of types of relevant and irrelevant information.

3. Remember that the goal is for students to take on the position of a decision maker in the real world. Students should interpret the information from the perspective of a disciplinarian and then use the decision-making tools of that discipline to ultimately reach a conclusion. You might want to construct cases around existing policies or social issues. Try to create a case that engages the learner as a disciplinarian with a real problem that needs a real solution.

4. Focus the case on incorporating the essential question. Using the essential question as a guiding framework will help students find meaning in the course content and show them how their new skills can be applied to real-life situations.

The components of a case include:

1. Background information to help students fully understand the issue. This could include definitions of terms and factual material. This part of the case helps students focus their attention on what really matters in the case.

2. A compelling narrative that fleshes out the human aspect of the story and offers a greater set of ambiguities. This is the meat of the case and should lay out the multiple dimensions of the issues involved.

3. Guiding questions to help students come to a conclusion. The questions should focus on:

   a. a summary of the case (What is this case about?)

   b. highlights of the various issues intertwined in the case (Example: What are the various concerns of each party involved in the case?)

   c. suggested resolutions from the various perspectives (Examples: Should this company settle the suit before going to court? Why or why not? Should the company seek a different location to build their plant? Why or why not? If the witnesses refuse to testify in front of Congress, should they be held in contempt? Why or why not?)

   d. the actions of the actors within the case (Examples: Did the police act in an ethical manner? Why or why not? Was the principal impractical in awarding the trophy? How did she do?)

Cases can be built from:
- current events
- historical documents
- news articles/reports
- editorials
- data reports
- research/scientific documents
- literary passages
- video/audio recordings
- ethnographies
- investigative reports
- documentary films
- online news reports/sources
- websites such as Google Scholar or TED Talks
- reality television shows

Case Method Examples

The intelligent pill

A major pharmaceutical company has developed a pill that can increase intelligence. Your school is considering testing the pill. What are the possible consequences of the testing that should be taken into account?

(Note: This case was based on true stories of pharmaceutical companies aiming to create pills to increase intelligence.)

Mimi gets sick!

Nasreen is a twenty-five-year-old aspiring actress living in New York City. She rents a small two-bedroom apartment on the Upper West Side, which she shares with her roommate, Toni. Nasreen met Toni through an apartment agency in the city. They have lived amicably in the apartment for nine months. Nasreen is devoted to her pet cat, Mimi. Recently, Mimi has become lethargic and disinterested in her normal play routine. Seeking to find a cause for Mimi's recent change in behavior, Nasreen took her to the local veterinarian. The veterinarian ran tests and identified that Mimi was suffering from liver damage. Nasreen would like to find the source of her cat's illness.

(Note: This case was developed based on information citing hazardous materials in homes and apartments that are dangerous to the health of pets.)

How to Teach Through the Case

Before case presentation

The case method requires teachers and students to be highly prepared before instruction. Prior to delivering the case to the students, you must be well versed in the details of case. It is important that you know the various nuances involved and work through the questions expected of the students, doing all the steps the students will be required to perform.

Also, it is helpful for students to have enough time prior to class for studying and understanding the case. The students should use the questioning guide (page 84) to help them prepare for classroom discussions. Encourage students to take notes in a way that will help them easily refresh their memory or make their point during class.

During case discussion

In case discussions there are three primary roles the teacher and students will play: questioner, responder, and listener. Before the discussions, inform students of the overarching goal or intended outcome of the case.

Using the I-FORD method of problem solving,[45] construct questions that guide students to a conclusion. Here is how the I-FORD method works:

I=Identify the problem: What is the situation?

F=Gather facts: What are the facts of this case? What do we know about each actor in the case?

O=List options for solutions: What can each person do? Why might that person choose that option?

R=Rank the possible solutions: list the consequences to each action.

D=Decide on the best course of action: Select one action and state why you believe it is the best solution.

See page 148 for more on the I-FORD method.

> In case discussions, the teacher and students will play three primary roles: questioner, responder, and listener.

You should also prepare questions that guide and coach students to review their own thinking and problem-solving skills. Those questions should:

- Focus the students on the facts of the case. (Example: "What information from the case gave you that idea?")
- Draw attention to important facts or information that may have been overlooked by the students. (Examples: "Note in the narrative that the company had chosen not to include the ingredients on the packaging. How might that fact change the judge's opinion?")
- Encourage students to question and debate each other. (Examples: "Sarah, please explain to Abdul why you believe the lawyer's actions were unethical.")
- Clarify and rephrase student questions and comments. (Examples: "Zak stated that the company had provided all the information required by law." "Addie asked how the plaintiff was liable for recognizing that peanuts were included in the cookie.")
- Compel students to support their claims and defend their views. (Example: "Mario, highlight the information that helped you come to your conclusion.")
- Allow students time to reflect on and provide an answer to the essential question based on what was learned in the case discussions. (Example: "What new information can we add to our answers of the essential question?")

---

45 Cash, 2011.

Be prepared for when students take the case in a direction you may not have considered. Be open to looking at the case from their point of view.

Create a classroom environment that encourages the exchange of ideas. For example:

- Use a seating arrangement that allows all students to see and hear each other and keeps the teacher out of the center of the discussion.
- Provide appropriate technologies and materials that support or allow the discussion to occur.
- Implement norms of discussion/debate behaviors.
- Encourage and allow intellectual risk taking.
- Use role playing to elaborate ideas or enhance understanding.
- Work from large to small groups.
- Offer opportunities for individuals to work independently.
- Provide time at the end of discussions for a student or a group of students to summarize the discussion.
- Require metacognitive reflection at the end of every session.
- Use the jigsaw technique to cover material more quickly.

After the case discussion

At the end of the case discussion (which can stretch out over several class sessions), provide highlights of the class discussions and conclusions. In this review, focus on the students' use of analytical thinking, creative idea generation, and problem-solving techniques used throughout the discussions. Note when students were effective in their thinking and in what ways they may be able to improve their strategies.

Also, it is beneficial to ask students to write a brief statement of what happened cognitively during the case discussions. Ask questions such as:

- What was the case really about?
- What was the general outcome of the case?
- What did you learn from this case?

- What did you learn from the class discussions about yourself as a thinker?
- How well did you perform during the class discussions?
- What might you change or improve for the next case?
- What did you like or dislike about the discussions held in class?
- In what ways can the method be enhanced or improved?

When to Use the Case Method

You can use the case method at numerous points in your schedule, including

- at the beginning of a unit to pique interest
- during a unit to add meaning to the students' skill development
- after a unit to check for understanding
- as an anchor activity
- to engage special interest groups
- to develop expert groups to reciprocally teach others
- at the opening of a lesson to stimulate the brain in thinking
- as a sponge activity (when you have a small amount of time near the end of a class session)

For more ideas on building a case, check out: serc.carleton.edu.

Ideas for Differentiating the Case Method
By readiness:

- For students who need more scaffolding, provide additional resources, highlighted text, or simplified text to gain the essential information.
- For students who are ready for a greater challenge, offer text that is more sophisticated and includes a greater degree of irrelevance and ambiguity.
- For those students who desire or require greater autonomy in their learning, allow them to perform a self-study on a topic that is especially important or of interest to them.

- To help students get started with a case, have them work through a KIQ (Know, Interested in, Question) to develop an idea for a case.

By interest:
- To engage the students, use topics that are relevant to the students' immediate lives, such as gaming, texting and driving, bullying, or the health benefits of organic food.
- For the unmotivated learner, provide an array of topics to choose from based on their personal interests.
- For the career-oriented student, create cases based on careers related to the discipline.
- As an anchor activity for all students, use the case method as a center, station, or website that students routinely and persistently work on throughout the term or course and that is based on a topic of interest.

By learning profile:
- Use a variety of information sources such as websites, news articles, videos, or music.
- Offer students opportunities to act out situations, draw out their ideas, blog about the topic, contribute ideas to a discussion board, or create poems or songs that articulate their beliefs about the outcomes of the case.
- Use simulations, debates, moot court, or role playing to help students gain an appreciation for the affective side of the case.
- For students who are more independent in their learning, offer a learning station or center that allows them to go through a case on their own.

By thinking levels:
Another way to add complexity in an honors class is through sophisticated degrees of the advanced levels of Bloom's Taxonomy. The upper levels of Bloom's Taxonomy include analysis, evaluation, and creation (or synthesis). The upper levels are often called the higher order thinking skills (HOTS). While all students can think at advanced levels, honors level students should be performing in more sophisticated degrees of HOTS.

In most cases, the standards are written for the general population. The general standard used in an honors level class can be made more sophisticated by highlighting the "be able to dos." Below is an example of a general social studies standard:

Sample Honors Course Standard: Ancient Civilizations

Students will analyze the geographic, political, economic, religious, and social structures of the early civilizations of Mesopotamia, Egypt, and Kush.[46]

Benchmarks:
- ✓ Locate and describe the major river systems and discuss the physical settings that supported permanent settlement and early civilizations. (6.2.1)
- ✓ Understand the relationship between religion and the social and political order in Mesopotamia and Egypt. (6.2.3)
- ✓ Trace the development of agricultural techniques that permitted the production of economic surplus and the emergence of cities as centers of culture and power. (6.2.2)
- ✓ Know the significance of Hammurabi's Code (Laws). (6.2.4)

In an effort to make this standard more sophisticated (and not more work), the main learning objective remains the same (analyze), but the following benchmarks are made more complex:
- ✓ Explain and illustrate why ancient civilizations would locate permanent settlements along the river systems that were used.
- ✓ Determine and articulate the specific elements of religion that supported the social and political order of Mesopotamia and Egypt, and the specific elements of the social and political order that supported the religions of those areas.
- ✓ Rank order and justify the agricultural techniques that permitted the production of economic surplus and the emergence of cities as centers of culture and power.
- ✓ Critique the impact of Hammurabi's Code (Laws) on the development of the ancient world.

---

[46] CA State Social Studies Standards, 6.2.

Using Common Core State Standards in Honors Courses

The Common Core State Standards have increased the rigor for all students by making the procedural level more sophisticated. (See Chapter 3 for more on how the standards affect gifted education.) Therefore, in an honors level course, since the procedural level is already more sophisticated, these standards are differentiated through the materials/content used. Additionally, since the standards are less grade-specific, they offer a greater opportunity for teachers to stretch into more advanced levels of the standards. For example:

Grades Nine to Ten

Cite strong and thorough textual evidence to support analysis of what the text says explicitly as well as inferences drawn from the text.[47]

Grades Eleven to Twelve

Cite strong and thorough textual evidence to support analysis of what the text says explicitly as well as inferences drawn from the text, including determining where the text leaves matters uncertain.[48]

In the case above, at the ninth- and tenth-grade honors level, students would be working with the eleventh- and twelfth-grade standard. Because they have addressed the standard in earlier years, students may now move into greater depth of a topic or move on to other studies.

Using the "Digging Deeper Matrix" in an Honors Course

Since honors level courses and regular level courses are often taught by the same teacher, consider using the Digging Deeper Matrix (DDM)[49] as a template for advancing all student performance into more sophisticated complexity and deeper content. The model provides a tiered system for creating activities at every level of Bloom's Taxonomy that are rigorous and complex, and respect the varying needs for academic difficulty in a mixed-ability classroom.

The model is designed so that the general education student would work through level 1 of the matrix, while students who need greater challenge in the inclusion classroom can work into level 2. In an honors classroom, all students would begin instruction in level 2 and advance into level 3 of the matrix. The intent behind this model is to:

1. Recognize that all students can and should be thinking at the most advanced levels of Bloom's Taxonomy

2. Respect teachers' time needed to create lessons at various levels by providing a structure to make the regular curriculum more sophisticated and deeper for both the regular and honors level classes

3. Support the idea that tiered assignments at all levels must be equally engaging, take about the same amount of time, and require students to use the same effort to complete the tasks

4. Provide a guide for assessments at each level of Bloom's Taxonomy and into greater depth

See **Figures 5.4** and **5.5** (pages 91 and 92) for examples of the DDM. A blank chart is also included in the digital download.

Alignment: Effective Practices in Student Selection

Once you have determined what an honors course is and the instructional practices and curricular methods used in the course, you are now ready to select students for honors courses. There are two basic methods for student selection: "open door" and identification through criteria.

Open-Door Method

In the open-door method of selection, students decide whether they would like to take on a more challenging course. No specific criteria is used other than a student self-selecting into the course. This method is beneficial for increasing the number of CLED students in advanced-level courses or allowing more students to be exposed to a greater level of challenge.

---

47 Reading for Informational Text 6–12, Key Ideas and Details, #1.
48 Ibid.
49 Cash, 2011.

Figure 5.4: Digging Deeper Matrix (DDM): ELA Example #1*

Unit: The Color Purple

Abstract concepts:
- awareness
- gender roles
- survival
- self-esteem/self-image

Essential questions:
- What roles do racism and feminism play in our society?
- Does society benefit from gender roles?
- What survival skills are necessary in American society?
- How does self-esteem and self-image affect our view of the world?

Common Core State Standards:
- Recall: 11.RL.10
- Understanding: 11.SL.1, 11.SL.4
- Apply: 11.W.1, 11.W.8, 11.RL.5
- Analyze: 11.RL.1, 11.RL.2, 11.W.4, 11.W.5
- Evaluate: 11.W.9
- Create: 11.SL.5

	Recall (R)	Understanding (U)	Apply (A)	Analyze (Z)	Evaluate (E)	Create (C)
Level 1 Assessment	Specific/Concrete Pages 1–130 Quiz Pages 131–221 Quiz Pages 222–295 Quiz	Translate Two Socratic Seminars • Survival Journal and question preparations • Gender Roles Journal and question preparations	Original Way Write a persuasive argument using The Color Purple; cite arguments for and/or against racism or feminism.	Individual Elements Write a two-passage analysis exploring two themes from The Color Purple novel, developing tweets the character might say.	Check Clarity Develop a Twitter page critically evaluating a presentation using the concepts of self-esteem/self-image.	Reorganize Create a multimedia presentation using the concepts of self-esteem/self-image.
Level 2 Assessment	Tools/Skills Pages 1–130 Quiz Pages 131–221 Quiz Pages 222–295 Quiz	Interpret Two Socratic Seminars • Survival Journal and question preparations • Gender Roles Journal and question preparations	Practical Way Using news and editorial articles from the same period as The Color Purple, cite situations where racism or feminism are supported or opposed in a persuasive argument.	Relationship Among Elements Identify two significant passages in The Color Purple and compare/contrast them using textual evidence to support your opinion.	Judge Accuracy Develop a Facebook page that critically evaluates a specific character's growth throughout the novel. Use specific references from the book.	Formulate Create a multimedia presentation/Public Service Announcement that takes the reader on a journey through the concept of self-esteem/self-image. Base the presentation on personally relatable experiences.
Level 3 Assessment	Abstract Information Pages 1–130 Quiz Pages 131–221 Quiz Pages 222–295 Quiz	Extrapolate Two Socratic Seminars • Survival Journal and question preparations • Gender Roles Journal and question preparations	Creative Way Search news and editorial articles from within the last year that support or oppose racism or feminism, and cite the authors use in a persuasive argument.	Principles Governing Elements Track a character and a page that critically evaluates a character throughout The Color Purple, choosing significant passages. Make connections between the passages and issues concerning 1910–1940 Southern culture.	Critique Validity Develop a Wikipedia page that critically evaluates a character from The Color Purple. Cite connections through relationships to other characters to support your opinion.	Innovate Using the concept of self-esteem/self-image in The Color Purple, create a Public Service Announcement/multi-media presentation that uses these concepts in a new and different way.

*Adapted from Cash, 2011; unit created by Kevin Konsler

Figure 5.5: Digging Deeper Matrix (DDM): ELA Example #2*

Unit: The Great Gatsby

Essential questions:

- What do I consider values and why is it important to have them as an individual and as a society?
- What is the American Dream and what values does it reflect?
- What does it mean to be a success?
- How does popular culture influence our values?

	Recall (R)	Understanding (U)	Apply (A)	Analyze (Z)	Evaluate (E)	Create (C)
Level 1 Assessment	Specific/Concrete Chapters 1–3 Quiz Chapters 4–6 Quiz Chapters 7–9 Quiz	Translate Discussion/Journal Questions in eBook Question Journal	Original Way Create a news article from *The Great Gatsby* novel that reflects the values of the 1920s.	Individual Elements Identify an element that supports a major theme in *The Great Gatsby*. Use textual evidence to support your opinion.	Check Clarity Develop a presentation and persuasive speech critically evaluating a significant scene in the novel.	Reorganize Choose a theme that has emerged and write a poem, short story, or personal connection about it, or create a graphic novel.
Level 2 Assessment	Tools/Skills Chapters 1–3 Quiz Chapters 4–6 Quiz Chapters 7–9 Quiz	Interpret Discussion/Journal Questions in eBook Question Journal	Practical Way Write a contemporary news article that compares modern values with values from the 1920s.	Relationship Among Elements Identify two major themes in *The Great Gatsby* and compare/contrast them using textual evidence to support your opinion.	Judge Accuracy Develop a presentation that judges the actions of at least two characters from the novel and how they either support or contradict a theme in the book.	Formulate Outline and design a short story, novella, or novel that takes the reader on a journey through the theme of the American Dream. Base the story on personally relatable experiences.
Level 3 Assessment	Abstract Information Chapters 1–3 Quiz Chapters 4–6 Quiz Chapters 7–9 Quiz	Extrapolate Discussion/Journal Questions in eBook Question Journal	Creative Way Write a futuristic news article that predicts or forecasts how values will change from the 1920s or how values may return to the standards of the 1920s.	Principles Governing Elements In what ways are *The Crucible* and *The Great Gatsby* similar/different thematically? Make these connections and use textual evidence to support your opinion.	Critique Validity Develop a movie that shows how various scenes in the book either support or contradict historical events that took place during the time of *The Great Gatsby*.	Innovate Using the idea's generated by *The Great Gatsby*, create a synopsis of a book you might propose to a publisher that uses the themes of the American Dream and popular social values in a new and different way.

*Adapted from Cash, 2011; unit created by Kevin Konsler

This method can only succeed if there is a support system in place before and during the students' participation in the honors course. Pre-support systems may include classes that prepare students for the challenge of an honors course, such as AVID. Another useful program that can prepare CLED students for advanced courses is the Pre-AP model.

It is extremely important that underrepresented populations or underprepared students in an honors course receive support throughout the course. Students should be offered tutoring before, during, or after schools, or one-on-one meetings with the teacher to review or ensure learning. Support sessions offered during class should be limited so that students who need the additional support don't feel "different" or highlighted for the lack of background experiences. Other ideas for support systems include:

- tutors
- mentors/role models
- guidance counseling
- test-prep classes/sessions
- study buddies
- family guidance and support sessions

Here are some other ideas to increase student diversity in honors courses:

- Ensure that the K–12 curriculum is used in a way that provides all students pathways into advanced-level courses.
- Provide career planning to all students early in their educational journey, focusing on the types and qualities of courses necessary for success in various fields.
- Train all teachers to recognize the characteristics of students who would be well served by an honors level course.
- Offer "tryout" courses or options (shorter versions of honors courses, perhaps three-week or nine-week courses).

Identification through Criteria

Unlike the open-door method of selecting students for honors level courses, this method relies on a set of criteria to determine which students would be best served in honors courses. The most effective way to identify students who would be appropriate for advanced classes is through multiple measures that correspond with the content and methods of the course. In most cases, summative tests/evaluations, classroom performances, and grades are used as the identifiers for honors courses. These may be supplemented with recommendations from:

- teachers
- the student
- parents or other family members
- other education professionals
- religious or community members
- employers

This method of selection should also include an "appeals process." Such a process allows students who have been declined placement or who don't meet the set criteria to appeal the decision, based on their desire, motivation, or aspirations to participate in the course. The appeals process could include:

- an interview with the student
- additional data, such as a personal narrative, portfolio assessments, or further testing
- abilities tests, such as an IQ test
- Nonverbal assessments, such as the *Naglieri Nonverbal Ability Test* (NNAT)

Exit Process

No matter which method is used to select students for an honors course, there needs to be an exit process. Exit processes should not be used as a punishment or be related to how well the students are prepared for the course. Rather, the process is used to ensure that students are placed in the course that is the right level for them. When students have a way out of the class that is not a good fit, then the course can proceed at its designed level and students are not unduly stressed by the academic workload. The process needs to be fair, equitable, and in the best interest of the child.

The process must have clearly defined procedures that all students and families are made aware of prior to course enrollment. Students should also know where they stand throughout the course, through either individual conferences or letters to the family.

> No matter which method is used to select students for an honors course, there needs to be an exit process.

Accountability: Continuous Review for Continuous Improvement

It is important to review all classes and courses annually to ensure their quality. Especially with an honors course, the instructional methods and curricular designs need to meet the needs of gifted learners. Administrators, gifted education coordinators, teaching peers, or educational specialists/consultants can help review honors courses. Reviewers should be well acquainted with the characteristics of gifted learners, advanced pedagogy, and deep content prior to observing the classroom.

A useful checklist for the reviewer is the **Accountability Chart** on page 95. Another form that can be helpful in reviewing honors courses is the **Professional Learning Communities Honors Worksheet** on page 96. What makes your honors class different? This form can be used in your PLC work to ensure that honors courses are truly designed and delivered for gifted learners. What makes the form most helpful is the citing of specific examples and being as honest as possible about your practice and curriculum. Use the form to help articulate and align your courses for accelerated pace, complex levels of thinking, and deep content.

The review of an honors course is intended to assist in continuous improvement. It should not be used to reward or punish a teacher or students. The teacher and reviewer should use the coaching methods (as described in Chapter 7) to reflect on the course offering.

Keep in mind, the honors classroom should offer:

- **an open environment** where students feel safe to take intellectual risks
- **flexible instructional grouping** that allows students to lead *and* follow **multiple approaches to information** beyond the textbook
- **multiple learning modes** beyond stand and deliver
- **a focus on student strengths** as a way to support areas of weakness
- **use of humor** to reduce stress and make learning fun
- **an atmosphere of inquiry** where questioning is the norm
- **acceptance, appreciation, and welcoming attitude of diversity** (in people and ideas)
- **independent research along with collaborative production**
- **innovative thinking and production of new thoughts, insights, or products**

Chapter Summary

Honors programming at the secondary level is meant to provide academically gifted students the opportunity to learn in an environment and curriculum that corresponds to their abilities. In some cases, honors classes have become the haven for "good students" or where we place the best teachers. All students have the right to a challenging learning experience. However, to ensure we are meeting the needs of our gifted secondary students, we need to provide programming and curriculum that are truly differentiated based on the cognitive and social/emotional needs of gifted learners.

◎ Accountability Chart

	Strong Evidence	Some Evidence	Little Evidence	No Evidence
Course Description: Highlights				
The difference between an honors and regular course				
The enhanced/enriched learning environment				
How the content is extended beyond the core curriculum				
The use of advanced levels of independence in learning				
The need for sophisticated, advanced levels of thinking, performance, and intellectual skills				
Instruction: Pace is accelerated				
More time on higher levels of information				
Instruction through big ideas				
Use of descriptive feedback				
Use of advanced levels of questioning				
Less teacher directed and more student directed				
Curriculum: Content is deep and complex				
Students work as disciplinarians				
Students are solving authentic problems				
Students are creating authentic products that have value to others				
Students are generating further questions beyond those offered by the teacher				
Materials are rich in language of the discipline				
Classroom discussions go beyond recall of facts to complex analysis of information/arguments or thesis development				
Issues are relevant, ambiguous, and provocative				
Assessments are authentic and produce products with value to others				
Students are encouraged to develop learning autonomy				
Students are developing advanced levels of self-regulation				

◎Professional Learning Communities Worksheet: What Makes Honors Different?*

Pace	Regular	Honors
How much time is spent **reviewing** at the beginning of the year?		
How are homework and assignments differentiated?		
How much time is spent on teacher-directed instruction?		
How much time is spent on student-led questioning?		
How are essential questions used in the class?		
In what ways are materials differentiated?		
Choose at least three representative chapters: How many days are spent on those chapters?		
Choose at least three representative topics: How many **teacher-led examples** are there before students work independently?		

Complexity	Regular	Honors
Choose a few representative topics: Give specific examples of the most difficult homework assignments on similar topics offered in regular and honors, and discuss how they are differentiated.		
Choose a few representative topics: Give specific examples of problems/questions that show the differing **levels of abstraction** between regular and honors.		

Depth	Regular	Honors
Choose a few representative topics: Give examples that show to what extent students learn **discipline-specific theories and vocabulary.**		
Choose a few representative topics: Give examples that demonstrate to what extent students have to apply learning in **new situations.**		

* Adapted from the work of Mr. Sean Foley, Secondary Curriculum Coordinator, Bloomington Public Schools, MN.

Chapter 6

Changing Roles for Educators of Gifted Students

Our collective years in the field of gifted education have taught us so many valuable lessons about gifted learners, particularly about their instructional needs and social and emotional development. In addition, we have both worked in regular education, and so we have a greater understanding of how to differentiate for both populations of students.

Gifted students learn in distinctly different ways from other learners, which call for vastly different instructional strategies. In general, gifted students learn basic information more rapidly, require less repetition to retain that information, are more independent or solo workers, and often enjoy being more self-directed in their learning. These characteristics can run counter to the educational tone in the general classroom. Thus, when gifted students are assigned to the general classroom, we are essentially setting them up for, in the worst case, underachievement or at least a sense of disengagement. This is most often due to the lack of match between the gifted student's learning characteristics and what a traditional class may offer.

Sometimes, when gifted students are placed in the general classroom without differentiation, the setting can inadvertently foster negative characteristics in gifted learners (see the list of negative behaviors provided in Chapter 4, page 39). When they are not challenged to a degree that requires them to stay focused or to put forth much effort, they can become highly unregulated. They do not learn how to study, set goals, make plans to achieve those goals, or monitor their plans for success. When challenge finally does come along, they may struggle to work through the process, fear attempting something that takes effort, fear making a mistake or failing, or work at something to perfection, not knowing when enough is enough.

Therefore, whether in a general classroom setting or in a specialized class, the role of the teacher of gifted students—and all students—must change from one of instructional leader *of* learning to one of instructional guide *for* learning. As stated previously, gifted students can be voracious learners; they don't need to be told to learn. They do need to be supported, guided, encouraged, coached, and directed toward fulfilling their desires to know, understand, and be able to do.

> Gifted students don't need to be told to learn. They do need to be supported, guided, and encouraged.

This chapter will clarify your role as the teacher in a differentiated classroom, whether general or specialized, when working with gifted learners. It will define the various levels that students pass through as they move toward mastery and success. We'll also present strategies and ideas on instructional practices and student actions throughout the chapter.

Defining the Role of the Teacher

Teachers can impact student learning in a wide range of ways, from setting expectations (unconscious or conscious) to providing direct training within various subgroups of students. Teaching is both an art and a science. Knowing the learners you have, setting appropriately challenging expectations, and having significant professional development with respect to various subgroups of students can all have an enormous effect on student achievement.

When working with gifted students, you need to be amply prepared to address their specific learning requirements as well as their social and emotional needs. Teachers of the gifted do not need to be gifted themselves, just thoroughly skilled in creating learning experiences that challenge and nurture the gifted child's academic, social, and emotional development.

Teacher as Mindset Shifter

As was mentioned earlier, some gifted students are not sufficiently challenged in the early years of learning and therefore don't learn how to face difficulties or lack of success. In other cases, they may have developed a skewed perception of their abilities because most educational experiences have required little effort. This lack of challenge in the early years can set in motion what psychologist Carol Dweck calls a "fixed mindset."

In research that spans over twenty-five years, Dweck found that "many of the most accomplished students shied away from challenge and fell apart in the face of setbacks . . . [These same students] questioned or condemned their intelligence, when they failed a task."[50] With this attitude of defeatism and self-doubt fixed, students believe their intelligence and talent are static, unchanging traits. They feel that their abilities have been proven through the documentation and assessments that assign them the classification of gifted. They also believe that their success (which required very little effort) is due to their verified intelligence or talent. Gifted individuals with a fixed mindset believe that things should just come easy. At the same time, these students are always fearful of being rendered "not gifted" if they fail

at a task or are unable to complete an assignment to their level of expectation. They are concerned with how smart they are and, therefore, may be reluctant to try new experiences in which they may fall short of being best. When learning becomes challenging, students with a fixed mindset may lose confidence in their abilities, their enjoyment of the task, their motivation to keep going, and, as a result, give up early.

Additionally, having a fixed mindset makes it difficult for students to admit to and correct their mistakes, and they may blame others or the situation when they actually put in little effort or failed to prepare. As a result, these students miss the opportunity to develop valuable life skills, or self-regulating skills, of learning how to fail, developing a locus of control (the ability to control events that affect them), learning effective study habits, and so forth.

On the personal development level, one of the roles of teachers of the gifted is to help students develop what Dweck defines as a "growth mindset." Students with this type of mindset learn that through effort, most things are doable. Gifted students with growth mindsets have an easier time facing obstacles and challenges and are more likely to persevere until they succeed. They are resilient to setbacks and are convinced that success will come with enough time and effort.

Knowing where you have weaknesses and how to overcome them is an essential learned trait of a person with a growth mindset. In order for fixed mindset gifted students to switch to a growth mindset, teachers will need to highlight their individual strengths as well as individual weaknesses.

This can be a difficult task, because no one really wants to be told what they are not good at, and some gifted students may never have had to look at their areas of weakness before. Yet developing a growth mindset can be an extremely valuable life tool, helpful in overcoming difficult situations, negative labels, or stereotypes and barriers. This is especially useful for CLED students in gifted programming.

---

[50] Dweck, 2000, p. 5.

◎ Ten Strategies for Developing a Growth Mindset in Gifted Students

How exactly do you help students switch mindsets? Here are some strategies that have proven effective for helping them make this transition..

1. Help students recognize their strengths and their weaknesses. Show them how to use their strengths to develop their weak areas or find learning partners who are strong in areas where they may be weak.

2. Provide descriptive, accurate, and constructive feedback that focuses on how students can develop themselves in specific tasks or skill areas.

3. Focus praise on the effort students put forth toward a goal.

4. Offer authentic challenges on issues they or others care about that will take time, effort, and persistence to solve.

5. Teach specific skills of studying, organization, metacognition, time management, goal setting, and monitoring.

6. Use preassessments to help students recognize what they already know/understand and are able to do, and what they don't know/understand and are not yet able to do. Be mindful that students may perceive preassessments as shameful (especially if they are in the fixed mindset). Reassure students that preassessments are meant to focus teaching and learning.

7. When teaching discrete strategies, show students how using the strategy will help them develop certain skills. Some gifted students are whole to part learners and may avoid practicing discrete strategies (part) if they don't understand how it leads to greater skill development (whole).

8. Structure time throughout the day when students can reflect on their learning process, talk with others about tasks that were easy or difficult, or take note of their personal feelings on the topic.

9. Create learning activities where students will need to rely on others to complete the tasks. In these "unlike" groups, students learn to appreciate other people's skills and realize they have skills unique to themselves.

10. Continually support students by showing them how their efforts lead to success.

Teacher as Knowledge Guide

In general, gifted students approach learning in a holistic manner. Most enjoy seeing the big picture first and then burrow down into the specifics or minutia of the content areas. This way of learning conflicts with the way teachers may approach a subject. With great frequency, teachers go from the factual level up toward the conceptual level—which can be frustrating for and discouraging to gifted learners.

When working with gifted students, keep in mind that accelerated movement from the factual level through the process level of learning can increase students' motivation to learn. Gifted students usually prefer to conceptualize information through the most advanced and abstract levels of the curriculum more quickly than does the general population. To support this desire teachers need to differentiate with gifted students during the learning process.

The Teaching and Learning Continuum

An effective instructional practice for working with advanced-level students to provide more instructional guidance at the coached and consultative level of the teaching and learning continuum that we developed is called the Cash-Heacox Teaching and Learning Continuum (TLC).[51] The TLC is intended to be a guiding framework to assist you and your students in developing learner autonomy. Gifted students need to become more independent learners to access advanced material more rapidly (see **Figure 6.1**).

Based on decades of research on the art and science of teaching and learning, the TLC was developed to synthesize the most effective strategies of instruction, learning, and assessment. Three theories were used to ground the TLC:

1. The Gradual Release of Responsibility Model, which scaffolds student learning to greater independence

2. Self-Determination Theory of human motivation, based on a hierarchy of psychological needs

3. Dweck's Mindset Theory, which encourages the belief that achievement is directly connected to the amount of effort put forth to the task

The guiding framework of the TLC can assist you and your students in developing greater learning autonomy. *Learning autonomy* is defined as the desire to learn without being persuaded to learn. Learning autonomous people are more intrinsically driven, find greater success, and continue to learn throughout their lives. We want this for all students, and most gifted students can move toward learning autonomy more quickly than others.

> *Learning autonomy* is the desire to learn without being persuaded to learn.

The model is divided into four levels, or phases, of the learning process. At the lowest level, teachers are primarily responsible for the teaching and learning process. At the upper levels of the model, students gain responsibility for learning new information. As the teacher's responsibility decreases from the bottom of the model up, the students' responsibility increases toward greater learning autonomy.

Figure 6.1: Cash-Heacox Teaching and Learning Continuum (TLC)*

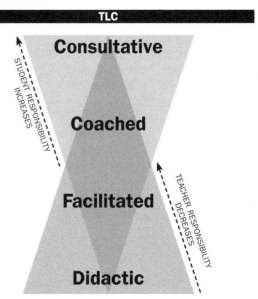

* Cash, 2011.

The lowest level of the model is described as "didactic." This is the level at which most of the factual and process information and strategies are defined and practiced. Here the teacher sets goals, determines student needs, plans instruction, forms groups, and develops prescribed assessments. Students may have choices in activities but are mainly directed into set tasks.

As students gain more skills and meet a certain level of mastery, they enter the "facilitated" level of the model. While the teacher is still mainly responsible for defining goals based on state/provincial standards and will use diagnostic data to determine where students need to focus attention, the student assumes a greater role in the learning process. Instruction becomes more flexible based on individual or group needs. Tasks stem from open-ended problems that require a deeper level of interaction and thinking. At this level, the practice of differentiation becomes much more apparent. While gifted students may stay at this level for only a brief time, here they'll develop the self-regulation skills that will be essential at the upper two levels.

At the "coached" level, the teacher observes students at work and provides descriptive feedback to enhance their performance or encourage them to greater proficiency. The teacher will act as a guide to higher levels of thinking, communicating, data collection, and group collaboration now. The primary goal for gifted students at the coached level is to build a greater sense of ownership in their learning. See **Figure 6.2** on page 102.

Goal Setting at the Coached Level

- The teacher provides the learner with information about strengths and weaknesses, and based on this information helps the student develop learning goals.
- Students are encouraged and provided opportunities to set and pursue additional goals that draw on their strengths and develop their weaknesses.

Instructional Practices at the Coached Level

- Students take on the primary role in pursing learning goals, by setting a learning pathway with the teacher.
- The teacher acts as an "encourager" of learning.
- Students and teachers work together to find resources necessary to complete tasks.
- The teacher and peers provide useful, critical feedback and guidance throughout the learning process.
- Based on teacher recommendations, students self-select lessons, tasks, and activities they feel will assist them in their development.
- The teacher often uses acceleration and compacting based on individual or group needs.
- Projects, discussions, and tasks are open-ended and authentic.

Assessment at the Coached Level

- The teacher and students confer regularly to monitor progress, evaluate work, and identify areas needing improvement or attention.
- Students are evaluated on project work by the teacher based on a mutually agreed upon set of criteria.

As students advance through the coached level, they become the initiators and designers of their own learning. They have now reached the "consultative" level of the TLC model. At this point, students determine the learning goals based on their personal needs and interests. The teacher works with the student to plan the course of action but allows the student to assume the primary responsibility for moving toward the goal. Now the teacher acts as a consultant to the student in the learning process. Students determine the criteria for evaluating their performance and provide their own critical reflection on what was learned and how well the learning process worked. See **Figure 6.3** on page 103.

Goal Setting at the Consultative Level

- Students assume the main responsibility for setting goals.
- Teachers work with the student to develop an appropriate course of action to achieve the goals.

Instructional Practices at the Consultative Level

- Based on goals, students define critical issues needing resolution and develop tasks to reconcile or solve the problems.

- Students work independently through tasks.
- Teacher takes on the role of consultant and counselor to the student.
- Students seek out resources, mentors, and materials within and beyond the classroom/school.
- Students attempt to develop new ideas and create new products.
- Teachers encouraged students to be creative and innovative in their approaches to solving authentic problems.

Figure 6.2: Example—Coached Level of the TLC *(also included in the digital download)*

Teacher Actions	Student Actions
Goal setting	
Provides student with a preassessment based on the standard	Takes preassessment
Reviews the preassessment and notes mastery and errors	Arranges to meet with the teacher to review preassessment
Provides descriptive feedback to the student related to areas of mastery and areas needing development or support	Notes areas of success and lists areas that require new learning, more practice, or deeper understanding
Asks student to create a goal and a timeline for meeting the goal	Defines specific goals that need to be met to achieve complete mastery of the standard and sets a timeline for complete/final assessment
Instructional practice	
Compacts and accelerates areas within the unit that the student can master quickly, providing time for deeper learning in areas not mastered	May work independently or through a self-study on the compacted or accelerated parts of the unit to buy time to work more in depth in areas not mastered
Highlights specific materials that can be useful to the student in pursuing his or her goal	Collects materials to achieve goal
Monitors and reviews student practice. Descriptive feedback meant to guide and encourage the student	Is responsible for managing goal attainment through daily and weekly work/practice
Groups students together to provide support, encouragement, and critical feedback	Works with others in the group to support, encourage, and offer critical feedback to group members
May offer suggestions of tasks that can be useful in developing areas requiring mastery	Chooses the resources and activities offered that are most effective in gaining deeper understanding, with assistance from the teacher
Assessment	
Meets with student regularly to monitor progress, assess understanding, and support achievement	Sets regular times to meet with the teacher to review progress, discuss areas of challenge, and ask questions
Works with student to choose a final project for evaluation of learning	Works through final project to be submitted to peers and/or teacher
Provides final assessment as well as reviews final product, offering feedback to the student	Utilizes descriptive feedback to modify product and resubmit to the teacher Submits a final reflection of the learning process

- Students routinely reflect on their thinking and learning process, analyzing, reporting, and recording ideas for improvement.
- Students must defend their work and practice to peers and experts in the field.
- Students take responsibility for what was learned and how it was learned, and accept feedback as a form of improvement.

Assessment at the Consultative Level

- Students determine and define the criteria and evaluation process of their performance.
- The teacher offers advice on the criteria and evaluation process.
- Students reflect, report, and act on evaluation feedback.

Chapter Summary

In our experience, working with gifted students can be the most rewarding, as well as the most challenging, of teaching endeavors. You will find yourself amazed by what these students know and how deep their interests run. However, they are learners who need our guidance, support, and nurturing to uncover or discover new interests and talents. A word of advice: never attempt to be the fount of knowledge for your gifted students. Your role is one of influence, suggestion, and advisement for further and deeper learning.

Figure 6.3: Example—Consultative Level of the TLC *(also included in the digital download)*

Teacher Actions	Student Actions
Goal setting	
Works with the student to craft goal based on unit of study and/or standard	Defines topic of interest and works with teacher to create a goal that addresses the standard or unit of study
Reviews student course of action and makes suggestions for additions/changes	Sets goal into discrete subcomponents/sub-goals and maps out course of action
Confers with student to define outcomes and assessments	Defines appropriate project outcomes and assessments
Instructional practice	
Confers with student on question and provides descriptive feedback on adaptations/changes	Identifies problem needing a solution or major question requiring an answer
Is available to student to counsel or confer on progress of work	Using goal map, works independently to solve problem or answer question; routinely meets with teacher to seek advice, suggestions, or ideas
Is available to student to counsel or confer on material needs	Locates and utilizes resources, experts, and materials within and beyond the classroom/school
Is available to student to encourage creative and innovative ideas and products	Develops innovative project to demonstrate learning
Routinely meets with the student to discuss the thinking and learning process and to offer descriptive feedback to improve performance	Keeps a journal of reflection on the thinking and learning process, shares challenges with peers, and consults with teacher to stay on track; acts on descriptive feedback to improve production or results
Assessment	
Advises student about timeline of project and members of review "jury"	Determines when the project is complete and assembles "jury" to review project
Advises student on criteria for jury review	Sets criteria for jury review
Acts as a "sounding board" for student's self-reflection, feedback report, and future course of action	Reflects and reports on feedback from jury and sets a future course of action

Chapter 7

Co-Teaching: A Collaborative Approach to Differentiation

By definition, *co-teaching* is two or more professionals delivering substantive instruction to a diverse group of students within a single physical space. Today, co-teaching is rather common with RtI interventions and inclusion classrooms that address the needs of special education and English language learners. However, more gifted education specialists are also taking on the role of classroom co-teachers and are finding the partnership advantageous to gifted learners. According to authors and educators Claire Hughes and Wendy Murawski, co-teaching can be viewed as a style of interaction between at least two co-equal professionals with diverse expertise.[52] When an inclusion classroom teacher and a gifted specialist interact in this way, they focus on providing appropriate learning experiences for all students, including those who are gifted. Dialogue, planning, shared and creative decision making, and follow-up are critical elements in this partnership that allows for differentiation of the "regular curriculum" and daily challenge for gifted learners.

Following are some reasons for co-teaching in gifted education. Co-teaching:

- ensures that the general curriculum is appropriately differentiated for gifted learners while not neglecting the needs of other students
- enables differentiated instruction to be more easily managed within the inclusion classroom or course
- brings the expertise of gifted educators into the planning for differentiation on a regular and consistent manner

- increases the classroom teacher's understanding that differentiation for gifted students differs from strategies used for other learners
- may encourage the use of compacting since support is available within the classroom
- provides individualized support to students who need guidance in extending learning
- reinforces that the responsibility for differentiation for gifted learners belongs to both classroom teachers and gifted education specialists

The Roles of Classroom Teacher and Gifted Specialist

In the context of gifted education, there are specific roles that are best suited for the classroom teacher and other roles best facilitated by the gifted specialist based on their differences in expertise. When classroom teachers and gifted specialists plan and teach together, they deepen and enhance their combined understandings about learning differences of gifted students as well as the grade level or course curriculum. See **Figure 7.1** for more detail.

Developing the Partnership

In the past, the interactions between gifted education specialists and classroom teachers have been limited. The gifted education specialist is typically expected to be the expert in the specific learning needs of gifted learners. The classroom teacher

---

[52] Hughes and Murawski, 2001.

Figure 7.1: Individual and Shared Roles of the Classroom Teacher and Gifted Specialist

Classroom Teacher Roles	Gifted Specialist Roles	Shared Roles
• Pre, formative, and summative assessment • Plan with standards up front • Structure curriculum content, process, and product around standards • Organize for differentiation	• Analyze relevant GT assessment data • Plan and organize for differentiation • Identify and/or organize instructional resource materials	• Analyze curriculum for depth, rigor, and variety • Analyze assessment data • Analyze/evaluate student work • Co-plan • Plan for instructional grouping • Co-teach • Facilitate looping • Curriculum compacting

Adapted from Mary Landrum Slade, 2002.

is considered the grade-level curriculum expert. Depending on the kinds of services offered, these two professionals may work completely separate from each other. Communication may be limited to establishing schedules when students can meet with the specialists or discussing issues related to a student's classroom performance. The two professionals rarely if ever discuss day-to-day differentiation for gifted learners.

Co-teaching demands working together in a collaborative, respectful way. Therefore, it is important that classroom teachers and gifted specialists establish a strong working relationship. Each teacher's particular expertise needs to be recognized and utilized. It is also important that the classroom teacher and the gifted education specialist come to co-teaching with an understanding of how it will benefit them both as well as make differentiation more practical and doable with two teachers in the room. Most important, the needs of gifted students will be better addressed and learning enhanced through this teacher collaboration.

Before you begin working with another teacher in the classroom, it is important that as partners you clearly understand each other's views and perspectives on co-teaching and discuss your "non-negotiables" in the management of students and the classroom. It is clearly better to agree on particular classroom issues up front.

You can get started by working through the questionnaire about co-teaching on page 106. Jot down your responses to the questions individually. Then share your ideas with your co-teacher by taking turns presenting each response. Talk through each response in turn without comment, taking notes if needed. Next share your reactions to the other teacher's responses. Your goal is to agree, compromise, or agree to disagree on views, perspectives, and expectations. It is important that you develop a level of understanding, comfort, and flexibility with each other's viewpoints and perspectives for the co-teaching partnership to be successful.

> Your goal is to agree, compromise, or agree to disagree on views, perspectives, and expectations.

Co-teachers should also create a workable schedule for co-planning as well as co-teaching and debriefing after a lesson. This is especially important since most gifted specialists are not in the same school five days a week. Please discuss the issues on page 107 prior to beginning your co-teaching.

◎ Co-Teaching Questionnaire

1. Do I believe that there is more than one way to facilitate a teaching/learning task?

▨ YES   ▨ NO

2. How comfortable am I giving up the lead on something in which I feel particularly skilled?

COMFORTABLE   NOT COMFORTABLE

▨ ▨ ▨ ▨   ▨ ▨ ▨ ▨

3. How willing am I to consider new approaches in my teaching?

COMFORTABLE   NOT COMFORTABLE

▨ ▨ ▨ ▨   ▨ ▨ ▨ ▨

4. What have been my challenges in meeting the needs of gifted students within my classroom?

_____

_____

_____

_____

_____

_____

5. How comfortable am I having someone in my classroom seeing all aspects of my teaching?

COMFORTABLE   NOT COMFORTABLE

▨ ▨ ▨ ▨   ▨ ▨ ▨ ▨

6. How comfortable am I in sharing responsibilities of the classroom with another teacher?

COMFORTABLE   NOT COMFORTABLE

▨ ▨ ▨ ▨   ▨ ▨ ▨ ▨

7. How willing am I to frankly share my concerns about a classroom or teaching issue?

WILLING   NOT WILLING

▨ ▨ ▨ ▨   ▨ ▨ ▨ ▨

8. What do I see as the challenges of a co-teaching relationship?

_____

_____

_____

_____

_____

_____

_____

9. In what ways do I believe co-teaching is going to enhance the learning of my students and my professional practices?

_____

_____

_____

_____

_____

_____

_____

10. I have expectations in a classroom regarding:

▨ discipline/behavior management

▨ in-class work

▨ homework

▨ differentiation for learning differences

▨ differentiation for gifted learners

▨ modifications for special education learners

▨ assessment and grading

▨ noise level during work time

▨ cooperative/collaborative work

▨ providing feedback to students

▨ other important expectations (or pet peeves!) not noted above

Adapted from Murawski, W., and L. Dieker. "Tips and Strategies for Co-Teaching at the Secondary Level." *Teaching Exceptional Children,* 36(5) (2004): 53–58; and the SCSU Teacher Quality Enhancement Center, 2012

◎Co-Teaching: Planning Decisions

1. How often will co-teaching occur: daily, a few times a week, several times a month or grading period, or for a specific curriculum unit?

_____

_____

_____

_____

_____

2. What schedule would best meet the needs of the students and the co-teachers?

_____

_____

_____

_____

_____

_____

3. When can we have consistent co-planning time?

_____

_____

_____

_____

_____

4. How will we find time to debrief after a co-taught lesson?

_____

_____

_____

_____

_____

_____

5. How will we maintain communication with each other?

_____

_____

_____

_____

_____

_____

a lesson on character development, one teacher may begin the lesson outlining key ideas to consider as students examine how characters change from the beginning to the end of a novel. After students meet in small discussion groups to study particular characters, the second teacher leads the summary discussion asking students to share their conclusions about how characters in their novels were developed. Each teacher has a significant role in the lesson in the eyes of students.

Following is an example of a team-taught lesson that includes multiple co-teaching approaches used in teaching a lesson on rocks and minerals. Note that each teacher has an equitable part of the co-taught lesson.

1. The classroom teacher provides background information on the classifications of rocks and minerals. The gifted specialist notes the responses of the students during the whole group instruction and discussion, and considers whether the initial grouping of students based on preassessment is appropriate. The teachers have agreed that they may reassign students to other instructional groups as necessary based on these initial observations. *(One teaching, one assisting)*

2. Students are matched to a particular sequence of labs based on the complexity of the tasks.

3. Students talented in science are assigned more appropriate lab experiences through differentiation of tasks. *(Workstation teaching)*

4. Each teacher facilitates one group's lab sequence. The gifted specialist works with the students engaged in the more complex tasks. *(Simultaneous instruction)*

5. The gifted specialist leads the final discussion that asks students to summarize what they learned through their labs; that is, what conclusions they drew about the classifications of rocks and minerals. The classroom teacher circulates the room noting students' success in recording and analyzing data. *(One teaching, one observing)*

Co-Planning Lessons for Gifted Learners

Classroom teachers and gifted specialists both have unique insights to contribute to lesson planning. The classroom teacher offers a substantive understanding of the curriculum for the grade level or course as well as personal strategies related to differentiation. The gifted education specialist offers knowledge related to the specific needs of the gifted learners within this particular classroom; plus the specialist understands how differentiation for gifted students needs to differ from the ways in which it is designed for average or struggling learners. During the co-planning process, consider addressing the questions on page 111.

If you cannot find a common planning time within your schedule, you'll need to be creative about finding time. Try using a "floating sub" scheduled throughout a day, rotating to classrooms to allow teachers and gifted specialists to meet. Could your principal cover your class occasionally for a short planning session? Consider whether you might be able to have students supervised by another teacher during a school assembly or program to provide some planning time. Take advantage of late-start or early-release days by asking for some time to be set aside for co-planning. As a last resort, set up a regular schedule around lunch or pre-school/after-school prep time. Finally, consider advocating that co-planning/co-teaching be a professional learning community (PLC) function.

Chapter Summary

Co-teaching reinforces that both classroom teachers and gifted education specialists are responsible for differentiating instruction for gifted learners. By creating partnerships between classrooms and gifted education services, teachers and gifted specialists bring their specific areas of expertise together. Collaborative planning for the diverse needs of gifted learners helps ensure that the regular curriculum is appropriately differentiated and that gifted students are experiencing challenging learning on a daily basis.

◎Co-Planning Questionnaire

1. What do we want the students to know, understand, and be able to do by the end of the lesson?

   _____

   _____

   _____

   _____

   _____

   _____

2. What learning differences should be considered in our planning? Are there differences in readiness? Is there need for deeper complexity? demand for greater abstraction? need for more sophisticated applications or techniques?

   _____

   _____

   _____

   _____

   _____

   _____

3. What co-teaching strategy is best suited for addressing learning differences within this lesson?

   _____

   _____

   _____

   _____

   _____

4. How will we actively and fairly engage all students in differentiated tasks?

   _____

   _____

   _____

   _____

   _____

   _____

5. How will we know if students have achieved or exceeded learning goals?

   _____

   _____

   _____

   _____

   _____

   _____

6. How will we respond to those who do not learn or who are reluctant learners?

   _____

   _____

   _____

   _____

   _____

7. How will we respond to those who demonstrate proficiency early in the lesson?

   _____

   _____

   _____

   _____

   _____

8. What would be "next step" goals for students who either demonstrate proficiency early or preassess out of the content, skill, or process? Will the lesson extend or enrich learning around the determined goals, or will we accelerate students to the next step in the learning progression?

   _____

   _____

   _____

   _____

   _____

◎ Ten Essential Elements for a Successful Co-Teaching Practice

There are specific elements that characterize successful co-teaching practices and partnerships in schools. Consider the following essential elements and then collaboratively work to make them part of your co-teaching practices.

1. Administrative support for co-teaching, including assistance in scheduling common time for co-planning and co-teaching.

2. Joint clarity on attitudes, responsibilities, and expectations related to co-teaching.

3. A teaching relationship built on trust, respect, and communication.

4. Shared roles and responsibilities within the classroom and during a lesson.

5. Equitable "workloads" so that one co-teacher is not doing significantly more work than the other. Consider how to fairly divide up lesson elements such as organization of student materials, review or evaluation of student work, and cleanup once a lesson concludes.

6. Flexibility, willingness, and an ability to resolve conflicts related to differences in personality, teaching style, time constraints, and curriculum priorities.

7. An established time for and commitment to co-planning.

8. A willingness and an ability to critically reflect following co-taught lessons.

9. Taking turns reviewing and/or grading student work.

10. A commitment to keep confidences for each other.

◎Tips and Cautions for Co-Teaching and Co-Planning

Here are some tips for getting started with successful co-teaching and co-planning:

- Establish consistent and shared student routines and procedures to aid in transitions, to gain the students' attention, to provide instructions, or to make announcements to the class.

- Set behavior expectations you both agree on.

- Consider each teacher's instructional style as you plan and how that may be used to benefit students.

- Post your KUDOs (learning goals) for each lesson to help you and the students stay on course.

- Establish subtle signals to communicate to each other when you need a short chat with your partner, when it is time to move on, and when you need more time.

- Vary teaching roles so that students don't consistently identify particular tasks or groups of students with particular teachers. This means that the gifted resource teacher may work with a small group of gifted learners (tiered instruction), with the whole class in a team teaching approach, with a flexible group that includes some but maybe not all gifted students, or with another group of students while the classroom teacher works with the group of gifted learners (simultaneous instruction or tiered instruction). A gifted resource teacher may also collaborate with the classroom teacher and be responsible for a workstation.

- Avoid overusing a particular co-teaching approach. Students need to experience both variety in instructional approaches but also shifts in the roles of the co-teachers.

- Carefully consider which approach is best suited for the particular content, skill, or process being presented in the lesson.

- Determine which approach could best facilitate differentiation of the lesson or task.

- Take steps to ensure that all students in groups perceive that the work they are asked to do is equally interesting and engaging.

- Group and regroup students for different purposes and in different manners so they are not "locked" into particular configurations.

- Clearly convey the sense of parity so students respond to both teachers as classroom equals.

Chapter 8

Understanding and Reversing Underachievement

Not all gifted learners are productive students. Not all are "A" students. Some perform exceedingly well in a single curriculum area but appear to be average in others. Some gifted students establish a perplexing pattern of either doing well or doing nothing. We also find that some gifted students seem to be happy when surrounded by non-achieving peers who also show little interest in learning and school. Some are reluctant and even resistant learners, refusing to play the school game. These gifted students are the ones who teachers, administrators, and even parents question whether they are indeed gifted.

If your school's process for identifying gifted students demands academic performance, the students described above will not be in your program. But if you identify students by looking for gifts and then focus on talent development (see Gagné's Model in Chapter 1), these students may be a frustrating part of your gifted program.

Defining Underachievement

Underachievement is most commonly defined as a discrepancy between potential (innate ability; gifts) and performance (achievement). Gifted education experts Sally Reis and D. Betsy McCoach view underachievement as a *severe and persistent discrepancy* between a student's expected achievement and his or her actual achievement that is not attributable to any diagnosed learning disability.[55] Expected achievement is often based on cognitive or intellectual ability assessments.

For example, if a student scores in the ninety-ninth percentile on a quantitative aptitude test, one would expect that student to do well in math. If the student's achievement tests or grades do not reflect similar data, the student may be an underachiever. Keep in mind that achievement test data indicates what has been learned; if a student does not engage in daily learning and/or routinely fails to achieve goals, it will eventually impact achievement scores.

> Underachievement is a discrepancy between potential and performance.

"Doing well" may be measured by achievement test data (Is the student learning as expected?) or by grades. However, since previous grading paradigms relied on wildly fluctuating teacher criteria, it was hard to view grades as totally accurate measures of learning. Today, if the teacher is using emerging grading paradigms—grades based on summative assessment and reflecting whether or not the student reached the term's learning goals—then grades may be considered more accurate reflections of learning.

Characteristics of Underachievers

Underachievers are a diverse population, so it's not easy to create a list of characteristics common among these learners. What characterizes one underachiever may not describe another. We consider the many risk factors and causes related to underachievement later in this chapter. However, when we examine the performance of underachievers, it is clear that they do not underachieve

---

[55] Reis and McCoach, 2000.

in every area, nor are they not learning. Two types of underachievers—nonproducers and selective producers—are still engaged in learning but their performance is erratic; this is what frustrates both teachers and parents.

Nonproducers are gifted students who refuse to do daily work or homework, yet are learning and perform exceedingly well on summative assessments or standardized achievement tests.[56] Nonproducers are frustrating to those teachers who believe that everything done in the class is critical work. The truth is, gifted students either knew the material before they walked in the door or simply did not need the amount of time, instruction, or practice that others need to learn it. If teachers use daily classroom work, homework, class notes, or participation in their grading formula, these students surely exhibit discrepancies between potential and performance.

Selective producers know they are smart, know they are capable of high performance, and they enjoy learning—but they engage in work only if it interests them.[57] They view school as a buffet table: you choose what you want to do based on your interests and leave the rest untouched. Selective producers know that learning can occur in lots of places outside of school. And grades, typically, do not motivate these gifted learners.

Factors That Influence Academic Achievement

Commonly known and researched factors related to achievement include academic self-perception; attitude toward school, teachers, and classes; motivation and self-regulation; and goal valuation.

Academic self-perceptions affect how students evaluate their abilities to do well in school, called their *academic self-concepts*. Perceptions that students have about their skills influence the types of activities they choose, the degree to which they challenge themselves in those activities, and how persistent they are in those tasks. In developing their academic self-concepts, students compare their performance to that of other students as well as to how they do in other areas. Academic self-concept may be accountable for as much as one-third of achievement discrepancies.[58]

Attitudes toward school appear to affect achievement, since students who do well in school tend to be interested in learning. Underachievers do hold more negative attitudes toward school than average or high achievers, but research does not conclude that one necessarily results in the other.

Attitudes toward teachers and classes are affected by a student's interests and motivation. Teacher personality and organizational skills may also affect achievement. In addition, many underachievers have problems with authority figures. Research suggests that students with a positive attitude toward their teachers and courses have higher achievement levels.

Motivation and self-regulation may separately or together affect achievement. Self-regulation refers to a student's thoughts, feelings, and actions related to attaining goals. However, students need to be motivated to use self-regulation strategies. How well students self-regulate can be observed in the degree of effort they exert toward reaching a goal.

Goal valuation reflects the degree to which students perceive a task to be important and of interest to them. Achievement is more likely when students view a task as enjoyable, important, and useful.

Together these factors create a picture of an academic achiever. They are students who have positive academic self-perceptions and strong academic self-concepts. The attitudes they hold toward school, teachers, and their courses are all positive. They possess and apply self-regulation skills; they are motivated and willing to work toward learning goals. And finally, they view learning tasks as important, interesting, useful, and worth their time and effort. So what is so different about some gifted students that sends them into a cycle of underachievement?

---

[56] Delisle and Galbraith, 2014.
[57] Figg, et al., 2012; Delisle and Galbraith, 2014.

[58] Lyon, 1993.

Differences between Achievers and Underachievers

Researchers D. Betsy McCoach and Del Siegle examined differences between achieving and underachieving gifted learners. They concluded that both groups of students had high academic self-perceptions. The researchers suggest that although gifted underachievers may fall behind in achievement, when these students compare their innate abilities across the classroom, they still feel confident in their academic abilities.[59]

The largest differences between the two groups occurred in motivation and self-regulation and in goal valuation. Underachievers were less motivated to use self-regulation skills. Therefore, they either didn't engage in the learning at all or their attempts were shallow, haphazard, or lacked effort. Goal valuation and motivation factors are also linked. If students value academic goals, they are more motivated to achieve. Students must either value the work they have been asked to do or value the outcome of the work. If they do not value either, they are not likely to put forth effort.

Potential Risks for Underachievement

What factors put gifted students at risk for underachievement?

Social-Emotional Risk Factors

When students underachieve in school, it's not always because they don't care for the curriculum or don't like learning. The following social and emotional challenges may be at play:

- *Perfectionism* is quite common among gifted students.
- *Fear of failure and poor risk taking,* along with perfectionism, may cause a gifted student to work and rework products, to give up when it is "not good enough," to procrastinate doing something that is new or challenging, or simply not to do the work out of fear of not being the best.

- *Lack of intellectual peer-ship.* When no one else has the same advanced interests or can compete with them intellectually *and* they may be teased or bullied for their advanced vocabulary or incessant questions, gifted students may choose to sit back and just be like everyone else.

Classroom and Curricular Risk Factors

A variety of classroom and curriculum factors may put gifted students at risk for underachievement. Such risks include failure to appropriately differentiate for gifted learners including:

- setting the same learning goals for all students and failing to plan for those who accomplish goals early
- conducting rerun lessons for all students when only some students need more instruction and practice
- failure to recognize and respond to advanced knowledge and skills
- not offering students the opportunity to act on their interests through choice
- a lack of depth and complexity in learning
- expectations that do not stretch and challenge gifted learners
- a focus on reaching minimal competencies rather than providing rigorous learning experiences

Suggested Causes of Underachievement within Gifted Populations[60]

Related to the more general risk factors are the particular causes that may lead to underachievement among gifted kids. These causes vary from one underachiever to the next. They include:

1. **An unusual or unexpected event** in the student's life, such as a move to a new school or neighborhood; a change in the family structure, such as a divorce or remarriage; a change in the family circumstances, such as unemployment or a health issue with a family member. For example, one gifted student tumbled into underachievement after being cut from the varsity hockey team.

[59] McCoach and Siegle, 2003.

[60] Adapted from Seigle and McCoach, 2013.

2. Power and control issues between students and their parents or between students and their teachers. Most experts in child rearing agree that power imbalances occur when parents or teachers do not set rules and guidelines, or do not consistently enforce the ones they set. Children test the limits of their power and may eventually gain control. Even when rules and guidelines exist and are enforced, students may test them as a way of getting attention from significant adults. Teachers or parents may insist that the child does well in school, and the student stays in control by refusing to comply with the adult's wishes . . . the power struggle is on!

3. Students who receive **conflicting or unclear messages from significant adults** may use the mixed or vague messages to justify their lack of effort and underachievement. The student's teachers should agree on expectations, and communication needs to be clear and specific about how those expectations play out in the classroom. "Turn in your lab notebook" is not as clear and specific as "Complete the activity log and write a summary of your conclusions related to the lab; turn in your notebook at the end of the class period." Parents or other significant adults at home need to agree on and communicate specific expectations; otherwise the student is likely to play one adult off the other.

4. Lack of an intellectually stimulating environment and support for students' passions may trigger underachievement. Without specific training in differentiating for gifted learners, teachers may be unprepared to provide experiences that address the particular learning needs of gifted students. When some gifted students in elementary school have already mastered an estimated 40 to 50 percent of grade-level content before they enter that grade, and the majority of gifted learners spend at least 80 percent of their school day in "regular" or inclusion classrooms, it is essential to modify their learning goals and differentiate their instruction.

5. Students who exhibit a **fixed mindset of intelligence** are at higher risk for underachievement. Again, gifted students with a fixed mindset believe that their intelligence is unchanging and that work should be effortless if they are "smart"; as a result, they may avoid difficult tasks where they risk "not being the best." They may choose to not engage at all rather than take the chance that they might perform and fail.[61]

6. Underachievers may hold **problematic beliefs,** such as:

- not believing that they have the skills to do well; fears that they may try and fail ("I'm just not good at this.")
- failing to see the work they are asked to do as meaningful ("This is dumb and a waste of my time.")
- believing that forces are working against them and any effort they make will be thwarted ("The teacher doesn't like me and does not want me to succeed.")

7. Gender affects achievement. The majority of gifted underachievers are male. For over fifty years and across numerous studies, male underachievers outnumber females at least two to one. Suggested reasons include:

- Male underachievers are more likely to act out and, therefore, are easier to recognize while more passive female underachievers may go unnoticed.
- Underachieving gifted females may never have been identified for services in the first place due to their lack of classroom accomplishments.

8. Family dynamics may also affect achievement. Although the empirical research on families of underachievers is limited, there do appear to be some common threads through the population. Risk factors may include inconsistent parenting techniques or parents who are overly lenient or overly strict.[62] It appears that families of underachieving students were no more likely to be dysfunctional than families of achieving students.[63]

---

[61] Dweck, 2006.

[62] Rimm and Lowe, 1988.

[63] Green, Fine, and Tollefson, 1998; Pendarvis, Howley, and Howley, 1990.

9. Underachieving students frequently report that ***their peers*** influence their school performance.[64] When students spend time with friends who engage in school and value doing well, they are less likely to succumb to peer pressure to diminish their school performance. Often, underachievers belong to social groups that share attitudes toward performance in school. Peer achievement levels do influence a student's academic achievement. However, we don't know whether associating with non-achievers causes underachievement or is the result of being an underachiever. After all, you choose your social group based on what you seem to have in common.

The Cycle of Success and Failure

Regardless of the particular reason for a gifted student's underachievement in school, or the reasons that a student is able to excel academically, it's important to note that either likely sets a cycle in motion.

Author Rosabeth Moss Kanter aptly describes the cycles of winning and losing that we have seen in gifted achievers and underachievers. Kanter suggests that individuals consider their confidence in particular situations, and whether students feel confident or not sets the cycle or "streak" in motion.[65] For example, students ask themselves, "Will the school (or teacher) support me or let me down?" and then determine whether it is worth investing their time, energy, effort, ideas, and the emotional commitment when the situation could produce either positive or negative results. If it seems worth the investment, a "winning streak" or cycle of academic success may follow; if the investment seems not to be worthwhile, however, a "losing streak" or cycle of underachievement may be initiated.

Winners or achievers are in a success cycle (**Figure 8.1**). They believe they deserve success and because of their confidence, they have positive feelings about school and learning. These positive feelings lead to desire or motivation to succeed. Given that these students commit the necessary time and effort, they most likely experience

success. This affirms that they deserve success and reinforces their beliefs that "I can do this!"

> Underachievers enter learning less confident and may believe that they do not deserve classroom success.

Underachievers, on the other hand, are in a cycle of failure (**Figure 8.2**). They enter learning less confident and may believe that they do not deserve classroom success. Their mental tapes say, "It's too hard. I'm not good at this. I don't get it. I don't know what she wants me to do." This lack of confidence and the negative mental tapes result in negative feelings about school and learning. Because of the negative attitudes, these students choose not to put in the necessary time, practice, and effort required for success. The result is like a self-fulfilling prophecy: they fail either on the

Figure 8.1: Cycle of Success

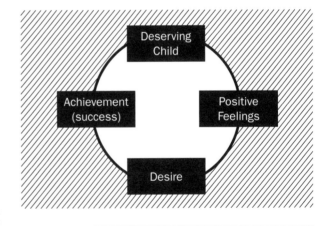

Figure 8.2: Cycle of Failure

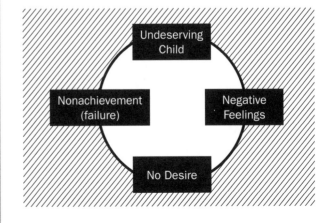

[64] Clasen and Clasen, 1995.
[65] Kanter, 2006.

short term with an assignment or on the long term, the course or class.

Kanter suggests that the dividing line between winning streaks and losing streaks is how students choose to respond to setbacks. "Winners" learn from their shortfalls and move on. They view their lack of success as a temporary glitch, not a permanent state. With extra effort, they are convinced that they will be successful next time. Their academic self-perceptions stay intact.

However, "losers" live in disappointment. These students do not believe they have control over whether they succeed or fail. Falling short only decreases their effort and the losses keep piling up. Their academic self-perceptions take a hit.

Following Kanter's line of thinking, winners have confidence in their ability to do well, maybe not the first time, but certainly in the end. Losers lack the confidence to take on new challenges and to bounce back from shortfalls.

Kanter notes three cornerstones of confidence: accountability, collaboration, and initiative. **Accountability** involves taking responsibility for your endeavors. Individuals who are accountable seek feedback and have the desire to improve; they put forth extra effort in order to live up to expectations. The **collaboration** part of confidence involves reaching out to others and seeking mutual support. Finally, we see **initiative** in individuals who are able to manage themselves. They understand that hard work matters and that effort leads to results. These students are often described as self-starters.

What happens when these cornerstones of confidence are lacking? Signs that trouble lies ahead is evidenced by weakened accountability, deteriorating relationships with others, and declining initiative.

Reversing Underachievement

Research indicates that when gifted underachievers are given challenging, engaging work that has been modified to focus on their individual strengths and interests, rates of underachievement may decrease.[66] This research supports the intervention strategy of McCoach and Siegle, who suggest a two-part process for reversing patterns of underachievement: *goal valuation* and *instructional interventions*. They conclude that developing trusting relationships with gifted underachievers, making school meaningful, and increasing student connections to school produced the strongest gains in academic grades and seem to be most viable strategies for reversing patterns of underachievement.

As such, they first suggest teacher interventions that target goal valuation. Here students meet with teachers to discuss their interests, values, and plans for the future. Based on these conversations, it may be appropriate for the teacher to help students understand how the work in school is useful both now and in the future, or the teacher may help students connect their interests to the course content.

Second, McCoach and Siegle suggest using instructional interventions. In particular, they recommend considering interest- and strength-based activities, which have the potential to reverse underachievement. Such activities, with the support of curriculum mentors, are considered an instructional intervention.

Daily Engagement as a Part of Instruction

We suggest using instructional interventions that go beyond interest- and strength-based activities and impact the day-to-day work of underachieving gifted students. Researcher Jennifer Fredricks suggests essential elements to help gifted students become more interested and passionate about the academics of school, including[67]:

- cognitively complex tasks that are both meaningful and challenging

- posing and solving real problems

- opportunities to incorporate outside interests and future plans

- choice over the kinds of activities they work on

- some control over how they complete their activities

---

[66] Emerick, 1992.

[67] Fredricks, 2010.

If Fredricks's essential elements increase students' interests and passion for their work, shouldn't they be applied to the "regular" curriculum in differentiating for gifted underachievers? Since many students in the United States must reach the Common Core State Standards as well as their state's academic standards in other subject areas, and all Canadian students must reach their provincial standards, how can we neglect to consider the day-to-day engagement of underachievers with the curriculum? We support a careful analysis and reflection on the degree to which daily curriculum and instruction reflects Fredricks's elements, and suggest that this be used to design instructional interventions for gifted underachievers. From our experience, reversing patterns of underachievement and breaking a failure cycle requires daily effort and focused adjustments in both the curriculum and instructional experiences and tasks.

In addition, we would like to return to the work of Kanter on confidence. She suggests that we begin to turn around losing streaks when we restore the three cornerstones of confidence: accountability, collaboration, and initiative. Let's consider how we can work on these turnarounds in our classrooms.

Restoring Accountability

Restoring accountability requires that students face the facts and accept responsibility. This means direct talk between the teacher and the student about specific problems shared in an open dialogue or interview.

Tips for successful student interviews concerning underachievement and possible questions for the interview are provided on pages 122–125. Our goal is for the student to own the problem. Once problems have been identified, then the teacher and student need to work together to establish clear priorities. Frequently, the student's low performance is related to more than one issue (such as no lab reports submitted, poor assessment results). From our experience, there are definite advantages to working on one goal at a time. When too much change is demanded at once, the student is more likely to neglect the plan

and give up. In addition, if students themselves determine the specific goal, they are more likely to be motivated to work toward it. (Ask: What one area would you really like to improve?)

Once a goal is determined, establish the steps to get there and schedule check-in dates. Students in first through third grade should have progress reviewed daily; students in fourth through twelfth grade should have progress checks weekly. The goal setting plan on pages 126–127 will walk you through this process. Note that questions are asked about what is good about reaching the goal (goal valuation). And students are asked to identify obstacles that may keep them from reaching the goal and how to overcome each obstacle. If you don't talk about this during the goal setting conference, you will likely hear about these obstacles in the form of excuses when the goal wasn't reached. Get it out ahead of time and solve it! Have students rewrite the goal and post it somewhere they will see it daily.

Finally, when the check-in dates arrive, provide descriptive feedback (see Chapter 9) on the student progress. Where are they now and what's next?

> Help the underachieving learner reconnect with same-age as well as intellectual peers.

Promoting Collaboration

Helping the underachieving gifted learner reconnect with same-age as well as intellectual peers is part of turning around problems with low confidence. Provide opportunities for students to work together collaboratively (refer to Chapter 4 for additional ideas on grouping). Keep in mind that the use of cooperative learning with gifted students has been an area of sustained concern. Specifically, the idea of grouping gifted students with nongifted students and the loss of opportunity for gifted learners to engage in appropriately complex and in-depth learning have been at the center of this.

In cooperative learning formats, where group members all work on the same task using the same content and pace, gifted students often cite the learning as boring and too slow. If they are also asked to tutor other group members, they may feel used. Second, much of the work done in cooperative groups often involves memorization of facts and low-level skill applications resulting in single correct answers. Such tasks do not promote more complex learning.

Remember that although giftedness is characterized by greater breadth and depth of knowledge and a faster pace of learning, gifted students are not advanced in all content areas or curriculum topics. In addition, they may hold misconceptions that limit their understanding much like what occurs with their same-age peers. Therefore, they should not be considered "experts" in all cooperative learning groups and tasks.

The Effectiveness of Mixed-Ability Grouping

Research suggests that cooperative or collaborative learning in mixed-ability groups can be effective with gifted learners when particular instructional formats are utilized.[68] There are two jigsaw grouping formats that, when structured and facilitated appropriately, show promise for use with gifted students. In both models, the student interaction appears to be more collaborative than cooperative. Cooperative learning typically focuses on the reproduction of knowledge. Collaborative learning encompasses both the reproduction and the production of knowledge; shared meaning develops through conversations and experiences.

Explorations of a Concept

As described by psychologist Elliot Aronson, providing explicit structures for the contributions of individual students may create a learning situation with enough openness for the curiosities of gifted learners.[69] In this format, a larger concept, such as freedom, is introduced. Students individually explore a subtopic related to the concept. We suggest that students be allowed to choose the subtopic of greatest interest to them. (Refer to Chapter 4 for ideas on expert and special interest groups.)

The exploration sets up a learning situation where all students have a unique experience guided by critical questions. These questions may be generated by the students with the teacher's support. Or, for students needing greater support, the teacher may provide the guiding questions for the exploration. Once students complete their individual exploration, they return to their collaborative group. Here, students share what they have learned and, therefore, learn about all subtopics of the concept. Teachers can further differentiate this experience by allowing students to determine how to present their work in their collaborative group.

Research and Discussion Groups

Educational psychologist Robert Slavin's version of the jigsaw incorporates the concept of a research group and a discussion group.[70] Particular tasks (A, B, C, and D) are assigned to individual members in each collaborative/ discussion group. Students leave their discussion group to meet with a new research group (all A's meet together, all B's meet together, and so on). Here they set research agendas and begin their work. Students continue to meet with their research groups to discuss sources, share insights, and suggest continued or new avenues for exploration. Each student prepares to become the expert on his or her assigned topic or concept. Finally, students return to their original discussion groups (joining A, B, C, and D together) to teach and learn from each other's expertise (reproduction and production of knowledge).

We believe that this process enables teachers to match gifted learners to topics, content, and resources most appropriate for them. It also encourages teachers to give gifted students tasks that call for greater complexity, depth, or degree of abstraction. In a research group composed of students similar, rather than different from them, gifted students would be more highly engaged.

---

[68] Patrick, et al., 2005.
[69] Aronson, 1978.

[70] Slavin, 1980.

◎ Tips for Successful Student Interviews

1. *Try to stay positive.* This lets the student know that you are concerned about him and want to hear what he has to say. If his responses are unrealistic, explore his point of view in a non-judgmental way. Don't just tell him that he is "wrong"; remember that he is probably expressing what he really believes to be true. Instead, ask questions that will lead him to see that there are other ways to perceive the situation. For example, you might ask, "What do you think the social studies teacher thought about the quality of your project?" This opens the door to dialogue. Introduce your questions with words such as, "What about," "What if," "What would you think, feel, or believe if."

2. *Avoid blaming.* Try to focus on the issues instead of finding fault. Carefully identify the problems, describe the situation, and work together to come up with alternatives.

3. *Practice active listening.* Active listening involves these specific skills:
    *   Be patient.
    *   Focus on really understanding the other person's point of view.
    *   Stay centered on the person, not just the words he or she is saying.
    *   Concentrate on what the other person is saying, not on what you will say next.
    *   Keep the discussion going slowly enough so that both of you can truly understand what is being said.
    *   Think before you respond, so your comments are relevant.
    *   Don't be afraid to say, "Just a minute; let me think."
    *   Restate what you believe to be the other person's ideas or perspectives. For example: "I think you are saying that . . . Is that right?"
    *   Convey empathy, respect, and acceptance of the other person's point of view through your posture, gestures, and facial expressions as well as your words

4. *Don't downplay the student's perspectives and feelings.* For example, try not to say, "You shouldn't feel that way." Validate the student's feelings by acknowledging them, then move on. For example, you might say something like, "I understand that you don't feel that your assignments are challenging enough. What would be your ideal independent project for the social studies unit?"

5. *Don't get defensive.* Remember that the student is presenting her point of view—her reality. If you are going to help her make a change, you need to really listen, not argue about who's right and who's wrong.

6. *Keep your questions neutral.* Avoid loaded words and phrases that convey your acceptance or displeasure, approval or disapproval. These may steer the student to say what you want to hear, which won't help either of you. Keeping your questions and observations neutral allows the student to express his true feelings and perspectives without getting defensive. ➔

Adapted from *Up from Underachievement* by Diane Heacox, Free Spirit Publishing, 1991.

7. *Give illustrations and examples whenever you can.* For example, you might say, "Some kids have a problem getting projects in when there are many steps involved and the timeline for getting them done is long. What about you? How do you feel about big projects?" Compare this to, "I hear you have a problem getting big projects done. Why is that?" Which question would you feel safer answering? The student feels the same way.

8. *Use simulation questions to introduce other points of view.* Try questions such as, "Why do you think your science teacher expects you to turn in your lab notebooks?" "What would you have done in that situation?" "What might be the consequences of not bringing your books to class?"

9. *Ask for elaboration.* Expect the student to clarify information she offers. Try questions such as, "Who was involved?" "What happened next?" "How did you feel about that?" "Can you tell me more about that?" "I don't quite understand; what else can you tell me?" "What do you specifically mean by using that word?" "Can you give me an example?"

10. *Summarize key points.* Go back to the main ideas or themes the student has presented and review them. You might say something like, "I think that what I'm hearing you say is . . . Am I right?"

11. *Avoid solving the problem yourself.* Let the student come up with a solution to try; that way, he will feel more committed. For example, you might ask, "What could you do in order to keep yourself from daydreaming during math class?" Then ask him to suggest some possible solutions. If necessary, help him out with ideas, such as, "Some kids find that taking notes helps them keep listening. Other kids have tried keeping track of how many times they stop paying attention in a particular class period. Then they try to cut down on that number each day."

Adapted from *Up from Underachievement* by Diane Heacox, Free Spirit Publishing, 1991.

◎ Questions for Student Interviews

Following is a preliminary list of questions for a student interview. These questions may be used by teachers and parents, since you are both trying to identify a student's school problems. Sort through the list to see which questions are appropriate for your particular student's age, grade, and circumstances. Ask those, and skip or modify the others.

The questions are grouped by problem area. As you do the interview, you should be able to begin identifying the major causes of your student's school problems, based on the responses he or she gives in each category.

Learning

1. What subject/class are you best in? What subject/class is the most difficult for you?

2. What do you like most about (your best subject/class)?

3. What makes (your most difficult subject/class) so hard for you?

4. What's the hardest thing for you to do: your daily work, the end-of-chapter tests, or independent projects?

5. Can you tell me what caused your grade in (the subject/class where you performed most poorly)?

6. Do you understand the material taught in (your most difficult subject/class)?

7. What school activities or projects do you enjoy the most?

8. Of all your subjects, which one do you think you could improve in? How could you improve your grade in that class?

9. If you feel you are behind in that class, do you think you could catch up? What extra help might you need?

10. What keeps you from being successful in that class? What could you do about it?

Developing Study Habits

1. How much time do you typically spend each day studying or doing homework at home?

2. Do you spend a specific amount of time studying and doing homework, or do you just work until you finish your assignments?

3. Do you have a particular place where you study at home? Describe it to me.

4. Do you have a set time to begin studying each night?

5. If you need to remember something for a test, how do you memorize it?

6. Tell me about your way of taking notes.

7. Can you usually predict what might be on a test? If yes, how can you tell?

8. Do you check over your work before you turn it in?

9. Do you sometimes get distracted during your home studying time? If yes, what kinds of things distract you?

10. How long can you study in one stretch? Do you give yourself a break during study time?

11. Do you reward yourself when your study time is over?

Adapted from *Up from Underachievement* by Diane Heacox, Free Spirit Publishing, 1991.

◎ Questions for Student Interviews (continued)

Managing Schoolwork

1. Are there any particular days of the week when it's more difficult to find time to study at home?

2. Is there a particular time of the school year when it's more difficult to study? (Examples: school play, athletic season.)

3. Do you keep an assignment notebook, folder, or calendar? Do you use it regularly? Does it work for you?

4. How do you organize your work for a big project that takes a long time to do? (Can you break down the project into small steps?)

5. If you have several deadlines at the same time, how do you decide what work to do each evening?

6. Each evening, when you start your study time, do you know what work needs to be done and what deadlines you have coming up?

Setting Goals

1. Where do you want to be and what do you want to be doing when you have completed school (or 5 to 10 years from now)?

2. What is the most important thing about school for you? What makes you (or could make you) want to come to school each day?

Dealing with Personal Issues

1. If you could change one thing about yourself, what would it be?

2. What do you do to handle stress?

3. Do you believe you are a perfectionist? (Does it bother you if things are not just right? Do you have problems getting your work in on time because it doesn't seem quite finished yet? Do you ever not try something because you don't think you'll be good enough?)

Adapted from *Up from Underachievement* by Diane Heacox, Free Spirit Publishing, 1991.

◎Goal Setting Plan

1. What is *one* area of your school performance you really want to improve? This is your *long-term goal.* It may take you several weeks, months, or even a whole school year to accomplish this goal.

   _____

   _____

2. What is *one* thing you can do to help you reach your goal? This is your *short-term goal.* You can accomplish this goal in 2 to 4 weeks.

   _____

   _____

3. What steps do you need to take to reach your goal?

   _____

   _____

   _____

   _____

4. What would be good about reaching your goal?

   _____

   _____

   _____

   _____

5. What things or people might keep you from reaching your goal? These are your *obstacles.* What can you do to get around your obstacles? These are your *solutions.*

Obstacles	Solutions
_____	_____
_____	_____
_____	_____

6. What special materials or help do you need to reach your goal? These are your *resources.*

   _____

   _____

   _____

   →

Adapted from *Up from Underachievement* by Diane Heacox, Free Spirit Publishing, 1991.

◎ Goal Setting Plan (continued)

7. How will you reward yourself if you reach your goal? These are your *incentives*.

_____

_____

_____

_____

8. How and when will you check on your progress? Who will help you do this—a teacher, a parent, a friend? Write down your check-point dates.

Check-Point Dates   Signature

_____   _____

_____   _____

_____   _____

Today's Date _____

Sign here _____

Have a parent, teacher, or friend sign here _____

Clip and Post

Write your goal below. Cut off this part of your Goal Setting Plan and post it somewhere you will see it every day.

Adapted from *Up from Underachievement* by Diane Heacox, Free Spirit Publishing, 1991.

Second, in their research group, gifted learners would be more likely to apply higher-order thinking skills and gain conceptual understandings through their exchanges. Interactions within collaborative groups encourage students to integrate information, explain it to others in their own words, consider different perspectives and opinions, evaluate conflicting ideas, and identify and resolve misconceptions. These analytical and reflective practices are particularly appropriate for gifted learners.

For collaborative learning to be successful, a climate of trust and respect is necessary. Students need explicit instruction on how to effectively engage in collaborative "sensemaking" and how to provide supporting evidence when making arguments. They also need to develop interpersonal skills that will help them with tasks such as questioning someone's perspective or argument without it seeming like a personal attack. There is a particular sense of urgency in developing these communication skills with some gifted students who lack these interpersonal skills or narrowly focus on their own perspectives, potentially shutting out those of others.

Collaborative formats that emphasize higher levels of understanding and require students to explain and justify their ideas can promote learning for both gifted and nongifted students as they interact.

> Grouping students only by their differences is not differentiation.

Benefits of Like-Ability Grouping

In typical cooperative learning formats, students are grouped together based on learning differences rather than likenesses. Grouping students only by their differences is not differentiation. However, if you differentiate the resources, materials, or tasks once the students are in mixed-readiness groups, elements of differentiation can be defended. It is important to understand that gifted learners need experiences with intellectual peers. Psychologist and cooperative learning researcher David Kenny and colleagues found that gifted students were more productive

and worked more quickly when grouped with other gifted students.[71]

The benefits of cooperative groups were evidenced for gifted students *only* when they worked in groups of other gifted learners. Under those circumstances, gifted students do tend to develop positive attitudes. They gain knowledge from other students who may have different talent areas. They are also able to work more effectively with other gifted students in the group. They communicate in relevant ways, form trusting relationships, and learn how to resolve conflicts and share leadership.

Increasing Initiative

There are a variety of ways in which teachers can increase student initiative in the classroom. Here are some guiding principles in this effort:

- Show underachievers their worth by paying attention to what matters most, not periphery issues.
- Comment on the things that matter to them.
- Always consider the new day; look forward not back.
- Because the underlying issues resulting in underachievement are complex, do not try to target all issues at once. Start small but start someplace by focusing on one area of concern at a time. Over time you will likely turn around the patterns of underachievement.
- Recognize even small victories (Getting one more assignment in this week is not there yet but it is on the way!).
- Use assessment to provide specific information to students on what they are doing well and what to do next to improve their performance.

Using Assessment to Build Initiative

Used appropriately, assessment can motivate students to strive for their best work. Assessments expert Richard Stiggins makes critical distinctions between assessment *of* learning and assessment *for* learning.[72] Many schools have initiatives around

---

[71] Kenny, 1995.
[72] Stiggins, 2005.

assessment for learning, also called "formative assessment." The ideas and principles of this kind of assessment can help rebuild the initiative of gifted underachievers.

Assessment *of* learning, also called "summative assessment," determines how much students have learned by a particular point in time. In contrast, assessment *for* learning examines how we might help students learn. This type of assessment tells us how the learning is going, what misconceptions or misinformation may exist, what skills are present and which are lacking, how deeply the student understands the concepts and generalizations of our curriculum. Assessment *for* learning, Stiggins contends, increases student confidence in learning because it provides specific information on how learning is going and, therefore, increases their initiative to take on tasks.

For further discussion of assessment and gifted learners, see Chapter 9.

Coaching for Success in Preventing Underachievement: Tips for Teachers

It has been said that the best way to address underachievement in the classroom is not to let it happen to begin with. Easier said than done! But here are some coaching tips for teachers that will support the success of gifted students in the classroom.

1. Focus on the positive. Remember that some gifted students are perfectionists. This means they "should" themselves to death! "I should have done … If I had more time, I should have …" They don't also need our criticisms since they have already gone way beyond what we might say. Second, many tend to focus on a negative comment and completely ignore positive remarks or even their grade on the task. In such cases, descriptive feedback will be welcomed—clearly note what went well and then provide direction (not criticism) on how to get better next time. What students are worried about is their performance; therefore, coaching them to higher achievement is exactly what they want.

2. Keep problems private. Gifted learners who are successful in school typically have higher academic self-confidence than personal self-confidence. They feel good about being good students. As a result, who they are may be bound up in being best and first. All too often students have relayed public statements made by their teachers along this line: "What do you mean you don't get this? You're gifted!" Such broadcasts place the vulnerable child in a hostile classroom. Hold private conferences with gifted students who are having difficulties. Replace any sort of public classroom encounter with personal one-on-one conversations.

3. Get them involved and interested. All students' motivation increases when they engage in learning that interests them. Begin by having your students take interest inventories. Provide opportunities for students to share what they know about a topic. Remember, some gifted learners are experts in some topics at very young ages. Also consider that gifted learners often have areas of passion that are not typical of their same-age peers. Are there opportunities to follow their curiosities and delve deeper into their passions? Could you compact them out of skills or content they have already mastered and replace that class time with a self-selected exploration outside your curriculum topics? See compacting forms and procedures in Chapter 4.

4. Provide variety and choice. Predictable daily or weekly routines are boring for students and teachers. If your fourth graders know that every Monday they will work on academic vocabulary, every Wednesday they will do some practice task or game with the words, and every Friday you will assess whether or not they have mastered the words, where's the suspense? If secondary math students know a daily routine of homework check, direct instruction, modeling, practice, and then independent work, what's new to look forward to? Variety in instructional strategies is important. With more instructional variety, we reach students with different learning styles or cognitive preference that may either limit or enhance their ability to learn new content, skills, or processes.

It is also important to provide variety in how students access *content*, how they will learn it (*process*), and how they show you what they learned (*products*). While a teacher would not be expected to do all this simultaneously, offering students a choice in whether they access content through online sources or eBooks; trap key ideas in a journal or graphic organizer; and create a podcast, a Smart Board presentation, or a simulation are welcomed by students. By providing choice, you are able to offer many more options and thus respond to a wider range of learning profiles and interests.

Whether they are kindergartners or high school seniors, all students want some power in the classroom. Letting them choose between options we have designed allows students to feel they have some control over how their learning happens. It is incredibly motivating! For some gifted students who seem to always want to do it another way or stretch the boundaries of a given task, this is a perfect learning scenario.

5. Keep your expectations high and the learning rigorous. With the implementation of standards-based learning in the United States over a decade ago, the focus in many classrooms shifted to minimal competencies and getting everyone to meet those goals. Gifted students were often the losers in such classrooms and schools, as resources and support focused on the most struggling learners. All students need, and teachers should expect that all students are engaged in, learning experiences that are rigorous and relevant. This book has provided a variety of lenses through which you can examine your curriculum in light of the needs of gifted learners. We have also provided a variety of classroom strategies to lift the rigor and complexity of learning in your classroom. Remember to continue to consider them as you plan your next curriculum unit or determine what you will do in the classroom tomorrow.

And, keep your expectations high. If work is too easy for gifted learners, they may get lazy about it. They learn over time that even doing the minimal will sometimes outshine other students' work. They can get by. We are not encouraging you to pile on more work for gifted learners, but we are suggesting that you do not accept less than a quality work effort. The use of tiered assignments matches students to tasks that are just right for them. Tiering does not allow gifted students to take the "low road."

6. Adjust your curriculum to make learning appropriate. In a differentiated classroom, pre-assessment and formative assessment are critical in determining both how and when to differentiate. These assessment strategies are even more essential for gifted learners who come to particular curriculum topics with extensive foundational knowledge. This is revealed through preassessment. Second, the pace of learning is accelerated for gifted students. This means that the time, instruction, and practice necessary for average learners to reach learning goals is inappropriate for gifted students. Formative assessment indicates who has reached the goal and who needs more time or a different instructional approach. Making these curricular and pace adjustments will help keep gifted learners engaged, motivated, and interested.

Chapter Summary

This chapter has defined underachievement and discussed its characteristics and potential risk factors and causes among gifted students. The challenges are considerable. However, we have provided a variety of considerations and strategies to try in your classroom to break the underachievement cycle. Finally, we have provided coaching tips for success. Implementing these strategies and tips can help you keep your gifted learners in a cycle of school success rather than falling into a cycle of failure and ceasing to reach their potential as gifted individuals.

◎ How to Use Formative Assessment to Increase Initiative and Deter Underachievement

- **Provide clear models** of work that does and does not meet quality criteria. When students examine this work, they better understand the quality called for and ask: Does my work look like the models for quality or not? How is mine different or the same? What improvements might I need to make in my product? This is particularly helpful when introducing a new type of project to the students, as it motivates them to reach for the higher standard.

- **Provide descriptive feedback.** As we've discussed several times in this book, when students know where they are and what's next, their initiative increases because they know how to improve.

- **Teach students to self-assess** and determine their own progress. Provide self-assessment checklists or rubrics in student-friendly language before a major task, refer to it while the work is in progress, and have students use it as the final check before submitting their work. This reflection helps students recognize "good" for themselves, a life skill worth cultivating.

You can also help students reflect on their learning and effort by having them evaluate their knowledge about the lesson's content before and after the lesson, and also consider the amount of effort they put into their work. First, teachers should share the goals for the lesson (KUDOs). Then students should write or summarize the goals on their logs. Students should also consider how much they believe they already know about the lesson's topics. Consider the following scale:

1. I do not know anything about this.
2. I think I know a little about this.
3. I know about this.
4. I know this so well I can tell others about it.

At the end of the lesson, students reflect on their learning using this scale:

1. I am just starting to learn this, but I do not really understand it yet.
2. I am starting to get this but may still need some help.
3. I get it but may still get stuck.
4. I understand this completely.

Finally, the students reflect on the effort they put into learning during the class period. Consider the following scale:

1. I didn't try very hard today.
2. I put forth some effort, but I wanted to quit.
3. I worked until I got it but had to push myself.
4. I worked hard until I got it, or I got it right away!

→

From *Differentiation for Gifted Learners: Going Beyond the Basics* by Diane Heacox, Ed.D., and Richard M. Cash, Ed.D., copyright © 2014. Free Spirit Publishing Inc., Minneapolis, MN; 800-735-7323; www.freespirit.com. This page may be reproduced for use within an individual school or district. For all other uses, contact www.freespirit.com/company/permissions.cfm.

- **Design mini-lessons** that focus on the qualities of "good," one element at a time. For example, if student book critiques reflect shallow thinking and unsupported conclusions, walk them through samples of "good" and "missed the mark," and list qualities of critiques. Have the students describe why one critique is more substantial than the other. Provide direct instruction in those specific skills that are affecting the students' end results.

- **Don't grade everything.** New paradigms for grading indicate that daily work, quizzes, and homework do not contribute to the end-of-term grade. As an alternative to grading these materials, have students do self-assessment of their work, or use peer evaluation guided by rubrics or checklists. Use check (met requirements), plus (exceeded requirements), minus (fell short on the requirements) to holistically respond to student work without grading it.

- **Use recovery, redo, and do-over points.** It is easy for students to just turn in work, get the grade, and move on. But what if we insisted on quality work and recognized that it takes some students longer to achieve a learning goal? Recovery points enable students to revise and resubmit work that has failed to earn full points. Descriptive feedback guides the revision process. New points are not averaged with the previous points but fully replace the previous grade/score. Recovery points increase initiative because students are given a chance to improve their work with guidance from the teacher.

- **Engage students in record keeping.** Students can maintain personal charts or graphs of their results. One teacher had students keep line graphs of their assessment results for academic vocabulary. This enabled students to see themselves getting better, a powerful motivator that increases students' initiative for doing the work and for making progress.

- **Consider one-on-one conferences** with your struggling students. Let them do the talking. Where are they now? What areas would they like to improve in? What obstacles, confusions, or frustrations are blocking their learning progress? How might we work together to get around, over, or through those obstacles?

◎ Elementary Student Reflective Log

Date _____

My name _____

Subject	Before the lesson	Today I learned ...	After the lesson	My effort in learning today
Math	1 2 3 4		1 2 3 4	1 2 3 4
Reading/ Language Arts	1 2 3 4		1 2 3 4	1 2 3 4
Social Studies	1 2 3 4		1 2 3 4	1 2 3 4
Science	1 2 3 4		1 2 3 4	1 2 3 4

◎ Secondary Student Reflective Log

Name _____ Date _____

Date	Goals for the Lesson	Before the Lesson (1–4)	After the Lesson (1–4)	Effort Today (1–4)

Chapter 9

Assessment and the Gifted Learner

Few issues in education stir as much controversy as that of assessment. Research and opinion abound as to what is and isn't quality assessment, the effects of assessment on learning, and the best ways to implement assessment to understand learning.

In the field of gifted education, assessment has taken on two main purposes:

1. To identify students for gifted services and programs

2. To measure results of and inform practice for learning within classroom, programs, and services

This chapter will focus on the second use: assessment of and for learning within classrooms, programs, and services.

We use Paul Black and Dylan Wiliam's definition of *assessment*: "all activities that teachers and students undertake to get information that can be used diagnostically to then adapt teaching and learning strategies to meet the students' needs."[73] In recent years, the system of assessment has moved away from judgmentally ranking and ordering students and toward making changes in instructional practices so that all students achieve greater learning.

Types of Assessment

Generally, there are three types of assessment:

Preassessments: Diagnostic assessments given to students prior to instruction. Preassessments allow the teacher time to plan activities and to differentiate based on the data collected. Preassessments identify:

- the student's degree of prior knowledge of skills or process (readiness)
- topics of personal interests or interests within the unit of study (interest)
- level of motivation or willingness to learn
- preferred ways of learning or gathering information (learning profiles)

Formative assessments: Also called assessment *for learning*, as discussed in Chapter 8, formative assessment refers to the ongoing assessments that checks student understanding and provides feedback to the learner and teacher on the learning process. Effective formative assessments offer students descriptive information that can help them move closer toward the learning targets. The assessments are timely—not too much information is given or time has passed before students are made aware of their progress or need for assistance. It is important that both the teacher and student respond to the formative assessment relatively quickly and that the assessment relates to the task at hand. Formative assessment identifies:

- the effectiveness of the instructional practices
- the effectiveness of the student's understanding of data and information
- areas where the student needs greater guidance and/or support

Summative assessments: Known as assessments *of learning*, summative assessments are final assessments or presentations that provide

---

[73] Black and Wiliam, 1998.

135

evidence on what was learned. Final assessments need to document the levels of growth and mastery achieved by the student. The assessment formats must match the learning objectives. A portfolio of performance, this type of assessment measures:

- goal attainment—whether students have met the learning goals
- final performance mastery or achievement—whether students have mastered the material and can demonstrate their knowledge and skills
- areas of future study—whether students are ready to move on to the next unit in the curriculum or whether more time, instruction, and practice are needed

Structured vs. Unstructured Assessment

For effective assessment practices, use a variety of assessment strategies. The strategies move along a continuum of structure from informal to formal assessments. Throughout this chapter, the assessment ideas highlighted in each of the three focus areas will be defined as either unstructured or structured. See **Figure 9.1.**

The most informal assessments are unstructured and are used throughout the instructional process to help guide teachers in creating future learning steps and goals. Unstructured assessments are not uniform like a test or a quiz (structured assessments) and take on many different forms.

Meanwhile, structured assessments are given at specific steps within the learning process. These forms of assessment are more calculated, are uniform in appearance, and are sometimes more "paper and pencil" friendly. Structured assessments are helpful when developing collaborative

common formative assessments—assessments that all teachers of the subject or grade level will give at a prescribed time during the instructional process. Also note that the more structured the assessment is, the more likely the assessment is to be summative to what a student has learned.

All assessments should be transparent—students know when they will be assessed, what they will be assessed on, and how that assessment will happen. The assessment should mirror the way in which the information was gathered or learned. The criteria being used to assess student learning should be clear and explicit to all involved (parents, students, and teachers).

Keep in mind, assessments should be:
- aligned to methods of assessment familiar to the student
- linked to instructional goals
- integrated into instruction
- descriptive to both student and teacher
- offered in a variety of methods
- a collection rather than a sample
- collaborative between the student and teacher
- from descriptive to performance-based (authentic)

Not only should the structure of assessments be varied; the format in which it is delivered should also be diverse. Using an array of styles or formats can benefit learners by allowing their preferred ways of doing to be maximized. **Figure 9.2** provides samples of both structured and unstructured formative assessments.

Figure 9.1: The Continuum of Assessment

Informal			Formal
Unstructured formative assessment	Structured formative assessment	Structured common formative assessment	Structured summative assessment

Integrating Assessment into Instruction

Part of using assessments effectively means seamlessly integrating them into the instructional process. Assessments are informative to all of the stakeholders in learning: students, parents, teachers, and administration. When we consider assessment for gifted students, we should also consider that program designers/administrators/coordinators have a stake in the learning outcome. Following is a step-by-step method for integrating assessment into instruction for gifted students. See **Figure 9.3.**

Step 1: Plan for Differentiated Instruction.

Before beginning any lesson or unit of study, you should fully investigate what the students will come to know, understand, and be able to do as a result of instruction. Clearly articulate the learning outcomes in specific terms to the three levels of learning. At this point, it is also wise to consider how to "modify up" the objectives for students who require a greater challenge. We do *not* recommend that you "modify down" the objectives, as all students should meet or exceed the standard. Also note that modifying up is rarely done at the "know" level—as being gifted should not require students to know more facts, but to do more sophisticated practice and gain a deeper understanding of the standards or objectives. In the following example, the modification up at the know level includes different facts for gifted students. It accelerates the standard from grade four to grade five for gifted students.

Figure 9.2: Quality Formative Assessment

Structured: Timed to specific steps within the learning process. This type of assessment works well when developing collaborative common formative assessments.

Examples:

- homework
- quizzes/performance tasks
- tests
- structured student reflections
- structured student self-assessment
- contracts
- Web postings
- peer assessments
- portfolio assessments
- content review study guides
- discussion boards
- Google groups
- exit slips

Unstructured: Used throughout the instructional process as a guide to learning and learning goals. This type of assessment adds to the "tool box" of instructional strategies that help ensure student success.

Examples:

- Observations of students during class sessions.
- Discussions of topics during class sessions.

- Fishbowl discussion. During a class session, form a small circle within a large circle of students. The students in the smaller circle discuss or debate a topic while the outer circle of students take notes on how the discussion progresses, ideas on how to resolve issues, or suggestions for clarifying opinions.
- 3-2-1. This strategy is often used as an entrance or exit slip format. Ask the students to write down 3 new ideas gained, 2 connections made to the new information, and 1 question that still remains.
- Thumbs up/thumbs down. Have students simply vote using the thumbs up/down whether they understand or comprehend the information.
- Red-Yellow-Green. Using three different color note cards, have students hold up the red card if the information is not making sense, yellow card if the information needs more explanation, or the green card if they completely understand.
- Questioning. This strategy involves asking questions that, through the way students answer, can help you gain an understanding of their level of comprehension.
- Reflections. Ask students to write a reflection after each class session to help you get a picture of how clearly they understand the material.
- Check-ins. This strategy involves simple one- to three-minute check-ins with individual students that can help you modify instruction.
- Online dialogues/postings.
- Exit/entrance slips.

Figure 9.3: The Integrated Assessment Cycle

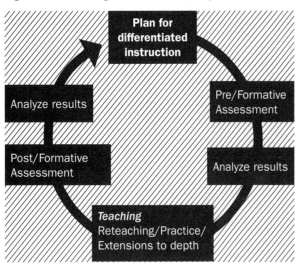

Example
(note the "modification up" for gifted learners)

As a result of this lesson/unit students will:[74]

Know the definitions of point, line, line segment, rays, angles (right, acute, obtuse), perpendicular and parallel lines; define two-dimensional figures, right triangles, and line-symmetric figures. [CCSS.Math.Content.4.G]

Modification up: Know how to define two-dimensional figures, square, and rectangle. [CCSS.Math.Content.4.G and 5.G]

Be able to draw points, lines, line segments, rays, angles (right, acute, obtuse), perpendicular and parallel lines; identify two-dimensional figures, right triangles, and line-symmetric figures; classify two-dimensional figures, and categorize right triangles. [CCSS.Math.Content.4.G]

Modification up: Be able to draw points, lines, line segments, rays, angles (right, acute, obtuse), perpendicular and parallel lines; identify two-dimensional figures, and square/rectangles figures; classify two-dimensional four-sided figures in a hierarchy based on properties. [CCSS.Math. Content.4.G and 5.G]

Understand that geometric shapes can be classified by properties of their lines and angles. [CCSS. Math.Content.4.G.A.2]

Modification up: Understand that attributes belonging to a category of two-dimensional figures also belong to all subcategories of that category. [CCSS.Math.Content.5.G.B.3]

Step 2: Conduct Preassessment.
Now that the goals have been set, deliver a preassessment to identify students' prior knowledge. For gifted learners the preassessment ensures they are prepared for the modified objectives. Suggestions of preassessment methods are offered on page 140.

Step 3: Analyze Preassessment: Considering Learning Differences.
Through reviewing the data collected from the preassessment, ready instruction to:

- move students through the unit
- group students based on readiness, interest, or learning profile for instruction
- provide or stimulate prior knowledge
- accelerate beyond or compact students out of components of instruction

Step 4: Respond Instructionally.
At this point, have students engage in direct instruction or practice. For gifted students whose preassessment shows the need for acceleration, be sure to provide instruction in the accelerated level. For students who have been compacted out of instruction, provide time for them to work on in-depth studies such as enrichment/extensions/ enhancements (E3).

Step 5: Conduct Formative Assessment.
At a point within the instruction where a chunk of information has been practiced, conduct formative assessments for:

- acquisition of learning development
- need for reteaching
- need for enrichment/extension/ enhancement (E3)

Step 6: Analyze Data.
Once again, review the data to determine whether you should:

- continue to move students through the unit
- reteach the material

---

[74] All standards from CCSS Math grades 4 and 5.

- regroup students based on readiness, interest, or learning profile for instruction
- accelerate beyond or compact students out of components of instruction

After step 6, the process begins again. Note how in **Figure 9.4** the cycle continues until students have met or exceeded the standard. At the end of a set of lessons or chapter, give students a formal summative assessment to identify their readiness for the next set of lessons or chapter. Such an assessment can also be considered a formative assessment for future studies or units.

Using Assessment with Gifted Students

For gifted students, assessment should be used for three main differentiated purposes:

1. **Preassessment** to determine whether compacting or accelerating instruction and learning is needed
2. **Formative assessment** to check for deep content knowledge and sophisticated levels of thinking

3. **Summative assessment** to identify purposes of future or further study

In general, assessment should focus on evidence of achievement rather than ability to regurgitate information. This is especially true for gifted learners. In all three phases of the assessment process, we will be looking for what the gifted students already know, where they may have "holes" in their learning (needing supports or fill to move forward), how they are processing information and gaining a deeper understanding of the complex ideas, and then how they have synthesized information to create new and unique ideas or products.

Figure 9.4: The Teaching and Learning Process of Assessment

The Teaching and Learning Process

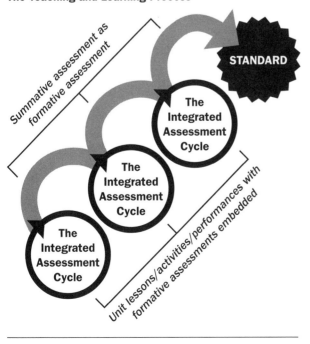

Value of Quality Assessment

For the Student

When well designed and implemented, assessment benefits students by:
- enhancing motivation to learn
- building student ownership of the learning
- reinforcing that effort will equal achievement
- producing significant learning gains
- encouraging collaboration with peers
- developing awareness of learning gaps

For the Teacher

Effective assessments allow teachers to:
- more precisely diagnose learning or gaps in understanding
- provide more detailed evidence of student progress
- distinguish the effectiveness of instructional strategies
- articulate the effectiveness of their curriculum.

Preassessment for Gifted Learners

Many gifted students come to the learning setting with a vast amount of preexisting knowledge in the content areas. Sally Reis and colleagues conducted a year-long study through the National Research Center on the Gifted and Talented that examined the effects of curriculum modification and compacting for gifted students in the inclusion classroom.[75] The study revealed that 60 percent of the students in the study were able to achieve 80 percent mastery of the content *before* school had even begun!

Three Ways to Preassess for Gifted Learners

Following are three ways we can use preassessments to avoid setting up gifted students for negative consequences—including poor learning habits and/or low motivation to persist at learning. Note that many of the assessments cross over the three areas of focus. You and the students must be clear about the intent of the assessment and how the results will be used. Here are the three ways that preassessments can benefit gifted students:

1. Identify holes in their learning; areas of the content that the student can demonstrate mastery and/or may be missing information or have misinformation.

Tools/Strategies:
- KWL—what I know, want to know, have learned (informal)
- questioning (informal)
- unit preassessments (formal)
- prior unit test (formal)
- standardized tests (formal)
- writing prompts (formal)
- student products and work samples (formal)
- concept map (formal)

2. Identify areas of the content where the student exhibits a natural tendency toward learning efficiency; information gathering and analysis comes easily.

Tools/Strategies:
- questioning (informal)
- KWL/KIQ—what I know, want to know, have learned; what I know, find interesting, and have questions about (informal)
- material preview to pique interest (informal)
- initiating activities (informal)
- informal survey/questionnaire/inventory (informal)
- turn and talk (informal)
- show of hands/fist to 5 (informal)
- interest or thinking journal (informal)
- student interviews (formal/informal)
- interest survey (formal)
- prior unit test (formal)
- standardized tests (formal)
- concept map (formal)
- student products and work samples (formal)
- self-evaluations (formal)

3. Identify areas of the content that excite or interest the student.

Tools/Strategies:
- questioning (informal)
- KWL/KIQ (informal)
- teacher observation (informal)
- student demonstrations and discussions (informal)
- material preview to pique interest (informal)
- initiating activities (informal)
- show of hands/fist to 5 (informal)
- informal survey/questionnaire/inventory (informal)
- games (informal)
- anticipation journal (informal)
- interest survey (formal)
- prior unit test (formal)
- standardized tests (formal)
- concept map (formal)
- student products and work samples (formal)
- self-evaluations (formal)

[75] Reis, Westburg, et.al, 1993.

Formative Assessment for Gifted Learners

Most gifted students learn factual information very quickly. You can use formative assessment to identify how well they understand the fundamental components of the curriculum, but do not spend too much time at this level. Where gifted students may need supports or modifications is in the procedural and conceptual knowledge areas. Therefore, gifted students should be practicing the strategies and skills using the tools of the discipline, as well as acting as disciplinarians. The tools of the discipline are considered both the thinking tools and the physical tools. Here are some examples of disciplinarians within subjects:

English/Language Arts Example:
Author's tools:
- Thinking examples:
  - voice
  - tone
  - patterns
- Physical examples:
  - computer/word processing
  - editing
  - voice recording

Math Example:
Statistician's tools:
- Thinking examples:
  - rules
  - laws
  - interpretation
- Physical examples:
  - calculator
  - graphs/charts
  - data systems

Social Studies Example:
Historian's tools:
- Thinking examples:
  - point of view
  - interpretation
  - analysis

- Physical examples:
  - original documents
  - maps, charts, graphs
  - interviews

Science Example:
Chemist's tools:
- Thinking examples:
  - research
  - questioning
  - experimentation
- Physical examples:
  - labs
  - safety gear
  - microscopes

The Importance of Descriptive Feedback

Assessing how well gifted students are using the discipline's tools and actions requires observation. Therefore, we suggest using feedback to coach gifted learners into higher performance. When gifted learners are in our classrooms, we want them highly engaged and always looking for the next challenge. We also want to consistently see learning progress. In order to support the growth of gifted learners as well as all other learners, teachers need to provide specific guidance for continual improvement. This is the purpose of *descriptive feedback*. Evaluative feedback, such as grades, is considered a critique. "This is what you got and now you are done" is the message of such feedback. Descriptive feedback, on the other hand, is constructive, helpful information that clearly answers "How can I do better?" It is best characterized as coaching.

Descriptive feedback affects both performance and motivation since it provides specific information on how students can improve. Descriptive feedback answers these questions for students:

Where am I?

What did I do well?

Where or how did I fall short?

How can I improve next time?

What is next?

This sort of feedback is linked to specific learning goals and/or criteria presented in a checklist or rubric.

> Descriptive feedback is constructive, helpful information that clearly answers "How can I do better?"

Nurturing a Growth Mindset with Descriptive Feedback

Descriptive feedback also reinforces students' view on intelligence. As we discussed in Chapter 6, Carol Dweck introduced educators to the concept of mindsets in relation to teachers' roles. She suggests that individuals have different views on intelligence. Some believe that intelligence is fixed—what you are born with is what you have to work with. Gifted students with a fixed mindset are convinced that if they have ability, they should not need effort. They believe that your ability ensures continued success.

Other people view intelligence as something that is not fixed but malleable; this is called a growth mindset—your abilities can be developed through effort and persistence.

When we have worked with gifted students who have a fixed mindset, they sometimes comment, "I used to be smart." When these students encounter content or skills that are new or experiences that are truly designed to challenge them, they cannot fall back on what they already know. At this point, they need to learn how to learn. With a fixed mindset, they can't figure out what to do when learning gets hard and so conclude that they are not smart anymore. Some students with fixed mindsets give up and become academic underachievers.

As their teachers, we need to help these gifted learners work through this changing image of who they are and offer strategies on how they can improve, learn, and succeed. Descriptive feedback provides specific guidance on how to get better. Its targeted coaching tells students what has been accomplished and what they need to do to improve the next time. Its goal is continual improvement. Descriptive feedback nurtures the growth mindset. It says, in essence, "You can get better and here is how."

Effective descriptive feedback provides students:

- ongoing, timely feedback
- explicit and focused feedback
- feedback in student-friendly language
- comments that are clearly connected to the learning goals and/or quality criteria ("Your use of descriptive language helped me clearly see your characters") rather than vague comments ("Good!")
- specifics about what they did well and where they are now
- specifics about how to improve and what is next
- small steps, if multiple improvements are necessary, the student can get overwhelmed (target a place or two to start)
- as appropriate, samples of exemplary work so they can see how it "looks" in comparison to their work

Teachers can provide written descriptive feedback directly on student work or noted on the rubric or checklist. This is particularly helpful if students need to refer to it as they revise their work. Or try offering oral feedback by stopping at student desks or having a two- or three-minute conference at a worktable or your desk. These short conferences can follow the model of speed dating, with students meeting with you one after the other during an independent work time.

If you discover that several students need identical feedback, consider meeting as a small group. If a critical mass of students need the same feedback, it is probably appropriate to present it to the class as a whole. You may ask students who were successful with the task to explain, demonstrate, or model strategies or approaches they used.

The Stars and Steps Method

Rick Stiggins suggests a two-phase process for presenting descriptive feedback called "Stars and Stairs."[76] The first phase involves commenting on strengths of the student's work (stars). This is followed by offering recommendations for improvement or specifics about what to do next (stairs).

---

[76] Stiggins, 2011.

When providing descriptive feedback, avoid making comments on the person ("You put a lot of work into this project"); these kinds of comments do not provide the specific information that students need to improve.

The chart on page 144 offers suggestions for what we call "stars" and "steps."

Remember that students need opportunities to apply descriptive feedback to their work. They either need a similar assignment in the near future or an immediate opportunity to revise their work so they can act on the insights provided in the descriptive feedback. Offering recovery points encourages students to revise their work and recapture any points they lost in the first submission. This process recognizes that some students simply need more time, practice, or feedback to reach a goal. When students have the opportunity to revise their work and gain recovery points, they are more likely to remember and apply what they learned from descriptive feedback.

Some gifted students will do just enough to get by or will slide into underachievement; we want to challenge them to commit to high-quality work. Gifted students with a fixed mindset need specific direction for improvement so they do not give up or give in to less than their best. Descriptive feedback provides all students constructive, specific information on how to improve. This feedback is essential for the continuous learning progress of all our students, including those who are gifted.

Assessing Thinking

Effective formative assessment can also be used with gifted students to assess their levels of thinking. An expert in assessing higher order thinking, Susan M. Brookhart describes three principles to follow when assessing students' thinking:

1. *Content should initiate the thinking process—* give students something to think about.

2. *Materials should be sophisticated and not subject to "recall"*—it should use ill-structured problems, the Case Study Method, or authentic/real-world issues that don't have easy or simple solutions.

3. *Assessments should range from lower order to higher order (complexity) and include a range of sophistication from simple to compound—* scaffold students up the ladder from recall to creating, and offer tasks of various levels, from single-step to multi-step actions.[77]

Following are strategies to use in assessing thinking.

Rubrics for Assessing 21st Century Skills

Use the rubrics on pages 148–152 to assess students' higher levels of thinking. Note on the assessments rubrics that a rating scale of 0, 1, 3, and 5 have descriptors provided. This offers a way for the teacher to suggest when a student is "almost there" or "not quite there yet," and assess the thinking at a rating of 2 or 4.

These rubrics provide guidance on what to look for as students develop their higher level thinking skills. Note that the descriptors in the 0, 1, 3, and 5 columns are as qualitative as possible. When giving feedback on thinking, be sure your comments are clear and specific. Nothing is more confusing to a student than nebulous statements that are hard to measure, interpret, or live up to.

Additional ideas for assessing students' critical thinking development are offered in **Assessment Questions for Critical Thinking** on page 153. We have designed questions, based on the work of Brookhart, that can help you better understand a student's level of critical thinking strategy development.[78] The questions can be used with text or graphic information. Graphics would include political cartoons, advertisements, photos, posters, or other non-text forms meant to persuade or provide information.

Digging Deeper into Questioning Matrix

Most every teacher has heard of and used Benjamin Bloom's Taxonomy of Educational Objectives to build learning activities.[79] In some cases, teachers have reserved the upper levels of the taxonomy (called the higher order thinking skills, or HOTS) for the gifted or the most

---

[77] Brookhart, 2010.
[78] Ibid.
[79] Bloom's Taxonomy of Educational Objectives, 1956.

◎ Stars and Steps*

Stars

Describe what was done well and why.

Comment on progress or improvement.

Describe the strengths of the work.

Note effective strategies or processes used.

Describe why an action or tactic was appropriate.

Connect the student's work to the learning goal.

Comment on the work related to quality criteria on a checklist or rubric.

Steps

Suggest a specific improvement.

Offer a new idea or perspective.

Comment on the limitations of the work.

Describe a next step in the improvement process.

Provide a better way or approach.

Suggest an alternative strategy.

Offer a comparison to previous work.

Provide a next step toward achieving the learning goal.

Specifically compare the student's work to quality criteria on a checklist or rubric.

* Stiggins, R., J. Chappius, and S. Chappius. *Classroom Assessment for Learning: Doing It Right, Using It Well, 2nd ed.* Upper Saddle River, NJ: Pearson, 2011.

advanced students in the classroom. Yet, in doing so, they misuse the taxonomy and undermine the educational opportunities for all those students who were never exposed to or allowed to work in the most advanced levels of the taxonomy.

We believe that all students have the right to think, perform, and be assessed in the most complex levels of Bloom's Taxonomy. For gifted learners, we need to encourage them to move into more sophisticated levels of higher order thinking (complexity). We have taken the Digging Deeper Matrix[80] for unit planning and organized it as an assessment tool. We are calling this the Digging Deeper into Questioning Matrix (DDQM); see page 155. At each stage of thinking (from recalling to creating), we suggest three tiers of assessment questions, from simple to sophisticated.

DDQM Tier 1: Complexity

At tier 1, the questions are basic and require reliance on the text, direct instruction, or materials that are readily available. Tier 1 provides a ladder to the higher order thinking strategies for those students who need more supports or scaffolding.

DDQM Tier 2: Increasing Complexity

Tier 2 assessment questions offer a bit more challenge. To answer these questions, students must rely on greater levels of practice, information gathering, inference making, and idea generation. This tier will also require students to complete more steps to find the answer. To achieve at this tier, many students may need to use the tier 1 questions to help them dig deeper into the difficulty of tier 2, while others may be able to answer the tier 2 questions outright without the support of tier 1.

DDQM Tier 3: Sophisticated Complexity

The most sophisticated tier of the DDQM is tier 3. This tier requires students to utilize significant amounts of prior knowledge, further data gathering, extrapolation of information, and unique idea production—the most sophisticated levels of complex thinking. Extrapolation of information means to project, extend, or expand upon information provided in cross-curricular or interdisciplinary

---

[80] Cash, 2011.

areas to develop new useful ideas. Some students may need to rely on both the tier 1 and 2 questions to stimulate their thinking into the tier 3 questions, while others may be able to move right into these deep and multifaceted questions.

See pages 156 and 157 for examples of the DDQM.

For additional ideas on formative assessment, see **FAST Ideas** on pages 158–161.

Summative Assessment for Gifted Learners

In general, summative assessment, which assesses the learning that has occurred, is considered the end point in the assessment process. Yet, even though summative assessment is performed at the end of the learning cycle, it can be used in a formative way to inform practice for the next unit of study.

> Even though summative assessment is performed at the end of learning cycle, it can inform practice for the next unit of study.

Some people may associate summative assessment only with standardized tests. However, there are many types of summative assessments; the most common are:

- state/provincial tests and CCSS assessments
- district or regional benchmark tests
- end-of-unit or chapter tests
- end-of-term or semester exams

All summative assessments are highly structured and formal. There is no informality in summative assessment because of the need to measure student performance or knowledge acquisition against a period of time and criteria set forth prior to the beginning of the learning process. Quality summative assessments must match the learning objectives and accurately reflect what students have learned, not just what they remember.

With gifted students, summative assessments can also alert students and teachers to the need for future study. For example, when a student performs exceptionally well in a particular course or unit, the teacher should recognize the student's unique abilities in that content area and suggest future studies or further investigations to deepen the student's knowledge. This could lead to:

- independent self-guided studies
- investigations into possible career or post-secondary pathways
- anchor activities for individual or small groups
- enrichment, extension, or enhancement (E3) ideas for the next unit

Summative assessments can also be used to assess how deeply gifted students understand the discipline. In this case, a student may be involved in what is called a "disciplined inquiry." This type of inquiry aims to develop an in-depth understanding of a problem rather than only a passing familiarity with it.[81] Disciplined inquiry requires the use of authentic assessments. In authentic assessments, students demonstrate whether they have mastered complex problems beyond a broad survey of topics. You may want to use the Case Study Method, as described in Chapter 5, as a format for developing authentic assessments.

Steps in constructing an authentic summative assessment for students include:

1. Based on prior experiences in a content area, students identify the problem.
2. Students work through a method (such as I-FORD) to find multiple options for solving the problem.
3. Students test and modify options until they find a viable solution.
4. Students select the best option for solving the problem.
5. Students present their solution to an authentic audience.

As cited in the formative assessment section of this chapter, many of the rubrics for thinking or the DDQM can be used as summative measures of learning. When using the rubrics or DDQM for summative assessment purposes, explain to students at the beginning of the learning cycle what they will be assessed on, when they will be assessed, and what is expected of them for product development.

Assessment That Builds Autonomy

In Chapter 6, we examined the Teaching and Learning Continuum (TLC) as a method for changing the role of teachers working with gifted students. The TLC can also be used as a model of assessments for developing learning autonomy in gifted students. Learning autonomy develops when students gain the confidence and competence to guide their own learning. The TLC provides teachers and students both an instructional and an assessment model for developing learning autonomy. As noted in **Figure 9.5**, lower level assessments encourage imitation and often relate to a singular discipline. The higher levels of the TLC Assessment Model, on the other hand, use more authentic assessments that require making connections between multiple disciplines and encourage the creation of useful, original products. Also, as students move upward in the model, their thinking expands from bilateral/convergent (closed, one right answer) to multilateral/divergent (open, many right answers) production. The TLC Assessment Model provides ideas for the preassessment/diagnostic, formative, and summative assessments options.

Chapter Summary

Quality feedback and assessment are essential for all students. For gifted learners, there can be a profound difference between doing what comes easy or natural to them and doing what truly meets their potential. Descriptive feedback and assessment are ways to coach gifted learners toward confidence and competence throughout the learning process. Additionally, using effective feedback and assessment practices helps us change students' mindsets from fixed to growth by nurturing deeper thinking.

---

81 Wehlage, Newmann, and Secada, 1996.

◎ Assessments That Build Autonomy

TLC Level	Knowledge Level	Type of Assessment		
		Diagnostic	**Formative**	**Summative**
Consultative Student designs assessment to develop, monitor, and evaluate own learning process	**Self-Regulatory** • Create • Produce • Hypothesize • Build • Compose • Critique • Extend • Invent • Originate • Transform	• Student-directed investigation to find problems • Personal goal setting • Proposal development	• Case study • Hypothesis development • Personal goal-setting update • Website • Progress report • Expert feedback	• Student-designed rubric • Student-designed product • Assessment by audience/expert
Coached Teacher and student collaborate to design assessment	**Conceptual** • Evaluate • Design • Support • Adapt • Discriminate • Analyze • Connect • Deconstruct • Differentiate • Examine • Infer • Integrate • Test for	• Interest survey • Contract • Self-preassessment	• Lab/experiment • Thesis statement • Self-assessment/progress report • Discussion forum • Simulation • Wiki • Reciprocal teaching	• Student- and teacher-negotiated rubric • Teacher- and student-negotiated product • Self-assessment • Peer review • Portfolio • Research report • Contract completion
Facilitated Teacher constructs assessment with options for individual learners or groups	**Procedural** • Construct • Perform • Solve • Reason • Understand • Analogize • Redesign • Predict • Map • Relate • Show • Examine • Inspect • Categorize • Classify • Clarify • Compare • Conclude • Contrast • Demonstrate • Distinguish • Explain • Illustrate • Interpret • Paraphrase • Predict • Represent • Reorganize • Summarize • Translate • Apply • Develop • Display • Execute • Implement • Model • Solve • Use	• KWL • Guided questioning • Group discussion • Mind map • Inventory of learning styles/modes/preferences	• Discussions • Reflections • Demonstration • Homework • Research • Exit cards • Oral presentation • Games • Check-ins • E-bulletin boards/e-chats	• Subjective assessment (open-ended essay) • Poster • Research paper • Teacher-designed rubric • Debate • Group project • Assessment stations
Didactic Teacher constructs assessment based on whole-group learning	**Factual** • Recall • Remember • Verify • Respond • Match • Choose • Define • Describe • Identify • Label • List • Locate/Find • Name • Recite • Say • Tell	• Teacher-constructed pretest	• Quizzes • Homework • Practice exams • Class participation • Performance assessments	• Objective assessment (multiple choice, true/false) • Standardized tests

Left margin (bottom to top): SINGLE DISCIPLINE → MULTIPLE DISCIPLINE

Right margin (bottom to top): IMITATION → AUTHENTIC

◎ The I-FORD Method for Assessing Thinking

Problem Solving: The I-FORD Method

	0	1	2	3	4	5
Identification of the problem	Did not identify the main problem	Incompletely identified the main problem		Completely identified the main problem		Described the problem in full detail, and identified why it is important to resolve the issue
Fact gathering	Did not gather any facts	Gathered a few facts about the problem		Gathered facts about the problem that will be helpful in resolving the issue		Gathered a significant number of facts to support the description of the problem and why it is important to resolve the issue
Options for possible solutions	No options listed	Offered a few options		Offered a number of options		Offered numerous options that were creative, divergent, or unique
Rank possible solutions	No ranking of solutions	Ranked solutions based on one criteria		Ranked solutions using at least three criteria		Ranked solutions using at least five criteria
Deciding the best course of action	No course set	Determined a course of action with little/no detail		Determined a course of action with steps included		Determined a course of action with well-defined steps for implementing the solution
Decision making	Does not identify who and what is necessary to implement the solution	Identifies some of the team members needed and some of what is necessary to implement the solution		Identifies all the team members needed and all of the materials necessary to implement the solution		Identifies all the team members needed and all of the materials, and includes why they are important to the solution

◎ The FFOE Method for Assessing Thinking

Creativity: The FFOE Method

Creativity: The FFOE Method	0	1	2	3	4	5
Fluency: idea generation	No ideas generated	Came up with a few ideas		Came up with several ideas		Came up with numerous unique and unexpected ideas
Flexibility: adapting situations or ways to approach	No ways to approach the problem	Came up with a few ways to approach the problem		Came up with several ways to approach the problem		Came up with numerous ways to approach the problem including ideas from different angles and perspectives
Originality: new ideas	No new ideas	Came up a new idea that was a reorganization of a past idea		Came up a new idea that took an old idea and made it better/ more efficient/ effective		Came up a new ideas that was unique and has great value to others
Elaboration: adding detail	Offered no details	Offered a few details		Offered several details that extend the idea		Offered refined details that enhance the outcome

◎ The Critical Thinking Method for Assessing Thinking

Critical Thinking	0	1	2	3	4	5
Question posing	Does not pose a question OR Poses an irrelevant question	Poses a simple question OR Poses a question that is easily answered		Poses an open-ended relevant question		Poses an open-ended complex question of high relevance
Gathering relevant data	Does not gather data	Gathers data that is biased, inaccurate, unreliable, irrelevant, erroneous, or assumptive		Gathers data that is free of bias, error, and assumption; accurate; reliable; relevant		Gathers data that is free of bias, error, and assumption; accurate; reliable; relevant; and articulated how the information can assist in answering the question
Effective interpretation of data	Does not interpret the data	Data interpretation is flawed, erroneous, unreliable, irrelevant, or assumptive		Data interpretation is free of bias, error, and assumption; accurate; reliable; and relevant		Data interpretation is free of bias, error, and assumption; accurate reliable; and demonstrates a use of logic, facts, graphs, questions theories, etc.
Impartially considers information, thoughts, and/or ideas	No consideration for other points of view, thoughts, and/or ideas	Expresses a narrow point of view or a view that is irrelevant or lacks a depth of understanding of other points of view, thoughts, and/or ideas		Expresses a point of view that is relevant, displays a depth of understanding of other points of view, thoughts, and/or ideas		Expresses an appropriately broad point of view or one that is significantly relevant and fairly articulates a deep understanding of other points of view, thoughts, and/or ideas
Develops well-reasoned conclusions or solutions based on information presented	Makes no inference based on the information presented and does not offer a conclusion or solution	Makes inaccurate, illogical, implausible inferences based on the information presented and offers conclusions or solutions that are unattainable, untested, and/or lacking a standard of judgment		Expresses accurate, logical, plausible inferences based on the information presented and offers conclusions or solutions that are attainable, tested, and/or based on a standard of judgment		Clearly and precisely articulates accurate, logical, plausible inferences based on the information presented and offers well-grounded conclusions or solutions that are attainable, well-tested, and/or based on a significant standard of judgment
Uses effective communication when working with others to solve problems	Does not articulate ideas, implications, personal line of thinking, and/or does not work well with others to solve problems	Is vague or ambiguous when articulating ideas, implications, and personal line of thinking, and at times works well with others to solve problems		Is clear and articulate when sharing ideas, implications, and personal line of thinking, and works well with others to solve problems		Is clear and precise when explaining or expressing ideas, implications, and personal line of thinking, and always works well with others to solve problems

From *Differentiation for Gifted Learners: Going Beyond the Basics* by Diane Heacox, Ed.D., and Richard M. Cash, Ed.D. copyright © 2014. Free Spirit Publishing Inc., Minneapolis, MN; 800-735-7323; www.freespirit.com. This page may be reproduced for use within an individual school or district. For all other uses, contact www.freespirit.com/company/permissions.cfm.

◎ The Collaboration/Communication Method for Assessing Thinking

Collaboration/ Communication	0	1	2	3	4	5
Contributes ideas to the team members	Does not contribute any ideas to the team	Contributes a limited amount of ideas to the team		Contributes ideas to the team		Contributes many useful and relevant ideas to the team
Contributes information or resources to team members	Does not contribute any information or resources to the team	Contributes a limited amount of information or resources to the team		Contributes information or resources to the team		Contributes a great amount of relevant and useful information and resources to the team
Shares the workload with team members	Does not share the workload with the team members	Shares some of the workload with other team members (either does most, if not all the work, or little to none of the work)		Shares the workload with other members of the team		Is aware of all members' duties, understands when others may need help, and offers help without being asked
Takes responsibility for duties as assigned within the group	Does not take any responsibility for duties as assigned	Takes limited responsibility for assigned duties or blames others when own duties are not performed or completed		Takes responsibility for duties as assigned		Takes responsibility for duties as assigned and keeps others aware of own progress. Seeks help when needed
Effectively participates in group discussion	Does not participate in group discussions	Participates in group discussions, but may control the conversation, offer little relevant information, or support or be a negative voice within the discussions		Effectively participates in group discussions using positive reinforcement techniques to encourage others' points of view or participation		Is an exceptionally effective group member who encourages, reinforces, and supports others during discussion, allowing others to think through ideas and suggestions. Is balanced in speaking and listening
Effectively uses and exhibits positive listening techniques	Does not exhibit listening behaviors or does not use positive listening techniques	Listens to group members but does little to support the group dynamic through negative body language or attitude		Effectively uses and exhibits positive listening techniques that encourage others to speak, generate ideas, or develop their thoughts		Is an exceptionally effective listener who uses body language, voice cues, and facial expressions to encourage and support others in their participation within the entire group process →

◎ The Collaboration/Communication Method for Assessing Thinking (continued)

Collaboration/ Communication	0	1	2	3	4	5
Cooperates with team members	Does not cooperate with other team members	Cooperates with some team members but not all		Cooperates with all team members		Cooperates with all team members and is considered to be a critical member of the team
Is prepared	Is never prepared	Is prepared some of the time		Is prepared for discussions, group activities, and projects		Is always prepared for discussions, activities, and projects
Is a positive influence on the team	Is a negative influence on the team	Is neither a positive or negative influence on the team		Is a positive influence on the team		Is a significantly positive influence on the team and is often the person others turn to for support, ideas, suggestions, or assistance
Respectfully considers others' ideas, points of view, and thoughts	Does not consider others' ideas, points of view, and thoughts	Considers others' ideas, points of view, and thoughts but may not be respectful		Respectfully considers others' ideas, points of view, and thoughts		Respectfully considers others' ideas, points of view, and thoughts and may even draw out other points of view that may be unique or different

From *Differentiation for Gifted Learners: Going Beyond the Basics* by Diane Heacox, Ed.D., and Richard M. Cash, Ed.D., copyright © 2014. Free Spirit Publishing Inc., Minneapolis, MN; 800-735-7323; www.freespirit.com. This page may be reproduced for use within an individual school or district. For all other uses, contact www.freespirit.com/company/permissions.cfm.

◎ Assessment Questions for Critical Thinking

Critical Thinking Strategy	Assessment Questions
Identifying main idea/argument	• What is the main idea, point, or argument the author is making? • What specific points support the main idea, point, or argument? • How does the author resolve the argument?
Analyzing arguments	• What evidence is used to support or contradict the argument? • What assumptions does the author rely upon? • What is the structure of the argument?
Compare and contrast	• What are the specific elements of each item? • How can the elements be organized into categories of similarity and difference? • What are the principles that govern each of the elements?
Sequencing and prioritizing	• In what way is the order or sequence important? • How might changing the order or sequence change the outcome? • Why is the order or sequence important?
Finding relevance and irrelevance	• What information is relevant or irrelevant to the argument? • What makes the information relevant or irrelevant to the argument? • How can relevant/irrelevant information be made irrelevant/relevant?
Discerning fact vs. opinion	• How can the facts be identified and validated? • How does the author use opinions to support or contradict the argument? • In what ways do the facts support or contradict opinions?
Investigating reliable and unreliable sources	• What sources does the author use? • In what ways do the sources support or contradict the author's point of view? • How is a source validated or invalidated?
Distinguishing assumptions and generalizations	• How does the author use assumptions in the argument? • What generalizations are made in the arguments? • How does the argument create assumptions or generalizations?
Identifying cause and effect	• What are the specific causes and effects? • What would happen if a cause or effect were changed? • In what ways do the causes/effects predict the effects/causes?
Understanding point of view	• How might the author's point of view develop? • How does the author's point of view affect the argument? • What is another point of view?
Recognizing bias and stereotype	• What bias or stereotype is used to support or contradict the argument? • Why did the author use bias or stereotyping in the argument?
Using deduction and induction	• How has the author used a sequence to generate a conclusion? (Deductive) • How has the author used individual events to generate conclusions? (Inductive)

◎Digging Deeper into Questioning Matrix (DDQM): Questioning Tiers

Questioning Level	Question Design
Tier 1: Complexity	To answer these questions, students will need: • prior knowledge • text, resources, and materials from the unit of study
Tier 2: Increased Complexity	To answer these questions, students will need: • prior knowledge • greater levels of practice • effective information gathering techniques (note taking, graphic organizers) • inference-making skills • patience, persistence, and perseverance
Tier 3: Sophisticated Complexity	To answer these questions, students will need: • significant levels of prior knowledge that is cross-curricular or interdisciplinary • expert practice • effective and efficient information gathering techniques (journals, files, data systems) • extrapolation skills

◎ Digging Deeper into Questioning Matrix (DDOM)

Unit: _____ Standard: _____

Students will know: _____

Students will be able to: _____

Students will understand: _____

	RECALL (R)	UNDERSTAND (U)	APPLY (A)	ANALYZE (Z)	EVALUATE (E)	CREATE (C)
Level 1 Factual:	*Tier 1 Questions* Factual questions: Who, what, when, where?	In your own words retell, recap, repeat	Use the text/factual information to support who, what, when, where; apply the strategy; and report the event	What are the individual elements? How do individual elements support the position? / Locate micro-level issues and identify the effect	Check information for clarity; what information supports understanding?	Reorganize, rearrange, and restructure information to create new
Level 2 Procedural:	Procedural questions: How? In what way? What are the steps? What are the criteria?	How can you say it in a different way? Use the information to give greater detail/clarify/describe	*Tier 2 Questions* Using text/facts expand to bigger effects; how can strategy be used in personal life; use strategy and reflect on effect	What are the relationships between the elements; how are those relationships affecting each other? / Locate issues and identify their effects; using greater information, how do they compare/contrast?	Judge information for accuracy; provide multiple sources to confirm understanding	Develop plans to change the outcome
Level 3 Conceptual:	Conceptual definitions: define the concept, theory; define the classification, theory; define the classification, periods, laws, principles; list the relationships, generalizations, and understandings	Using the text/factual information: Expand, elaborate, illustrate, frame, extend	*Tier 3 Questions* Using text/facts elaborate on much greater effects; how can strategy be used in a creative way to solve authentic problems? Use strategy and suggest improvements	What principles govern the outcome/effects; what are the systemic level issues; using all the information, how do all the parts affect the whole?	Critique information for validity; scrutinize understanding from multiple perspectives	Using both current and new information create a uniquely different product

From *Differentiation for Gifted Learners: Going Beyond the Basics* by Diane Heacox, Ed.D., and Richard M. Cash, Ed.D., copyright © 2014. Free Spirit Publishing Inc., Minneapolis, MN; 800-735-7323; www.freespirit.com. This page may be reproduced for use within an individual school or district. For all other uses, contact www.freespirit.com/company/permissions.cfm.

◎ Digging Deeper into Questioning Matrix (DDQM): ELA Example

Unit: Hamlet Standard: Analyze how particular lines of dialogue or incidents in a story or drama propel the action, reveal aspects of a character, or provoke a decision.

Students will know: Lines of dialogue, key events, actions and characteristic of key players in Hamlet; scene, setting, plot of Hamlet; key vocabulary

Students will be able to: Analyze how particular lines of dialogue, key events, and character actions and characteristics propel the action within the story of Hamlet

Students will understand: how authors use dialogue, setting, plot, and characters to propel action within a story or drama; How authors represent the human condition (fatal flaws) through literature

	RECALL (R)	UNDERSTAND (U)	APPLY (A)	ANALYZE (Z)	EVALUATE (E)	CREATE (C)
Level 1 Factual:	*Tier 1 Questions* Specific/Concrete (1R) List up to 6 players in *Hamlet* who have significant effect on the actions of the play. (5 pts)	Translate (1U) What are the major characteristics of the 6 key players you selected? (5 pts)	Original Way (1A) What dialogue supports your list of characteristics for each player? (10 pts)	Individual Elements (1Z) Using two of your key players, how do their flaws influence their actions over the course of the play? (20 pts)	Check Clarity (1E) In what ways did Shakespeare successfully represent Hamlet's fatal flaws? (30 pts)	Reorganize (1C) How might the play have ended differently if one of your key players had not existed in this play? (30 pts)
Level 2 Procedural:	Tools/Skills (2R) Why do you believe the characters you identified are essential to the movement of the play toward understanding human's fatal flaw? (5 pts)	Interpret (2U) Why would Shakespeare use the character trait of fatal flaws in *Hamlet?* (5 pts)	*Tier 2 Questions* Practical Way (2A) How did Shakespeare structure those scenes to highlight the fatal flaws of the key players you selected? (20 pts)	Relationship Among Elements (2Z) Using 3 of the key players, how are their flaws alike and different? (30 pts)	Judge Accuracy (2E) Why might audiences find Hamlet's fatal flaws appealing or appalling? (40 pts)	Formulate (2C) In what ways would the play have been different if all the characters were commoners/non-royalty? (50 pts)
Level 3 Conceptual:	Abstract Information (3R) Provide lines of dialogue from each character that helps you understand their fatal flaws. (5 pts)	Extrapolate (3U) How does Shakespeare use these players to help the viewer understand their own fatal flaws? (10 pts)	*Tier 3 Questions* Creative Way (3A) What additional literary techniques might Shakespeare have considered to highlight either the players' fatal flaws or propel the actions within the drama? (30 pts)	Principles Governing Elements (3Z) Using your 6 key players, in what ways do their fatal flaws propel the actions within the drama? (50 pts)	Critique Validity (3E) In what ways did Shakespeare use the human condition effectively to propel the plot and actions to a conclusion or resolution? (60 pts)	Innovate (3C) Using your 6 key players, and a period in history (other than the time used in *Hamlet*), write an abstract of an idea for a new drama based on human fatal flaws. (70 pts)
Assessment: Examples	Students must do all three boxes (max 15 pts)	Students choose at least 2 boxes (max 15 pts)	Students choose at least 1 box (max 30 pts)	Students choose at least 1 box (max 50 pts)	Students choose 1 box (max 60 pts)	Students choose 1 box (max 70 pts)

◎ Digging Deeper into Questioning Matrix (DDOM): Science Example

Unit: Electrical Engineering: Designing a Circuit. Standard: The engineering design process involves defining a problem, generating ideas, selecting a solution & testing it, making it, evaluating it, & presenting results.

Students will know: materials used in making things, properties of different materials, the steps in the design process, signs and symbols, the definitions of the key terms

Students will be able to: define problems, generate ideas, select solutions, plan, construct an object based on the plan, evaluate it, improve the object, present results, ask questions, troubleshoot, follow directions

	RECALL (R)	UNDERSTAND (U)	APPLY (A)	ANALYZE (Z)	EVALUATE (E)	CREATE (C)
Level 1 Factual	*Tier 1 Questions* Specific/Concrete (1R) Write a definition for the 10 key terms used in this unit. (5 pts)	Translate (1U) Why is it important to know the key terms used in this unit? (5 pts)	Original Way (1A) How did you apply the EDP to solving the alarm problem? (10 pts)	Individual Elements (1Z) Why are signs and symbols used in schematic diagrams? (20 pts)	Check Clarity (1E) What made your electrical circuit work or not? (30 pts)	Reorganize (1C) Using the materials provided, create an alarm circuit system that can help alert Emily when the water runs out. (30 pts)
Level 2 Procedural	Tools/Skills (2R) What are the steps in the Engineering Design Process (EDP)? (5 pts)	Interpret (2U) Why is it important to know the steps in the EDP? (5 pts)	*Tier 2 Questions* Practical Way (2A) How might you use the EDP in your daily life? (20 pts)	Relationship Among Elements (2Z) Why is it important that in *A Reminder for Emily* she learned about electricity and electrical engineering? (30 pts)	Judge Accuracy (2E) Did Emily use all of her resources effectively? (40 pts)	Formulate (2C) Draw out a plan for creating an alarm circuit system for Emily. (50 pts)
Level 3 Conceptual	Abstract Information (3R) What does it mean to solve problems? (5 pts)	Extrapolate (3U) Why would scientists/engineers use the EDP to solve problems? (10 pts)	*Tier 3 Questions* Creative Way (3A) How might an author use the EDP when writing a story? (30 pts)	Principles Governing Elements (3Z) Compare and contrast the roles of an electrician to that of an electrical engineer? (50 pts)	Critique Validity (3E) Why is it important for us to use an effective problem solving method? (60 pts)	Innovate (3C) Create a new circuit system that could be helpful to a person with a disability. (70 pts)
Assessment: Examples	Students must do all three boxes (max 15 pts)	Students choose at least 2 boxes (max 15 pts)	Students choose at least 1 box (max 30 pts)	Students choose at least 1 box (max 50 pts)	Students choose 1 box (max 60 pts)	Students choose 1 box (max 70 pts)

◎ FAST Ideas*

NAME	DESCRIPTION	WHAT TO DO WITH THE DATA	BEST WHEN USED
Background knowledge probe	Measures student's preexisting knowledge of course material via a short, simple questionnaire.	Used to determine what students already know to determine a starting point for new instruction.	P
Focused listening	Focuses student attention on a single important term and/or concept and requires students to list closely related ideas.	Used to discover what learners recall as most important points related to a particular topic and helps to center attention on key concepts.	P, D
Misconception/ preconception check	Examines prior knowledge and beliefs that may interfere with the ability to correctly learn new information.	Used to identify misconceptions so that modifications can be made that facilitate the acquisition of new knowledge.	P, D
Empty outlines	Students are provided with an empty or partially completed outline of course material and required to fill in the missing components in a limited amount of time.	Used to discover what learners recall and can organize into appropriate knowledge structure; promotes organization of information.	P, D
Minute paper	During the last few minutes of the class period, ask students to answer on a half-sheet of paper: "What is the most important point you learned today?" and, "What point remains least clear to you?" The purpose is to elicit data about students' comprehension of a particular class session.	Review responses and note any useful comments. During the next class periods emphasize the issues illuminated by your students' comments.	A
Muddiest point	Determines conceptual errors by asking questions such as "What is/was the muddiest point in this lesson?"	Used to identify what learners find least clear or most confusing.	D, A
Memory matrix	Students fill in cells of a two-dimensional diagram for which instructor has provided labels. For example, in a music course, labels might consist of periods (Baroque, Classical) by countries (Germany, France, Britain); students enter composers in cells to demonstrate their ability to remember and classify key concepts.	Tally the numbers of correct and incorrect responses in each cell. Analyze differences both between and among the cells. Look for patterns among the incorrect responses and decide what might be the cause(s).	D, A →

P= Prior to the lesson   **D**= During the lesson   **A**= After the lesson

* Adapted from Formative Assessment Strategies and Techniques. Park University: www.park.edu; National Teaching & Learning Forum: www.ntlf.com.

◎ FAST Ideas (continued)

NAME	DESCRIPTION	WHAT TO DO WITH THE DATA	BEST WHEN USED
Chain notes	Students pass around an envelope on which the teacher has written one question about the class. When the envelope reaches a student he/she spends a moment to respond to the question and then places the response in the envelope.	Go through the student responses and determine the best criteria for categorizing the data with the goal of detecting response patterns. Discussing the patterns of responses with students can lead to better teaching and learning.	P, D, A
Directed paraphrasing	Ask students to write a layman's "translation" of something they have just learned—geared to a specified individual or audience—to assess their ability to comprehend and transfer concepts.	Categorize student responses according to characteristics you feel are important. Analyze the responses both within and across categories, noting ways you could address student needs.	D, A
Categorization grid	Students are given a grid containing 2 or 3 important categories and required to sort a scrambled list of terms, images, equations into these categories.	Used to discover how students categorize information and how well learners understand "what goes with what."	D, A
Pro and con grid	Pros/cons, costs/benefits, advantages/disadvantages are listed in relationship to a specific concept, theory, or idea.	Used to discover the depth/ breadth of a student's analyses and their capacity for objectivity.	D
Content, form, and function outlines	Students are given a short instructional message and required to identify the what (content), how (form), and why (function).	Used to discover how learners analyze new information; also helps students focus on form and purpose.	D, A
Analytic memos	Learners write a structured 1–2 page analysis of and response to a specific problem or issue.	Used to examine the ability to analyze problems using discipline-specific approaches, methods, and techniques.	D, A
Word journal	Learners summarize information into a single word, then write a short paragraph explaining the word selection.	Used to examine the depth of reading comprehension, creativity in summarizing information, and skill at defending selection.	D, A
Approximate analogies	Instructor provides the first half of an analogy and students are required to fill in the remaining analogy component.	Used to promote the connection of newly learned relationships to ones that are more familiar; enhances the overall cognitive network.	P, D, A

→

P= Prior to the lesson   **D**= During the lesson   **A**= After the lesson

* Adapted from Formative Assessment Strategies and Techniques. Park University: www.park.edu; National Teaching & Learning Forum: www.ntlf.com.

◎FAST Ideas (continued)

NAME	DESCRIPTION	WHAT TO DO WITH THE DATA	BEST WHEN USED
Concept map	Focuses student attention on patterns of association, mental connections between a major concept and other learning while requiring them to diagram relationships.	Used to assess the students' understanding of the relationships between concepts and degree of "fit" between a concept map and the larger discipline.	P, D, A
Invented dialogues	Learners are required to either weave together original quotes or invent their own dialogue based on a specific theory or historical period.	Used to discover the learner's creativity in adapting information and expanding beyond basic knowledge.	D, A
One sentence summary	Students summarize knowledge of a topic by constructing a single sentence that answers the questions *"Who does what to whom, when, where, how, and why?"* The purpose is to require students to select only the defining features of an idea.	Evaluate the quality of each summary quickly and holistically. Note whether students have identified the essential concepts of the class topic and their interrelationships. Share your observations with your students.	D, A
Exam evaluations	Select a type of test that you are likely to give more than once or that has a significant impact on student performance. Create a few questions that evaluate the quality of the test. Add these questions to the exam or administer a separate, follow-up evaluation.	Try to distinguish student comments that address the fairness of your grading from those that address the fairness of the test as an assessment instrument. Respond to the general ideas represented by student comments.	A
Application cards	After teaching about an important theory, principle, or procedure, ask students to write down at least one real-world application for what they have just learned to determine how well they can transfer their learning.	Quickly read once through the applications and categorize them according to their quality. Pick out a broad range of examples and present them to the class.	A
Student-generated test questions	Allow students to write test questions and model answers for specified topics, in a format consistent with course exams. This will give students the opportunity to evaluate the course topics, reflect on what they understand, and what good test items are.	Make a rough tally of the questions your students propose and the topics that they cover. Evaluate the questions and use the goods ones as prompts for discussion. You may also want to revise the questions and use them on the upcoming exam.	A

→

P= Prior to the lesson   **D**= During the lesson   **A**= After the lesson

* Adapted from Formative Assessment Strategies and Techniques. Park University: www.park.edu; National Teaching & Learning Forum: www.ntlf.com.

◎ FAST Ideas (continued)

NAME	DESCRIPTION	WHAT TO DO WITH THE DATA	BEST WHEN USED
Annotated portfolios	Students select a few pieces that highlight their work and provide a short written prose explaining why each piece was selected.	Used to encourage critical self-evaluation of work as well as the connection between creative work and course content.	A
Problem recognition tasks	Instructors provide students with a range of problems from which they must identify the type of problem that each example represents.	Used to examine how well students can identify problem types and match problem with possible solution methods.	A
What's the principle?	Students are given examples of problems from which they must identify what principle or theory is at work.	Used to assess the ability to relate problems with the strategies or principles used to solve them.	A
Documented problem solutions	Learners are asked to document the steps in the problem-solving process as they work through real-world type issues.	Used to encourage critical self-analysis and self-awareness of problem-solving strategies.	D, A
Audio and videorecorded protocols	Instructors audio- or videorecord students working through a problem-solving task.	Used to review how students actively problem-solve; encourages an in-depth analysis of the process involved in problem-solving.	D, A
Directed paraphrasing	Focuses student attention on summarizing and restating important information or con-cepts in their own words directed to a particular type of audience.	Used to discover the learner's ability to understand and communicate newly learned information.	A
Human tableau or Class modeling	Learners use their bodies to create "living" scenes or model processes to kinesthetically show their knowledge.	Used to discover how learners demonstrate knowledge through performance.	D, A
Paper or project prospectus	Students write a brief, structure first-draft plan for a term paper or project.	Used to examine understanding of an assignment and topic; encour-ages planning while there is still time for project modifications.	D
321 exit ticket	After a lesson have the students record on a small piece of paper: 3 new ideas they gained during the lesson, 2 connections they have made from the lesson to other content areas, and 1 question that still remains.	Analyze the tickets to learn how many of the students got the big ideas, what resonated with the students, how they made connec-tions to other content areas, and what further studies can come from this lesson/unit of study.	D, A

P= Prior to the lesson   **D**= During the lesson   **A**= After the lesson

---

* Adapted from Formative Assessment Strategies and Techniques. Park University: www.park.edu; National Teaching & Learning Forum: www.ntlf.com.

Chapter 10

Leadership

A variety of school professionals may provide leadership when it comes to differentiation for gifted learners. Certainly the building principal plays a crucial role in supporting teachers using differentiation. In all schools, teacher leaders—either those formally assigned to a role or those who informally influence classroom practices—also need to be part of an implementation team.

Other professionals who lend critical support for this endeavor include lead teachers, encompassing those who are teachers on special assignment (TOSAs), grade-level or department chairs, or curriculum specialists. Finally, gifted education teachers, specialists, coordinators, or facilitators take a lead role in assisting classroom teachers in this important work. Most educators who hold a position of responsibility for gifted services are considered teacher leaders.

Effective teacher leaders exhibit particular skills, values, and dispositions that enable them to be successful in their roles. Key is the ability to collaborate with others. As teacher effectiveness expert Charlotte Danielson states, "Teacher leaders must enlist colleagues to support their vision, build consensus among diverse groups of educators, and convince others of the importance of what they are proposing and the feasibility of their general plan for improvement." She continues, "Effective teacher leaders are open-minded and respectful of others' views. They display optimism and enthusiasm, confidence and decisiveness. They persevere and do not permit setbacks to derail an important initiative they are pursuing. On the other hand, they are flexible and willing to try a different approach if the first effort runs into roadblocks."[82]

This chapter provides ideas on how school leaders can encourage and support gifted education specialists as they work to embed the strategies of differentiation for gifted learners in classroom practice. First, we will explore the role of gifted education specialists as teacher leaders. Next, we'll examine critical elements in getting teacher support for differentiation for gifted learners. The chapter will conclude by describing two models for supporting teachers as they strive to better meet the needs of gifted students through instructional coaching and lesson study.

Gifted Education Specialist: Administrator or Teacher Leader?

Although many gifted education teachers, facilitators, or coordinators are considered gifted specialists and have similar responsibilities to school administrators—including managing budgets, hiring new team members, and overseeing and evaluating student services—most specialists by job title are directors, facilitators, or coordinators of gifted services. Some specialists are teachers on special assignment. Most are on teacher contracts, sometimes but not always with an extension to the contract that increases their number of duty days or that "rewards" them for taking on additional responsibilities.

Many gifted education specialists could be called teacher leaders. Using Charlotte Danielson's definition of this term, specialists would be considered formal teacher leaders since individuals typically apply for these positions and are chosen through an official selection process. Formal teacher leaders manage projects,

---

[82] Danielson, 2007.

facilitate study groups or task forces, provide professional development, and manage materials and resources. Some may also evaluate teacher performance and are thus regarded as "pseudo administrators" by teachers. Fulfilling this role is sometimes both confusing and challenging. Since formal teacher leaders' roles and responsibilities suggest some sort of power and decision making, teachers may be perplexed over what decisions these individuals can and cannot make on their behalf.

Many gifted education specialists could be called teacher leaders.

There are many attributes of good teacher leaders that are also attributes of good teachers. However, the ability to develop and support a vision, to call others to action and energize them, and to determine a course of action and monitor progress—all part of the work of many gifted specialists—are not typically included in teacher preparation coursework.

Danielson suggests that there are particular conditions that promote and support teacher leaders. School administrators play a critical role in supporting the work of teacher leaders. Gifted education specialists should consider whether these conditions are present in their current school settings.

Conditions That Support Teacher Leaders

Two conditions in particular are key for supporting teacher leaders:

1. A safe environment for risk taking. Innovation has long been a hallmark of gifted education. Specialists must feel confident that they can express ideas and take professional risks without being criticized. Creativity in thought and action can only be nurtured in settings that welcome new ideas and approaches. A principal once said, "Bring me any new idea you have. I'll consider it as long as you have done your homework." Indeed, when we offer new initiatives or ideas, we must be overly prepared to support them with research and evidence related to their likelihood to solve a problem or issue, to enhance our professional

practices, or to improve teaching and learning for students. Does your school environment nurture and support your passion for innovation?

2. Opportunities to develop leadership skills and administrators who encourage teacher leaders. As stated previously, colleges do not necessarily prepare educators for school-wide or district-wide leadership. Therefore, we need to work with school administrators who are willing to help us develop leadership skills and who promote our involvement at the school and/or district level.

Involvement in school or district-level committees and task forces, for example, enable you to learn leadership skills through firsthand experiences on a more limited scope. Are you part of leadership cabinets or the decision-making groups in your school? If not, are you professionally connected to someone who can keep you informed about issues that are being discussed or pending decision that will affect the work you do in gifted services? It is always better to be the person who informs a leadership group or directly participates in its agenda than the person who reacts to decisions handed down that have negative consequences for gifted students and services. Being at the table ensures that gifted education will have a voice in decisions made at the school or district level. If you are not involved in leadership-level activities, consider ways in which you can access these opportunities not only to develop your leadership skills, but also to influence school or district-level decisions that have implications for gifted learners. This is a key element in your advocacy for the needs of these students!

Embedding Differentiation for Gifted Learners into Classroom Practice

Although many schools still rely on single-day professional development sessions either during the school year or in the summer, we surely recognize that hearing does not mean doing. Our overall goal to change teaching and learning practices often is not accomplished through such professional development endeavors alone.

Studies suggest that effective teacher learning embodies two distinct realms: the individual and interpersonal. During the individual realm, teachers are provided new ideas related to content and pedagogy; they consider whether they agree or disagree with these new concepts; and then they decide whether or not they will implement them in their classrooms. In the interpersonal realm, teachers discuss the concepts with colleagues and then may choose to collaborate with others in order to further develop and support continued work with the concepts.

Educational researcher Cynthia Coburn calls the coming together of individual and interpersonal realms *sensemaking,* which she defines as: "The process by which teachers notice and select certain messages from their environment, interpret them, and then decide whether or not to act on those interpretations to change their practice."[83] Coburn's research indicates that, when it comes to new strategies, teachers fall along a continuum of acceptance from outright rejection to acceptance and use based on sensemaking. As they learn more about how the strategy works, teachers who were initially on the rejection end of the continuum shift toward the acceptance end—*if* the strategy better meets their students' learning needs. Therefore, in promoting differentiation for gifted learners, we need to introduce strategies that even the reluctant teacher will see as worthwhile to students.

Coburn also suggests that teachers have varying levels of commitment to using a particular strategy. Some teachers may apply the strategy in a halfhearted manner; it "looks" like they are using it but it may be in an inconsistent or even a faulty manner. Others fully and deeply adapt the strategy and use it consistently and in the way it was intended.

Coburn's research shows us that teachers' learning is an ongoing process; they continually take in new ideas and strategies on teaching and then actively work through them using personal

---

83 Coburn, 2001, 2004.

> Teachers' learning is an ongoing process as they continually take in new ideas and strategies and actively work through them to construct their classroom practices.

reflection and interpersonal interactions to construct their classroom practices. So what does this mean for those of us in leadership positions who are looking for "buy-in" from teachers and maybe even administrators?

Nine Tips for Achieving Buy-In from Colleagues

Your colleagues are more likely to buy in to using differentiation strategies with gifted students if you make it easy to adopt the strategies and clearly communicate the benefits of doing so. Following are some tips for getting their buy-in.

1. Provide information on new strategies in *multiple ways.*

- Provide articles or summarize key points or strategies in both online and offline print.
- Facilitate large and small group training sessions that cover teacher-selected topics and interests.
- Offer online learning opportunities, such as podcasts or webinars.
- Set up your training as a WebQuest so teachers can proceed at their own rate.
- Try brown bag lunches or coffee and dessert sessions to make the best use of available teacher time.
- Promote the exploration of differentiation for gifted through professional learning community agendas.
- Suggest books on educational practices appropriate for gifted learners to the school or grade level's book study group.

2. Provide opportunities for *teacher choice.*
Choice is a powerful motivation in adult learning. Determine particular differentiation strategies related to gifted learners and create a menu of choices for teachers (see **Essential Foundations**

for Classroom Teachers of the Gifted on page 166). Consider whether there are teachers in your school or district who are "experts" in using a particular strategy. If possible, create a list of teacher experts who, along with you, can offer a variety of mini-training sessions on the recommended strategies.

Ask teachers to select a strategy that interests them and sign up for a strategy training session either online or at a faculty meeting. Consider providing some pre-reading material prior to each session so teachers have a general introduction to the strategy. Encourage teacher experts to invite participants into their classrooms to observe the strategy in action. Also consider asking teacher experts to observe the classrooms of training participants and to provide descriptive feedback on their use of the strategy, or visit these classrooms yourself as part of your work in the role of instructional coach (see details later in this chapter). Here's where hiring a single roving substitute will provide release time for teachers to make classroom visits.

3. Make *collaborative discussion* a part of all learning approaches.

Teachers need time for the interpersonal realm to hear, absorb, understand, and discuss the new strategies or approaches. Consider offering a list of questions to frame and focus their discussions. The section on instructional coaching and lesson study offers discussion formats you may wish to review and adapt to your particular needs.

4. Solidly and explicitly *ground teacher learning in examples of practice* to illuminate the direct benefits to students.

- Model the strategy in one of your school's classrooms, and videorecord the session for review by teachers.

- Provide teachers with instructional coaching (details later in this chapter) to support their classroom applications.

- Use co-teaching (see Chapter 7) as a way to actively engage with the teacher to integrate the strategy into classroom practice.

- Encourage teachers to visit each other's classrooms to see the strategy in action.

- Try lesson study (see details later in this chapter) to collaboratively implement a strategy into classroom practice.

5. Create a *bank of best practices*.

Members of various professional communities not only get new ideas from each other but share ideas that work. Consider establishing a share file on your school's or district's intranet site. Create and label the specific file, such as "grade one" or "middle school social studies." Teachers, as they have time, can then look for ideas in the file as well as submit what works in their classrooms. Consider including digital video and web-based streaming video samples of differentiation in action. Teachers can also suggest resources, including websites and tablet applications, that they have used successfully with their students. They can also swap samples of student work so others in the group have quality examples to share with their students. Educators can also share pre-assessment or formative assessment tasks and evaluation rubrics for the others to consider.

Teachers in larger school districts may start a blog to enable teachers with common grade or course assignments to communicate ideas, concerns, and insights as well as solve problems collaboratively. Teachers truly value collaboration time; however, with differing school schedules and shrinking professional development time, we need to consider how technology can link us.

6. *Build in time* for teachers to reconvene *to share and discuss* their use of the strategy with their students.

Encourage them to bring samples of their students' work to share and be examined by other teachers. Discuss what worked and what you would change in using the strategy again. Try to provide time during the school day for teachers to collaboratively plan differentiated tasks that respond to the needs of their particular learners.

One school district held a "share fair" on a professional development day where teachers brought examples of differentiation used in their classroom and then met in grade-level or department groups to discuss their work.

◎Essential Foundations for Classroom Teachers of the Gifted

✓ Define for yourself what it means for students to be gifted and understand the definition used by your district or school.

✓ Understand rationale for the program model used in the district or school.

✓ Locate students for the program services (identification).

✓ Understand learning and affective characteristics and differences.

✓ Differentiate through content, process, and product for gifted learners.

✓ Design tiered assignments appropriate for gifted learners.

✓ Use grouping patterns that enhance the learning of gifted students.

✓ Add complexity and depth in learning.

✓ Understand compacting rationale and process.

✓ Use self-selected, self-directed learning including contracts.

✓ Recognize special populations: ELL, twice exceptional, ADHD, Asperger's, CLED.

✓ Understand nonproducers, selective producers, and underachievers in gifted populations.

Menu (for teacher choice of topics)

☐ Extend questioning strategies into creative and critical thinking.

☐ Embed creative thinking strategies.

☐ Embed critical thinking strategies.

☐ Use defensible enrichment strategies.

☐ Support talent development.

☐ Use acceleration practices (use the CCSS to guide acceleration decisions).

☐ Offer simulations: in class and online.

☐ Use technology to better differentiate and manage instruction.

☐ Implement pacing strategies.

☐ Differentiate lesson routines.

☐ Assign projects, presentations, and performances (engaging products).

☐ Use student inventories (modality, cognitive preference, interest).

☐ Create a learning profile.

☐ Examine data to determine readiness levels.

☐ Differentiate interest centers.

☐ Develop academic competitions.

☐ Work with parents/significant adults of gifted learners.

7. *Provide descriptive feedback* on the work that the teachers are undertaking.

Descriptive feedback both identifies the strengths of the teacher's work and gives them next steps to further develop their professional practices. This topic is discussed in Chapter 9 and taken to greater depth later in this chapter.

8. Reaffirm that differentiation is the *purpose of professional learning community* activities.

Many schools have established professional learning communities (PLCs) of teachers to both model professional development and to increase student learning. However, even Richard DuFour, the recognized authority on PLCs, expresses concerns that the term is used so ubiquitously that it is in danger of losing all meaning. It's time to remind ourselves of the stated purpose for PLCs. The professional learning community model flows from the assumption that the core mission of formal education is to ensure not simply that students are taught but also that they can learn. Shifting our focus from teaching to learning has profound implications for schools. As such, PLC teacher teams meet on a regular basis to explore four questions:[84]

1. What do we want each student to learn?
2. How will we know when each student has learned it?
3. How will we respond when a student experiences difficulty in learning?
4. How do we respond when a student already knows it or achieves mastery early?

The consistent focus of PLCs is to improve student learning. This cannot be a preoccupation with only students who struggle to learn, take longer to learn, or learn in different ways. We also need to be concerned about the continual learning of those students whose pace of learning and curiosities can take them beyond grade- or course-level learning goals and who need learning experiences whose rigor, complexity, or depth extend beyond the norm for their grade-level peers. This broadened focus on the learning needs of *all* students as the primary work of PLCs necessitates embedding strategies for differentiating for gifted learners into classroom practice.

Education expert Sonia Nieto suggests teachers take three actions to revitalize their classroom work and their personal energy for teaching.[85] By making these reflective actions part of their preparation for PLCs, teachers are better able to focus on specific student learning needs. If you are a classroom teacher:

Learn about yourself. Consider your current work in differentiation. Are you just *beginning* to understand and apply the practices of differentiation? Do you have a well-developed toolkit of best practices in differentiation in your teaching repertoire but want to *extend* your practices? Do you believe you have a deep understanding of differentiation and that it has become a habit in how you plan for differences in your classroom; are you *refining* your practices? Finally, determine the degree to which you consider and preplan differentiation for specific gifted students in your classroom. Are these students consistently in your mind as you consider content, activities, and tasks? Do you have preassessment or formative assessment data on which to base your instructional decisions for them? Do you understand and apply best practices in differentiation for your gifted learners?

Learn about your students. It's important to consider readiness (in content, skills, and understandings), interest, and learning profile (cognitive preference or modality strengths) when responding to learning differences. Then make "in course" adjustments based on formative assessment.

Many schools have extensive student data from standardized tests available for use. These data provide information on student learning progress and often include reading readiness levels (Lexile scores) and skill-by-skill analysis of student learning. However, this type of data is only valuable *if* teachers use it to guide their instructional decisions. (Refer to Chapter 9 on assessment.)

---

[84] DuFour and Eaker, 1998.

[85] Nieto, 2009.

In one school, analyzing previously unused data helped eighth-grade teachers understand why their students struggled so mightily reading grade-level text. They discovered that most of the students' reading readiness levels were far below the level of the text they were being asked to read. In another case, middle school math teachers used general math data to identify which students were scoring far above grade level in the subject, but when they drilled down to more specific data, they discovered one of their highest scoring math students had scored at the lowest level in geometry. Without examining this data, they might have assumed that she excelled in all aspects of math and made inappropriate instructional decisions for her as they considered differentiation in math unit by unit.

Let's not overlook the data gathered in "on your feet" work in the classroom. What you observe and know from responses in discussion, what you overhear as you monitor partner or small group work, and what you deduce from stopping at desks during individual work time helps you determine when and what instructional adjustments are necessary.

> Learning about your students includes knowing their general interests as well as specific curricular interests.

Learning about your students also includes knowing their general interests as well as specific curricular interests. See pages 170–171 for a general interest inventory. **Figure 10.1** is an example of a student interest inventory that should be completed prior to a new curriculum unit and used to guide your planning. Adapt the inventory to fit the age range of your students. Remember that the key to motivation is interest. If you want your students to more actively engage in a unit, find out what curricular topics and instructional activities they are most interested in and use those topics and tasks to pull students into the learning.

It's also helpful to remember that not all gifted students are spectacular performers or passionate about all curricular areas. What are the strengths and limitations of your gifted learners? Which gifted learners are high performers? Selective performers? Academic underachievers? (See Chapter 8 on underachievement.)

Develop allies. The final element in revitalizing your classroom work and boosting your energy is to develop allies. Nieto suggests, and we agree, that teaching can be a lonely profession. Collaboration, she contends, keeps teachers fresh, committed, and hopeful. Explore ways to form grade-level or department-level groups around common interests. If this is not possible, find a learning buddy who is willing to discuss best practices, read and discuss a common book, or collaborate on classroom applications. Remember that with today's technology, your buddy does not need to be down the hall from you—and can even be across the country!

Professional learning communities are a place to naturally form allies. They provide a systematic process for teachers to work together to analyze and improve classroom practices and thereby increase student learning. Established protocols for PLC meetings include collaborative work that should result in more focus on individual and small group learning needs, distinctive and appropriate differentiation, and higher levels of achievement for all students, including those who are gifted. When you carry out Nieto's three actions either individually, with a partner, or in a professional learning community, you will energize your work and further embed student-centered differentiation into your classroom practice.

9. Foster an *open, supportive climate.*

A climate of openness and shared problem solving and decision making encourages teachers as they work to embed differentiation into their classrooms for gifted students. Teachers are professionals who need to be respected for their instructional knowledge and classroom experiences.

In promoting differentiation for gifted learners, gifted specialists need to use care to both respect and acknowledge what teachers are doing already to respond to learning differences.

The next step is to assist teachers in building on or extending their particular foundations and instructional practices for gifted learners and to support their efforts.

In addition, consider how well your building principal or district administrator understands and supports differentiation for gifted learners. Does your building leader believe that "general" classroom-based differentiation is enough to meet the needs of gifted students? Or does the leader understand that differentiation with this population needs to go beyond the basics? Your principal or district administrator's attitudes, beliefs, and priorities influence the perceived climate of openness and support for teachers' efforts in differentiation. If your building principal or district leader is not on board, it is best to get this person on board as swiftly as possible!

Figure 10.1: Poetry Interest Inventory

These are some of the topics we will be studying and activities we will be doing in our poetry unit. I want to know what you are most interested in learning and doing.

1. Do you have a favorite poem? If so, what is the name of it?

2. Do you have a favorite poet? If so, what is his/her name?

3. Have you ever memorized a poem? If so, which one?

4. Below is a list of poems. Tell me if you have written this kind of poem before (yes/no) and tell me if you enjoyed writing this kind of poem by putting an "X" in the final column.

	Yes	No	X
a. Haiku			
b. Acrostic			
c. Cinquain			
d. Diamante			
e. Epitaph/elegy			
f. Limerick			
g. Free or blank verse			
h. Couplet			
i. Triplet			
j. Alphabet poems			
k. Ballads			
l. Raps			
m. Musical lyrics			
n. Slogans, jingles			

5. Which do you like better?
   a. Poems with rhymes (such as couplets or triplets)
   b. Free verse
   c. Blank verse

6. Please number your topic choices from 1 to 4. "1" is the topic you are most interested in.
   ___ learning about poets
   ___ learning about and writing different kinds of poems
   ___ discussing ways that poetry is used such as in song writing or advertising slogans.
   ___ learning about and participating in either competitive or noncompetitive poetry slams

7. Rate the following in order of what you would most enjoy (1) to least enjoy (5)
   ___ writing original poetry
   ___ reading poetry to myself
   ___ reading poetry to others
   ___ listening to others read poetry aloud
   ___ participating in a poetry "slam"

8. On a scale of 1 to 10. How interested are you in poetry? "1" is very interested, and "10" is not interested.

   1   2   3   4   5   6   7   8   9   10

9. What are some things you hope we do in this unit on poetry?

◎ Interest Inventory

Name _____ **Date** _____

1. What is your favorite activity or subject in school? Why? Your least favorite? Why?

_____

_____

_____

2. What are your "best" subjects? What makes them the easiest for you?

_____

_____

_____

3. What subjects are difficult for you? What makes them the hardest?

_____

_____

_____

4. What subject makes you think and work the hardest? Why is it the most challenging?

_____

_____

_____

5. Rate the following topics according to your interests. (1=very interested, 2=somewhat interested, 3=not interested)

___ dance

___ music

___ drama, including improvisation

___ sports

___ writing

___ math

___ technology

___ history

___ politics/law

___ geography

___ advertising, media

___ world languages

___ science (such as biology, chemistry, or physics)

___ science, technology, engineering, and math (STEM)

___ art, including visual art, cartooning, architectural design, and digital graphic design

6. What are your favorite games, sports, or apps?

_____

_____

7. If you could learn about anything you wanted to, what would you choose to learn about? Be specific. (For example: Film making, meteorology, architecture, Steve Jobs, Africa, social networks)

_____

_____

_____

8. What are three things you like to *do* when you have free time (besides seeing friends)?

_____

_____

9. What clubs, groups, teams, or organizations do you belong to? Include both school activities and those not sponsored by the school.

_____

_____

_____

10. What things have you collected in the past? What, if anything, are you currently collecting?

_____

_____

11. Have you ever taught yourself to do something without the help of another person? If so, what?

_____

_____

_____

→

◎ Interest Inventory (continued)

12. If you were going to start an eBook club, what kinds of books would your club read?

_____

13. If people were to come to you for information about something you know a lot about, what would the topic be?

_____

14. If you could plan a field trip for learning, where would you go? Why would you choose that place?

_____

_____

_____

15. When you're using your computer or tablet, are you usually playing games, doing homework, researching a topic, visiting websites, using chat rooms or discussion boards, shopping, exchanging email, using group sites such as Google group, using apps, social networking, watching videos/movies/TV shows, or some other activity?

_____

_____

_____

16. If you could interview an expert on any subject, what subject would you like to talk to someone about?

_____

17. If you could interview one significant person from the present and one from the past, who would you interview? Why would you choose these two people?

_____

_____

_____

18. What careers or jobs are you currently interested in?

_____

_____

19. Complete the following sentence: In school, I _prefer_ to work:

▨ alone ▨ with one other person

▨ in a small group ▨ in a larger group

20. Complete the following sentence: In school, I _learn_ best:

▨ alone ▨ with one other person

▨ in a small group ▨ in a larger group

21. What helps you learn? (For example, a hands-on activity, reading, taking notes, sketching out ideas, or discussing ideas with someone)

_____

_____

22. What makes learning more difficult for you? (For example, lectures, lots of writing)

_____

_____

23. Think of a great teacher you've had. Describe what made this teacher so amazing.

_____

_____

_____

24. What past school assignment, project, or activity are you proudest of? Why?

_____

_____

_____

25. What project or activity done outside of school are you proudest of? Why?

_____

_____

_____

26. What else would you like me to know about you as a learner?

_____

_____

_____

Instructional Coaching

How can we ensure that the strategies related to differentiation for gifted learners are actually embedded in daily classroom practice? Instructional coaching helps gifted education specialists to thoughtfully and actively engage classroom teachers in applying their new knowledge and instructional practices to benefit gifted learners. Although instructional coaching has been used in some classrooms to implement general education initiatives as well as new curriculum adoptions, coaching specific to improving practices for gifted learners has been limited.

> Instructional coaching helps gifted education specialists engage classroom teachers in applying their knowledge to benefit gifted learners.

Also, although instructional coaches are being used more and more in our schools, we do not yet have a standard definition of this type of coach. For our purposes, we will define an *instructional coach* as:

> Someone whose primary professional responsibility is to bring practices that have been studied into classrooms by working with teachers rather than with their students. Coaches may offer collaborative planning, classroom modeling, descriptive feedback on instructional plans or classroom visits, or specific observations of individual teaching practices.[86]

Gifted specialists may serve as instructional coaches, helping teachers recognize their individual teaching strengths and limitations, and supporting them as they revise, refine, or implement new strategies to better meet the needs of gifted learners in their classrooms.

Coaches can be collaborators or consultants or both. Coaches work with teachers to help them improve their classroom practices by *modeling instructional strategies*, by *co-teaching* (see Chapter 7), *co-planning* lessons or units, or by *observing teachers* and *providing descriptive feedback* on their work. When gifted specialists serve as instructional coaches, they have the potential to greatly influence the frequency and depth of differentiation for gifted learners as well as focus attention on the specific needs of such students within the inclusion classroom or course.

If you are a gifted education specialist, determine how you use your time at a particular school and consider the ways in which instructional coaching may enhance your relationships with teachers and better meet the instructional needs of gifted learners within their classrooms.

Advantages of Coaching for Gifted Education Specialists

When gifted education specialists provide coaching to classroom teachers, the specialists "win" in these ways. The coaching:

- establishes a collaborative relationship with classroom teachers
- allows for advocacy for the instructional needs of gifted learners within specific classrooms
- deepens the classroom teacher's understanding of the specific needs of individual gifted students within their classroom
- supports the use of strategies specific to the needs of gifted learners
- extends practices of differentiation into the regular grade-level curriculum
- encourages co-planning for differentiation for gifted students
- enables specialists to observe how gifted students engage in the classroom
- provides opportunities to directly model gifted strategies within the classroom context

---

[86] Adapted dfrom Center for Comprehensive School Reform and Improvement, 2007.

Advantages of Gifted Coaching for Classroom Teachers

Classroom teachers also benefit immensely from receiving coaching on differentiating for their gifted students. The process:

- establishes a collaborative relationship with the gifted education specialist

- encourages co-planning differentiation with the gifted specialist, thus lightening the "workload"

- provides descriptive feedback on instructional strategies as they are embedded into practice

- deepens understandings of the specific needs of gifted students within their classrooms

- enables gifted instructional strategies to be directly modeled within their classrooms with their students

- supports the ongoing professional development of individual teachers

Advantages of Instructional Coaching for Gifted Students

The benefits of coaching extend directly to the gifted students themselves. It:

- increases the likelihood of daily differentiation for gifted learners

- enhances students' learning experiences with the regular curriculum as differentiation for gifted becomes embedded into practice

- engages gifted students in more authentic differentiation as classroom practices are extended and enhanced

- deepens the classroom teachers' understanding of their specific learning differences and needs

- brings the gifted specialist into the classroom to provide connections between the classroom and gifted services

- provides an advocate for their needs in the inclusion classroom and within the required curriculum

What Teachers Want from an Instructional Coach

Teachers have different ideas on what they want from an instructional coach. Some teachers want an idea generator (Give me an idea for how I could make this task more complex for my gifted students). Some want an encourager and supporter (Should I try differentiated homework since my advanced math students would not be challenged by these problems?). Others want a mentor (Help me plan for my small group discussion. How can I better engage my talented learners in thought provoking, rigorous thinking?). Finally, some teachers want an expert (Help me understand why my most talented writer consistently produces work well below her capabilities.). The gifted specialist serving as an instructional coach must be both open and ready to respond to the specific needs of the classroom teacher. We need to be ready to tailor our responses and support to the needs teachers make known during our conversations. Use the questions on page 174 to reflect on and consider the individual needs of each classroom teacher you will work with.

Using Descriptive Feedback in Coaching

Chapter 9 described how descriptive feedback can help improve student performance. Descriptive feedback can also be used with teachers to enhance their performance. It's important that gifted specialists in the role of instructional coaches use descriptive feedback to provide specific information for teachers on what was done well and why, and on how to improve. Using descriptive feedback in coaching is a way to offer constructive and helpful information on instructional strengths plus ideas for improving teaching methods or approaches. This specific guidance also helps teachers learn to use instructional practices that better respond to the learning differences of gifted students. To use descriptive feedback effectively, the gifted specialist must be able to critically reflect on current classroom or lesson practices in light of best practices for gifted learners. Effective coaching prompts teachers to better align their practices

◎ Teacher Needs Questionnaire

1. What are the teacher's individual strengths and needs that will determine where we will start our work together?

_____

_____

_____

2. What is the teacher's depth of knowledge and understanding related to the learning and socioaffective differences of gifted students?

_____

_____

_____

3. Does the teacher generally recognize the need for differentiation specific to the needs of gifted learners?

_____

_____

_____

4. Does the teacher see the value of changes in instructional practices?

_____

_____

_____

5. Will instructional changes be difficult or easy for the teacher to implement?

_____

_____

_____

6. What does the teacher want from my coaching (idea generator, encourager/supporter, mentor, or expert)?

_____

_____

_____

7. To what degree will descriptive feedback be welcomed by the teacher?

_____

_____

_____

8. What kind of descriptive feedback will be most effective with this teacher?

_____

_____

_____

9. What modeling, examples, or resources will need to be provided?

_____

_____

_____

10. What coaching strategy does this teacher most value:
- ▨ collaborative planning
- ▨ classroom modeling
- ▨ descriptive feedback on units or lesson plans
- ▨ classroom visits to observe lessons and provide descriptive feedback
- ▨ combination:

_____

_____

11. What coaching strategies do I believe will be most effective in my work with this teacher:
- ▨ collaborative planning
- ▨ classroom modeling
- ▨ descriptive feedback on units or lesson plans
- ▨ classroom visits to observe lessons and provide descriptive feedback
- ▨ combination:

_____

_____

to those supported by research as essential for the gifted.

In providing descriptive feedback to teachers, consider the stars and steps strategy presented in Chapter 9. Always comment on a strength and then provide guidance to enhance the teacher's professional skills related to gifted learners. See **Figure 10.2.**

Characteristics of Successful Instructional Coaches

There are particular characteristics common to successful instructional coaches. Most important, they need to have substantial knowledge of pedagogy, possess content expertise, and have strong interpersonal skills.

Knowledge of Pedagogy

Being an effective instructional coach requires substantial knowledge of pedagogy. Successful coaches thoroughly understand how all children learn, from those who struggle in school to those who are gifted. An instructional coach in differentiation for the gifted must also have deep understanding of best practices in gifted education. You'll have more credibility with teachers if you also have demonstrated success in the inclusion classroom. Having "been there" yourself establishes a level of trust with teachers. You'll also need a large repertoire of instructional strategies that you can offer. Teachers need lots of ideas, from questioning strategies to classroom

management tips—all suggested to improve student learning. Finally, coaches need skills in both developing and implementing instructional strategies with teachers. Professional development expertise and confidence in applying new ideas in the classroom are important.

Content Expertise

Second, successful coaches possess content expertise. Coaches need to be familiar with the Common Core or state/provincial academic standards for grade-level subjects or courses as well the as curriculum that teachers are responsible for. This can be challenging at both the elementary and secondary levels. For elementary school coaches, the breadth of curriculum can be difficult, as teachers are responsible for all subject areas. For secondary coaches, the depth of expertise is what's daunting, since the teachers are typically subject area specialists. In best-case scenarios, coaches are assigned to teachers in the same content area. However, this typically is not possible. We have found it works best to consider the coach as the instructional consultant and the teacher as the content expert. Coaches need to have at least a general understanding of the required curriculum but then rely on the classroom teachers to provide the depth of content expertise as they plan and work together. Therefore, the instructional coach is responsible for embedding new strategies and practices into the curriculum content with the guidance of the classroom teacher. When coaches focus on

Figure 10.2: Stars and Steps: Descriptive Feedback to Teachers

Stars	Steps
• Note instructional strategies that were done well and explain what made them effective for gifted students.	• Offer an alternative strategy that would deepen the degree of differentiation in the lesson.
• Comment on improvements in instructional practice.	• Provide insights on better approaches.
• Note the strengths of particular strategies utilized.	• Offer ideas on how to better differentiate the lesson in light of the needs of gifted students.
• Connect their practices to best practices for gifted learners.	• Suggest ways in which a particular gifted student might be more appropriately engaged in learning within the lesson.
• Describe the ways in which the lesson addressed learning needs of particular gifted students.	• Suggest a strategy more aligned to best practices for gifted learners.
• Identify examples of depth and complexity within the lesson.	• Provide specific examples of how the lesson could be designed to reflect greater depth, complexity, or rigor.
• Describe examples of rigorous learning represented in the lesson.	

differentiation for gifted learners, a key skill is being able to think and plan for using the curriculum in ways that go above and beyond the regular use. Finally, instructional coaches need experience in and a deep understanding of data analysis as it is used to guide instructional planning.

Interpersonal Skills

The interpersonal skills of instructional coaches are also key to success in their collaborative role with teachers. Teachers need to understand that coaching is not supervision or evaluation of their performance. Care must be taken to clearly convey this to teachers and to work at developing a trusting relationship. Coaches need to be skilled in establishing respectful relations with their teaching colleagues that promote trust and build their credibility. Successful coaches are also flexible. This allows them to respond to differing classroom circumstances, a variety of teaching styles, diverse beliefs about teaching and learning, and teachers with particular preferences on what they need and want from coaching.

How to Prepare for a Coaching Session on Lesson Observation

1. Confer with the teacher. It is often helpful for teachers to submit at least a draft of a lesson prior to this conference. (See the **Differentiated Lesson Plan** on pages 180–183 and **Figure 10.4.**) The teacher must have specific learning goals in mind when you meet. Also remember that the purpose of this instructional coaching concerns differentiation. Therefore, the lesson must represent one way to apply differentiation and specifically be an instructional response to giftedness.

This conference should focus on student learning. Teachers may bring preassessment or formative assessment data to consider as you work together to further develop the lesson. In the meeting, you may refine the lesson by adding particular elements of differentiation or adjust the lesson to better respond to learning differences. Consider the elements in the lesson plan flowchart **(Figure 10.3)** as you continue to map out the lesson.

Figure 10.3: Lesson Plan Flowchart

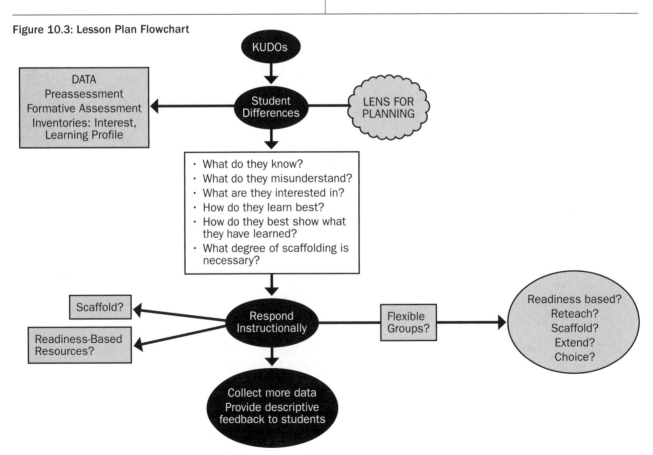

If you are working from a lesson plan provided in a teacher's guide or one you have used in previous years, consider using the **Review a Lesson for Differentiation** template (page 184) to guide your planning. Share additional ideas or strategies, consider alternative ways to engage the students, and determine how evidence of student learning will be represented (in-class task or exit slip—a brief writing reflection on the learning?). Decide how and when you will meet together after the lesson.

2. Observe the lesson. The instructional coach watches the plan in action. We have found it helpful to take thorough notes. This provides reference points as you consider what descriptive feedback to provide the teacher after the lesson. It is also helpful to be able to offer specific comments on what you saw and heard during the lesson. For example, "When you provided the data on shrinking ice caps, Devone was particularly engaged and anxious to share what he knew. You encouraged him to add to the discussion." You may wish to take notes on the **Classroom Observation Form** (pages 185–187). As you observe the lesson, consider what guidance will enhance the teacher's professional growth.

3. Debrief together. Schedule the debriefing conversation as soon as possible after the classroom visit. Meeting immediately after the lesson is best. This can be accomplished if roving substitutes are utilized. Once a teacher has completed the lesson, the teacher and the coach leave the classroom for their debriefing session, and the substitute takes over the class. Once the teacher returns, the substitute moves on to the classroom where the next observation will occur. Using a roving sub allows debriefing sessions to quickly follow the lesson. In addition, hiring one substitute to cover several classes in rotation over the day is cost effective.

During the debriefing, ask the teacher to begin the conversation. You may want to prompt that discussion by inquiring, "What went well? How do you know?" Next you may ask, "If you were to change some element of the lesson, what would that be?"

> Schedule the debriefing conversation as soon as possible— immediately after the lesson is best.

Discuss the goals for the lesson and determine whether they were accomplished. Seek any needed clarifications from the teacher for what you saw or heard. Provide descriptive feedback, following the stars and steps protocol suggested earlier.

Examine any evidence of student learning, including exit slips, which may have been collected during the lesson. Then determine the instructional course of action for the next day. Do we move on in the curriculum? Do we reteach? Do we form instructional groups for purposes of differentiation?

Finally, reflect on what each of you learned from the process of lesson planning, observation, and debriefing. Did your collaborative planning makes a difference in student engagement, learning, and performance?

Lesson Study

Lesson study is a professional development process initially developed in Japan and now practiced in schools in the United States and Canada. Designed to improve teaching and learning, the process engages teachers in systematically examining their classroom practices through small group interactions. Teachers work in groups with others who generally teach the same or similar grades or subjects. During a lesson study cycle, the teachers work together to collaboratively plan a lesson. One member of the group agrees to teach the lesson with his or her students, and the other group members observe the lesson. Once the lesson is completed, the group reconvenes to discuss it. Teachers consider modifying or changing the lesson plan based on their observations. They also consider whether the lesson might need to be adjusted to meet the needs of students in their particular classrooms. The teachers who were the observers then present the revised lesson in their classrooms. In Japan, teachers carry out two to three lesson study cycles per year.

As we've discussed, many schools have professional learning communities (PLCs). This format works well for facilitating lesson study. Gifted education specialists as well as instructional coaches may be part of a lesson study group. Lesson study, like instructional coaching, can be used to embed differentiation strategies most appropriate for gifted learners into classroom practice.

Also like instructional coaching, the intent of lesson study is not to evaluate teacher performance. It is to improve instructional practices.

The Lesson Study Cycle

Following are the typical steps in the lesson study cycle:

1. Teachers meet to discuss the specific needs of their students and identify a topic, process, or skill that might benefit from a differentiated lesson.

2. Teachers collaboratively plan the lesson, including at least one element of differentiation. Teachers pay particular attention to the learning needs of gifted students in the design of the lesson. (Teachers may use the **Differentiated Lesson Plan** format, pages 180–181.)

3. One teacher agrees to present the lesson to his or her students. The other teachers observe the lesson.

4. The teacher who is using the lesson provides relevant information to the observers in order to help them best understand the particular students in the classroom. (See **Pre-Observation Discussion About the Classroom to Be Visited,** page 188.)

5. The lesson is presented; teachers follow specific guidelines for the observation (see **The Observation,** page 189) and allow time to complete a reflection on the lesson (see **Observation Notes and Reflections,** page 190). Unlike coaching debriefings, which we suggest doing directly after a lesson, participants in lesson study need time to reflect on the lesson before debriefing. Our preferred schedule is to visit classrooms

in the morning and then hold the group discussions in the afternoon. Again, use roving substitutes to free up educators to teach or observe the lesson and then to meet for their discussions.

6. The teachers meet to discuss their observations of the lesson following the discussion protocols. (See **Post-Observation Discussion,** page 191.)

7. Teachers determine whether there are any steps or parts of the lesson that would benefit from some modifications or changes.

8. The teachers who were the observers now teach the revised lesson in their classrooms.

9. Teachers meet to discuss the results of their lesson presentations.

10. Teachers complete a summary evaluation of the process. (See **Feedback on the Lesson Study Process,** page 192.)

There are many benefits of lesson study. First, it fosters a collaborative effort toward embedding strategies of differentiation into classroom practice. Since the needs of all students are considered, this process highlights ways in which a lesson needs to be differentiated for gifted learners. Lesson study can potentially bring together classroom teachers, gifted specialists, instructional coaches, and teacher leaders in conversations about teaching and learning. All are involved in critically examining best practices and determining how they can be utilized in lesson design. Lesson study builds community and respect for the work of all teachers as they become more aware of each other's strengths, teaching beliefs, and expertise in the classroom. It opens up communication about the ways in which we can promote success for all learners through our critical reflection and collaborative planning. Finally, lesson study moves school communities toward greater autonomy in implementing and extending the practices of differentiation. Teachers become more independent and confident about using differentiation as they support each other in this work.

Chapter Summary

A variety of professionals within a school community may provide leadership in supporting teachers as they embed practices of differentiation for gifted learners in the classroom. However, if there are individuals with specific responsibilities for gifted students, they are usually the ones who need to be highly involved in this work. It is assumed that educators who serve in a variety of capacities as gifted specialists are trained in authentic differentiation for gifted learners. This enables them to provide support and leadership in this work.

This chapter presented critical elements in encouraging "buy-in" from classroom teachers when it comes to differentiating for gifted students within the classroom. We also presented two models—instructional coaching and lesson study—for encouraging teachers to embed these practices into their daily planning and instruction. To truly meet the needs of gifted learners in the classroom, differentiation strategies need to extend from the training session to thoughtful and active classroom practice.

◎ Differentiated Lesson Plan

Your name _____ *Grade level* _____

Curriculum area(s) _____

Lesson topic _____ *Date and time for lesson* _____

Rationale for differentiating this lesson (Why did you decide to differentiate this lesson?)

Preassessment or formative assessment data (What information/data did you use to determine that this lesson needed to be differentiated?)

Common Core or state/provincial academic standards addressed in this lesson

As a result of this lesson, students will . . . *(Consider using student language so these can be shared with the students at the beginning of the lesson.)*

Know . . .

Understand that . . .

Be able to do . . .

Assessment for learning strategy (How will you know if students have accomplished the goals of this lesson?)

→

◎ Differentiated Lesson Plan (continued)

Instructional groupings (Will you use whole group and/or small groups, partners, or quads? Will the students be purposefully grouped by *likeness?*)

What will I differentiate? (circle)

▨ Content (how they will *access* content)

▨ Process (*how* they will learn it)

▨ Product (how they will *show what they have learned*)

How will I differentiate? (circle)

▨ By readiness differences

▨ By cognitive preference (multiple intelligences)

▨ By learning need (level of challenge or complexity, abstractness, degree of structure)

Steps in the lesson: Include whole group instruction as well as differentiated activities and application of learning (assignments, homework).

Closure/wrap-up (How will you remind students what they learned today? This may be statements of learning as well as formative assessment strategies.)

Next steps (What are your thoughts now that the lesson has been taught? What will you keep in mind as you think about your plans for tomorrow?)

Critical reflection (What went well in this lesson? If you were to do this lesson again, what would you change and why would you change it?)

Figure 10.4: Sample Differentiated Lesson Plan

Your name Kayla   *Grade level* Grade 8

Curriculum area(s) Media literacy

Lesson topic Analysis of information presented in media   *Date and time for lesson*

Rationale for differentiating this lesson *(Why did you decide to differentiate this lesson?)*
The students vary in their critical thinking skills. Some students need a more complex task to keep them engaged in learning.

Preassessment or formative assessment data *(What information/data did you use to determine that this lesson needed to be differentiated?)*
Students have already identified differences in how a single story is presented in three different media: local newspaper, national newspaper, and television news broadcast. Their assignments indicate differences in their critical thinking related to analysis of the media message. Some students need additional time and practice with this content.

Common Core or state/provincial academic standards addressed in this lesson:
CCSS.ELA-Literacy.RH.6-8.6 Identify aspects of a text that reveal an author's point of view or purpose (e.g., loaded language, inclusion or avoidance of particular facts).

CCSS.ELA-Literacy.RI.8.9 Analyze a case in which two or more texts provide conflicting information on the same topic and identify where the texts disagree on matters of fact or interpretation.

CCSS.ELA-Literacy.RI.8.8 Delineate and evaluate the argument and specific claims in a text, assessing whether the reasoning is sound and the evidence is relevant and sufficient; recognize when irrelevant evidence is introduced.

As a result of this lesson, students will . . . *(Consider using student language so these can be shared with the students at the beginning of the lesson.)*

Know . . .

· media techniques

Understand that . . .

· media text uses particular techniques to influence our viewpoints or perspectives.

· we must critically analyze what is presented in the media text.

Be able to do . . .

· identify media techniques used to influence viewpoints or perspectives.

· critically analyze media text to determine their intended message, purpose, and audience.

· make informed decisions based on analysis of media messages.

Assessment for learning strategy *(How will you know if students have accomplished the goals of this lesson?)*
Products (essay, poster, or diagram) share their conclusions related to media messages.

Students complete individual exit slips to select three strategies that they will use to critically analyze media messages. They will also note why they believe these three to be the most effective.

Instructional groupings *(Will you use whole group and/or small groups, partners, or quads? Will the students be purposefully grouped by likeness?)*

· Students will complete tiered assignments in instructional groups based on likeness.

· Students will share their conclusions with someone who completed a different task (paired by difference).

What will I differentiate? *(circle)*

· Content (how they will *access* content)

· Process (*how* they will learn it)

· Product (how they will *show what they have learned*)   ➔

Figure 10.4: Sample Differentiated Lesson Plan (continued)

How will I differentiate? *(circle)*

- By readiness differences
- By cognitive preference (multiple intelligences)
- By learning need (level of challenge or complexity, abstractness, degree of structure)

Small group tasks are tiered by level of complexity.

Steps in the lesson: *Include whole group instruction as well as differentiated activities and application of learning (assignments, homework).*

1. Hook: Show students two editorial cartoons featuring the same political figure. Ask students to consider the characteristics of the figure presented and identify the message that has been chosen to send to the public with the cartoon. Whole class discussion. Compare and contrast both the representation of the figure and the media message. Suggest that television news programs also present individuals and their stories in ways to influence the audience's perspectives and viewpoints.

2. Remind the students of the work they did previously in examining the same news story in a variety of media sources.

3. Present video clips of the same story being presented on a commercial network, a cable station, and a public television broadcast. (If possible and appropriate, include a *Saturday Night Live* or Jon Stewart version also.)

4. As they watch the clips, ask students to consider the ways in which the facts and messages were alike and different in the clips and also consider why the messages may be different.

5. Tiered assignment (*differentiated by process*)
   Group one: Compare and contrast the facts presented and the manner in which they were presented in each clip. Consider why the messages from news sources may differ.

   Group two: Through an analysis of facts, identify the intended message, its purpose, and what the media source wants the audience to conclude.

6. Students may *choose* to share their conclusions in an essay, poster, diagram, or chart, based on learning preference (*differentiated by product*).

7. Students partner with someone who completed a different task (group one member meets with a group two member). Students present their products and suggest their conclusions related to the differences among news sources.

8. Closure: Large group debrief and discussion. What techniques did the media use to influence our viewpoints or perspectives on this issue? What "do's" can we recommend to help people critically analyze what they see and hear in the media? Compile a class list of ideas.

9. Individual exit slips: Select three strategies that they will use to critically analyze media messages. Note why they believe these three to be the most effective.

Closure/wrap-up *(How will you remind students what they learned today? This may be statements of learning as well as formative assessment strategies.)*

Class will compile a list of ways to critically analyze what they see and hear in the media.

Individual students will complete exit slips.

Next steps *(What are your thoughts now that the lesson has been taught? What will you keep in mind as you think about your plans for tomorrow?)*

Products showed students' conclusions related to their analysis of media messages.

Exit slips indicated that students were able to identify ways to better analyze media messages.

Critical reflection *(What went well in this lesson? If you were to do this lesson again, what would you change and why would you change it?)*

The students were enthusiastic about the tasks that they engaged in.

One student seemed to be misplaced in his task, so I moved him to the other group. This worked well for him.

If we didn't do block scheduling, this would probably be a two-day lesson plan with sharing in day two.

◎Review a Lesson for Differentiation

1. Review the goals for the lesson and consider the students in your classroom.

2. Ask, "Will some students already know this?"

3. Consider where some students might struggle.

4. As appropriate, plan and design a preassessment or formative assessment aligned with the goals.

5. Administer the assessment to all students.

6. Consider "grouping strategies" and goals for each group based on data (focusing on "like" needs).

7. Review materials provided by the text or your own resources, evaluating which tasks would best match the needs of each instructional group. Consider level of challenge or *complexity* of tasks, *concrete or abstract* applications, and degree of structure provided in light of the specific students in each group.

8. Determine which materials/tasks each group would utilize.

◎Classroom Observation Form: Coaching for Differentiated Instruction

Coach _____ Teacher _____

School _____ Grade _____ Date/time _____

Topic of lesson _____

Common Core/State or Provincial Standards	Learning Goals (KUDOs)

Indicate the degree to which a particular lesson element was observed:

3 = Observed; clearly demonstrated   **2** = Somewhat demonstrated   **1** = Not observed in this lesson

Preparation/Context for the Lesson

	1	2	3
1. Established clear goals related to knowledge, skills, understandings			
2. Stated or posted goals; shared them with the students			
3. Connected prior learning or experiences to new subject matter			
4. Opened the lesson with a "hook" to engage student curiosity and/or interest			
5. Provided rubrics/checklists to establish a focus on the goals and the quality of their work			
6. Ended the lesson by summarizing or asking students to summarize learning with a focus on the lesson's goals			

Comments/notes:

→

* Adapted in part from Carol Tomlinson for Strategic Research, LLC.

From *Differentiation for Gifted Learners: Going Beyond the Basics* by Diane Heacox, Ed.D., and Richard M. Cash, Ed.D., copyright © 2014. Free Spirit Publishing Inc., Minneapolis, MN; 800-735-7323; www.freespirit.com. This page may be reproduced for use within an individual school or district. For all other uses, contact www.freespirit.com/company/permissions.cfm.

◎Classroom Observation Form:
Coaching for Differentiated Instruction (continued)

Assessment	1	2	3
1. Used results of preassessment or formative assessment to inform plans for differentiation			
2. Used formal or informal formative assessment during the lesson to adjust plans			
3. Responded to observations and/or student questions, comments, or confusion during the lesson			
4. Used formal or informal formative assessment during the lesson to consider student learning progress			

Comments/notes:

Classroom Community Building/Individual Interactions	1	2	3
1. Established a sense of respect, comfort, and safety for student intellectual risk taking			
2. Talked with individual students during practice or independent work time; provided descriptive feedback prompts to improve student work			
3. Circulated in the classroom during the lesson to convey a sense of teacher presence as well as to observe work in progress			
4. Brought forth individual students' strengths, interests, and experiences during the lesson, creating a sense of awareness and connectedness to the students			
5. Involved students in sharing, reflecting, and evaluating their thinking and/or work			

Comments/notes:

→

* Adapted in part from Carol Tomlinson for Strategic Research, LLC.

◎ Classroom Observation Form:
Coaching for Differentiated Instruction (continued)

Instructional Practices	1	2	3
1. Utilized varied work arrangements: individual, partners, and small groups			
2. Used multiple modes of instruction (such as cognitive preference, auditory/ kinesthetic/visual, integration of technology, or inductive/deductive)			
3. Actively engaged the broad range of students in learning			
4. Organized students by likeness, utilizing flexible instructional grouping			
5. Was aware of and provided necessary scaffolding to support the learning of special needs students, including those who are ELL or are involved in RtI interventions; considered ways for gifted students to proceed with greater independence			
6. Utilized gradual release of responsibility to prepare students for independent work with new skills or processes			
7. Was aware of and responded to the needs of gifted learners as well as those who attained the goals of the lesson early			
8. Demonstrated an awareness of the various cultural/ethnic communities represented within the classroom			
9. Communicated clear and specific directions for multiple tasks through prompts and/or work cards			
10. Provided for those who completed work early through anchor activities			
11. Communicated effective rules and routines so that the lesson went smoothly			
12. Established and maintained effective management of time, instruction, and materials/resources			
13. Established and maintained effective management of student behavior			

Comments/notes:

➔

* Adapted in part from Carol Tomlinson for Strategic Research, LLC.

◎ Classroom Observation Form:
Coaching for Differentiated Instruction (continued)

Evidence of Differentiation	1	2	3
1. Showed evidence of preplanning for *anticipated* learning differences			
2. Showed evidence of preplanning for special needs students including those who are ELL or involved in RtI interventions			
3. Showed evidence of preplanning for students with physical or behavioral challenges			
4. Showed evidence of preplanning for the needs of gifted learners by providing the necessary levels of rigor, complexity, and/or depth as well as adjusting the pace of instruction as appropriate			
5. Applied *content* differentiation; for example, used readiness or interest-based materials or resources, provided multiple pathways for accessing information, or adjusted depth or complexity of information based on prior knowledge or experience			
6. Applied *process* differentiation; for example, used tiered assignments, utilized flexible instructional groups based on likeness, provided choice in tasks based on interest, used tasks reflecting a variety of cognitive preferences, provided varied levels of scaffolding, or provided choice in work arrangements			
7. Applied *product* differentiation; for example, utilized products reflecting a variety of cognitive preferences, offered products with varied degrees of complexity, offered students an opportunity to make a choice on how to demonstrate their learning, or utilized student interests in determining products			

Comments/notes:

→

---

* Adapted in part from Carol Tomlinson for Strategic Research, LLC.

Quality Curriculum

	1	2	3
1. Addressed one or more Common Core or state/provincial academic standards			
2. Focused on significant ideas, concepts, issues, or problems			
3. Engaged students in tasks clearly aligned with the learning goals			
4. Actively engaged students in applying their learning in relevant ways			
5. Engaged students in reflecting on their learning			

Comments/notes:

Summary of Target Instructional Groups

1. Did the lesson meet the needs of students with a variety of readiness levels related to knowledge, skills, or understandings? ▨ yes ▨ no

2. If not, what students' needs were best met with this lesson? (Check all that apply.)
▨ struggling learners ▨ average learners ▨ gifted learners

Explanation: _____

_____

_____

Descriptive Feedback on the Lesson

Strengths of the lesson:_____

_____

_____

Considerations/ideas/resources: _____

_____

_____

Next steps determined by the teacher: _____

_____

_____

* Adapted in part from Carol Tomlinson for Strategic Research, LLC.

◎ Pre-Observation Discussion About the Classroom to Be Visited

1. What do you want us to know about your classroom?

_____

_____

_____

_____

_____

2. Who are your students? What individual differences in learning needs, preferences, or interests are represented in your classroom?

_____

_____

_____

_____

_____

3. What motivates your students?

_____

_____

_____

_____

_____

4. What personal knowledge do you want to share with us so that we can best understand what is going on with individual students? What might we expect to see or hear related to particular students in your classroom?

_____

_____

_____

_____

_____

5. Given our lesson plan, is there anything we might anticipate related to your students' thinking, reactions, responses, interactions, and work during the lesson?

_____

_____

_____

_____

_____

◎ The Observation

The purpose of the observation is to carefully consider the elements in the lesson plan. The observer does not comment on or discuss other elements of the classroom, such as student behavior or demeanor of the teacher. Remember, the purpose of the observation is never to evaluate teacher performance.

Observing the Lesson

1. When observing the lesson, do not interfere with the process of the lesson (such as stepping in to help a student). Observing teachers should sit or stand at the back or sides of the classroom. During times when students are working independently, you may circulate around the room to observe the students' work.

2. You may wish to take notes on the lesson plan itself. This will help with the discussion.

3. It would be helpful if students wore name tags so observers can refer to specific students by name in the discussion. (For example, "The opening question really got the attention of Terrell.")

4. You may choose to interview a student or group of students at the end of the lesson for two to three minutes. Suggested questions:

   - *What did you especially enjoy about this lesson?*

   _____

   _____

   _____

   _____

   - *What did you learn?*

   _____

   _____

   _____

   _____

   - *What else do you want to learn about or do in other lessons?*

   _____

   _____

   _____

   _____

   - *Other:*

   _____

   _____

   _____

   _____

5. Review and complete the **Observation Notes and Reflections** sheet before the group discussion.

◎ Observation Notes and Reflections

Please consider the following before we meet.

1. What went well?

_____

_____

_____

_____

_____

2. Were the goals for the lesson addressed?

_____

_____

_____

_____

_____

3. How well did the sequence of activities or experiences work?

_____

_____

_____

_____

4. What was the high point of the lesson for you? For the students?

_____

_____

_____

_____

5. What was the level of motivation for learning exhibited by the students?

_____

_____

_____

_____

6. How actively were the students engaged in the lesson?

_____

_____

_____

_____

_____

7. Do you believe the students achieved the learning goal for the lesson? Explain.

_____

_____

_____

_____

_____

8. What is something new you learned about the lesson topic, activities, or the students in the classroom from observing this lesson?

_____

_____

_____

_____

9. What immediate changes in the lesson come to your mind?

_____

_____

_____

_____

10. How might the lesson need to be modified for use with your students?

_____

_____

_____

_____

◎ The Post-Observation Discussion

Preparing for the Discussion

1. Think through the lesson before meeting to discuss it.

2. Use the **Observation Notes and Reflections** page to collect your ideas and thoughts.

3. For the discussion, choose a timekeeper and a recorder.

Guidelines for the Discussion

- Speak for yourself.

- Consider the needs of the group in balance with your individual needs.

- Make sure all members have an opportunity to share their perspectives and ideas.

- Focus only on the design and implementation of the lesson. Be sure to discuss the lesson; do not critique other teaching issues or student behaviors.

The Discussion Process

1. Remind the presenting teacher and the observing teachers to join equally in the discussion of the lesson.

2. Share reactions to the lesson. The teacher who taught the lesson should be the first to do this. (What worked? What improvements could be made?)

3. Considering the goals for the lesson, take turns commenting about specific observations of the lesson and allow others to comment on the point. (I noticed that . . .)

4. Raise questions/issues regarding the lesson plan design, the ways in which the students engaged in the lesson, the lesson's effectiveness in addressing differing student needs including those of gifted learners, and the results of the lesson related to achieving the learning goals. Remember, the purpose of the discussion is to engage in problem solving in order to maximize student learning through the lesson.

5. Offer suggestions on ways to improve the lesson to better meet the goals and effectively model a differentiated lesson.

   As a group, revise the lesson plan based on the discussion. Also consider specific changes that may benefit the particular students in the classroom.

◎ Feedback on the Lesson Study Process

Your name _____

1. What did you learn through the lesson study process?

_____

_____

_____

_____

2. How did lesson study help you better understand and apply differentiation in your classroom?

_____

_____

_____

_____

3. What new questions do you have as a result of our lesson study?

_____

_____

_____

_____

4. What is something you would like to learn or better understand related to differentiation?

_____

_____

_____

_____

5. On a scale of 1–5 (1=poor, 5=excellent), rate the quality of your learning experience in lesson study. Explain your rating.

_____

_____

_____

_____

_____

6. What's one thing that you learned through lesson study that you will now apply in your teaching?

_____

_____

_____

_____

Chapter 11

Next Steps

As we developed this book, we considered the current status of gifted students in general classrooms as well as in school programs and services, and we listened to teacher concerns, questions, and even anxieties about such practices. We worked to make differentiation practical, doable, and less time consuming yet significant and sustainable. We hope that as you read our words and put the suggested ideas and strategies into practice, one new concept at a time, that differentiation will become a habit for you. At that point, when you think about what your students will do tomorrow, you will automatically consider whether, how, when, and in what ways you might need to differentiate. We assure you that this will happen and that differentiation will eventually become on-your-feet planning.

In an effort to create an easy-to-use reference to guide your planning of differentiated learning experiences, we offer this summary of strategies (**Differentiation Based on Student Need** on pages 196–198). We know that thinking about differentiating content, process, and product across readiness, interest, and learning profile differences can become complicated and even overwhelming. Based on an initial idea presented by researchers David Sousa, Carol Ann Tomlinson, and Marcia Imbeau, we have extended and sorted differentiation strategies across these elements with a focus on the needs of gifted students.[87] The first table provides ideas for **differentiating content** (how students access content) based on *readiness*, *interest*, and *learning profile*. Although strategies can be used across the student learning spectrum, please note that strategies marked with an asterisk* are those we consider most appropriate for gifted learners.

The second table addresses **process differentiation,** how students actively work with the content, again across readiness, interest, and learning profile differences.

The final table considers how students demonstrate their learning; this is called **product differentiation.** Keep in mind that products may also represent summative assessment. Products are also differentiated across readiness, interest, and learning profiles. Use this menu of differentiation strategies to quickly scan for workable ways to differentiate without feeling either overwhelmed or struggling for ideas.

Finally, page 199 offers a brief summary of what distinguishes differentiation for gifted learners. Use this as you engage in discussions related to differentiation, as you plan or co-plan experiences for gifted students, or as you advocate for the day-to-day needs of gifted learners in the classroom and in your programs and services.

We encourage you to take the next steps in your own journey as an educator of the gifted. We are certain that your efforts will be rewarded by gifted students who are enthusiastically engaged, who stretch what is possible into the amazing, who continue to ask the hard questions, and who never fail to give you an "aha" moment each day. Please share your insights, applications, remarks, and questions with us through our publisher:

Free Spirit Publishing
help4kids@freespirit.com

We look forward to hearing from you!
Diane Heacox, Ed.D., and Richard M. Cash, Ed.D.

---

[87] Sousa, 2011; Tomlinson, 2010, 2011; Imbeau, 2010.

◎ Differentiation Based on Student Need

Asterisks denote strategies most appropriate for gifted learners

	Readiness	Interest	Learning Profile
CONTENT *How students will access content.*	Provide materials at varied reading levels.* Provide access to content through various degrees of scaffolding. Provide targeted small group instruction.* Front-load academic vocabulary. Use highlighted text. Use video images to augment complex text. Use demonstrations during lecture so students can see concrete applications. Summarize key ideas for ELL students before you start a lesson. Use bookmarked websites for students who are experts to supplement text.* Offer graphic organizers for notetaking. Audio-record texts as necessary. Use flexible groups based on likeness matched with appropriate tasks.* Offer more abstract materials, representations, ideas, or applications.*	Provide materials that connect key ideas and skills to real applications. Include lessons to respond to students' curricular interests and curiosities. Provide additional resources (videos, websites, podcasts, articles) related to KUDOs that respond to student interests.* Show examples of real applications of content, skills, or processes.* Use examples, analogies, and applications that reflect the cultures, languages, and experiences of your students. Share curious, unusual, or intriguing elements of your curriculum topic.	Use varied teaching modalities: visual, auditory, kinesthetic. Use varied teaching strategies to respond to MI preferences. Expand the ways in which you present content to the students: scenarios, photos, video, labs, diagrams, podcasts, explorations, demonstrations, or small group dialogue. Engage students in discussions that ask them to think analytically, creatively, and identify "real" applications.* Include both whole-to-part and part-to-whole teaching. Offer graphic organizers to organize ideas visually. Use a range of websites so students can explore topics based on their curiosities.*

Adapted from Tomlinson and Imbeau. *Leading and Managing a Differentiated Classroom.* Arlington, VA: ASCD, 2010; and Tomlinson and Sousa, *Differentiation and the Brain.* Bloomington, IN: Solution Tree, 2011.

◎Differentiation Based on Student Need (continued)

Asterisks denote strategies most appropriate for gifted learners

	Readiness	**Interest**	**Learning Preference**
PROCESS *How the students will actively work with the content.*	Use tiered assignments.* Provide mini-sessions. Use learning contracts.* Differentiate homework.* Provide tiered, targeted choice boards.* Increase or decrease the complexity of a task while holding the goal steady.* Increase or decrease the number of facets or variables in a task.* Use "like" partners.* Provide additional modeling or scaffolding. Use more advanced (but not more criteria) rubrics for highly able students.* Use flexible groups based on likeness matched with appropriate task.* Increase or decrease the amount of practice applications based on readiness.* Pace instruction based on the learning rates of the students.* Accelerate and "compact" learning as appropriate to the needs of the advanced learners.*	Group students by interest. Provide supplementary materials based on interests.* Provide choices in how students will do the work. Use independent explorations to encourage them to pursue answers to their questions.* Provide opportunities for students to apply skills in areas of interest (such as self-select an article and write a summary). Use relevant simulations to actively engage students in using their learning. Enable students to choose a perspective or viewpoint they want to represent.	Allow students to choose how they wish to work: alone, with a partner, or in a small group. Use multiple modalities when you teach a process. Provide multiple "ways to learn" based on MI preferences. Develop tasks with a more concrete focus as well as ones with a more abstract focus.* Encourage students to suggest other modes for their work.* Assign group roles based on learning profile or strengths. Provide both sequential and more open graphic organizers.

Adapted from Tomlinson and Imbeau. *Leading and Managing a Differentiated Classroom.* Arlington, VA: ASCD, 2010; and Tomlinson and Sousa, *Differentiation and the Brain.* Bloomington, IN: Solution Tree, 2011.

◎ Differentiation Based on Student Need (continued)

Asterisks denote strategies most appropriate for gifted learners

	Readiness	Interest	Learning Preference
PRODUCT *How the students demonstrate their learning.* *This may be a summative assessment.*	Use tiered products.* Require varied resources and references. Provide more complex, in-depth resources based on readiness.* Use flexible groups based on likeness and matched with appropriate tasks.* Invite experts or mentors for those who can go to more complex or sophisticated representations.* Provide models representing different levels of sophistication of the product.* Scaffold, as necessary, the processes for completing a product. Provide mini-lessons on elements of the product.	Determine unit products based on student interests. Encourage students to use new forms of digital technology to represent learning. Encourage students to choose products to represent their learning. Develop products that represent real applications of content, skills, or processes.*	Provide varied unit or lesson products representing MI preferences. Allow student choice in completing the product: individual, partner, or small group. Encourage varied modalities in representing their learning: auditory, visual, or kinesthetic. Provide options on how to share products (such as with a partner, in a small group, or in front of the class).

Adapted from Tomlinson and Imbeau. *Leading and Managing a Differentiated Classroom*. Arlington, VA: ASCD, 2010; and Tomlinson and Sousa, *Differentiation and the Brain*. Bloomington, IN: Solution Tree, 2011.

◎ Ten Critical Elements in Differentiation for Gifted Learners

Use any of the elements below to create defensible differentiation for gifted students.

1. Present content related to broad-based issues, themes, or problems.

2. Integrate or connect more than one discipline.

3. Create comprehensive, in-depth, and complex learning experiences.

4. Facilitate in-depth, self-selected individual learning experiences for students based on their interests, curiosities, or passion for going deeper or further, using compacting as a way to find time for the work.

5. Engage students in open-ended, complex, abstract learning experiences that focus on higher order thinking skills.

6. Focus on products that are innovative and present new ideas, perspectives, and thoughts.

7. Engage students in experiences that will help them develop self-understanding (such as recognizing and using one's abilities, becoming self-directed, or appreciating one's uniqueness).

8. Make provisions for the development of the student's particular talents and interests.

9. Provide access to information, ideas, perspectives, and viewpoints not bound by grade level.

10. Provide detailed descriptive feedback to encourage review, revision, and refinement of ideas and engage students in self-appraisal.

References and Resources

Ames, C. "Motivation: What Teachers Need to Know." *Teachers College Record, 91* (1991): 409–421.

Aronson, E., et al. *The Jigsaw Classroom.* Beverly Hills, CA: Sage, 1978.

Association for Middle Level Education. *This We Believe: Keys to Educating Young Adolescents.* AMLE, 2010.

Bacharach, N., and T. Washut Heck. *Mentoring Teacher Candidates through Co-Teaching.* St. Cloud, MN: St. Cloud State University Teacher Quality Enhancement Center, 2011.

Ball, D. L., and D. K. Cohen. "Developing Practice, Developing Practitioners: Toward a Practice-Based Theory of Professional Education." In *Teaching as the Learning Profession: Handbook of Policy and Practice,* edited by G. Sykes and L. Darling-Hammond. San Francisco, CA: Jossey-Bass, 1999.

Bandura, A. "Self-Efficacy: Toward a Unifying Theory of Behavioral Change." *Psychological Review, 84* (1977): 191–215.

———. *Social Foundations of Thought and Action: A Social Cognitive Theory.* Englewood Cliffs, NJ: Prentice-Hall, 1986.

Baum, S., and S. Reis, eds. *Twice-Exceptional and Special Populations of Gifted Students.* Thousand Oaks, CA: Corwin, 2004.

Baum, S., J. Renzulli, and T. Hebert. "Reversing Underachievement: Creative Productivity as a Systemic Intervention." *Gifted Child Quarterly, 39* (1995): 224–235.

Betts, G. T., and J. K. Kercher. *The Autonomous Learner Model: Optimizing Ability.* Greeley, CO: ALPS Publishing, 1999.

Bloom, Benjamin, et al. *Taxonomy of Educational Objectives: The Classification of Educational Goals: Handbook I: Cognitive Domain.* New York: Longman, 1956.

Bransford, J. D., A. L. Brown, and R. R. Cocking, eds. *How People Learn: Brain, Mind, Experience, and School (expanded ed.).* Washington, DC: National Academy Press, 2000.

Brookhart, S. M. *How to Assess Higher-Order Thinking Skills in Your Classroom,* Alexandria, VA: ASCD, 2010.

Callahan, C., and H. Hertberg-Davis. *Fundamentals of Gifted Education.* New York: Routledge, 2013.

Cash, R. M. *Advancing Differentiation: Thinking and Learning for the 21st Century.* Minneapolis, MN: Free Spirit Publishing, 2011.

Chappuis, J. *Seven Strategies of Assessment for Learning.* Boston, MA: Pearson Education, 2009.

Clasen, D. R., and R. E. Clasen. "Underachievement of Highly Able Students and the Peer Society." *Gifted and Talented International, 10 (2)* (1995): 67–75.

Coburn, C. E. "Collective Sense-Making About Reading: How Teachers Mediate Reading Policy in Their Professional Communities." *Educational Evaluation and Policy Analysis, 23(2)* (2001): 145–170.

———. "Beyond Decoupling: Rethinking the Relationship Between the Institutional Environment and the Classroom." *Sociology of Education, 77(3)* (2004): 211–244.

Colangelo, N., S. A. Assouline, and M. Gross. *A Nation Deceived: How Schools Hold Back America's Brightest Students (The Templeton National Report on Academic Acceleration, Volumes 1 and 2).* Iowa City, IA: University of Iowa Press, 2004.

Colangelo, N., and G. Davis, eds. *Handbook of Gifted Education.* Boston, MA: Allyn and Bacon, 2003.

Common Core State Standards Initiative (n.d.). *Common Core State Standards.* www.corestandards .org.

Cook, L., and M. Friend. "Co-Teaching: Guidelines for Creating Effective Practices." *Focus on Exceptional Children, 28* (1995): 1–16.

Dabrowski, K. *Psychoneurosis Is Not an Illness.* London: Gryf, 1972.

———. *Personality Shaping Through Positive Disintegration.* Boston, MA: Little, Brown, 1967.

Danielson, C. "The Many Faces of Leadership." *Educational Leadership, 65(1)* (2007): 14–19.

———. *Enhancing Professional Practice: A Framework for Teaching.* Alexandria, VA: ASCD, 2007.

Daniels, S., and M. Peichowski. *Living with Intensity: Understanding the Sensitivity, Excitability, and Emotional Development of Gifted Children, Adolescents, and Adults.* Tucson, AZ: Great Potential Press, 2008.

Davis, G. *Gifted Children and Gifted Education: A Handbook for Teachers and Parents.* Tucson, AZ: Great Potential Press, 2006.

De Lisi, R., and S. L. Goldbeck. "Implications of Piagetian Theory for Peer Learning." In *Cognitive Perspectives on Peer Learning,* edited by A. M. O'Donnell and A. King. Mahwah, NJ: Erlbaum, 1999.

Delisle, J., and J. Galbraith. *When Gifted Kids Don't Have All the Answers: How to Meet Their Social and Emotional Needs.* Minneapolis, MN: Free Spirit Publishing, 2002.

Dix, J., and S. Schafer. "From Paradox to Performance: Practical Strategies for Identifying and Teaching Gifted/LD Students." In *Teaching Gifted Students with Disabilities,* edited by S. K. Johnson and J. Kendrick. Waco, TX: Prufrock Press, 2005.

Dixon, F. A. & Moon, S. M., eds. *The Handbook of Secondary Gifted Education.* Waco, TX: Prufrock Press, 2006.

Dowdall, Cynthia, and Nicholas Colangelo. "Understanding Gifted Students: Review and Implications." *Gifted Child Quarterly 26 (4)* (1982): 179–184.

DuFour, R. "What Is a 'Professional Learning Community'?" *Educational Leadership, 61(8)* (2004): 6–11.

DuFour, R., and R. E. Eaker. *Professional Learning Communities at Work.* Bloomington, IN: National Education Service, 1998.

Dweck, C. *Mindset: A New Psychology for Success.* New York: Ballantine, 2006.

——. *Self-Theories: Their Role in Motivation, Personality, and Development.* Philadelphia, PA: Taylor and Francis, 2000.

Emerick. L. "Academic Underachievement Among the Gifted: Students' Perceptions of Factors That Reverse the Pattern." *Gifted Child Quarterly, 36* (1992): 140–146.

Figg, S., et al. "Differentiating Low Performance of the Gifted Learner: Achieving, Underachieving, and Selective Consuming Students." *Journal of Advanced Academics, 23 (1)* (2012): 53–71.

Fredricks, J., C. Alfeld, and J. Eccles. "Developing and Fostering Passion in Academic and Nonacademic Domains." *Gifted Child Quarterly, 54* (2010): 18–30.

Frey, N., D. Fisher, and S. Everlove. *Productive Group Work: How to Engage Students, Build Teamwork, and Promote Understanding.* Alexandria, VA: ASCD, 2009.

Friend, M., and D. Hurley-Chamberlain. "Is Co-Teaching Effective?" Online article available at www.cec.sped.org.

Friend, M., et al. "Co-Teaching: An Illustration of the Complexity of Collaboration in Special Education." *Journal of Educational and Pscychological Consultation, 20* (2010): 9–27.

Gagné, F. "Transforming Gifts into Talents: The DMGT as a Developmental Theory." In *Handbook of Gifted Education, 3rd edition,* edited by N. Colangelo and G. Davis. Boston: Allyn & Bacon, 2003.

——. "Ten Commandments for Academic Talent Development." *Gifted Child Quarterly, 51 (93)* (2007): 93–118.

Geake, J. "High Abilities at Fluid Analogizing: A Cognitive Neuroscience Construct of Giftedness." *Roeper Review, 30(3)* (2008), 187–195.

Gentry, M. L. *Promoting Student Achievement and Exemplary Classroom Practices Through Cluster Grouping: A Research-Based Alternative to Heterogeneous Elementary Classrooms (RM99138).* Storrs, CT: The National Research Center on the Gifted and Talented, University of Connecticut, 1999.

Gentry, M., et al. *Total School Cluster Grouping.* Waco, TX: Prufrock Press, 2014.

Gosfield, M. W., ed. *Expert Approaches to Support Gifted Learners.* Minneapolis, MN: Free Spirit Publishing, 2008.

Grabner, R. H., A. C. Neubauer, and E. Stern. "Superior Performance and Neural Efficiency: The Impact of Intelligence and Expertise." *Brain Research Bulletin 69* (2006): 422–39.

Green, K., M. J. Fine, and N. Tollefson. "Family Systems Characteristics and Underachieving Males." *Gifted Child Quarterly, 32* (1988): 267–272.

Harris, C. R. *Identifying and Serving Recent Immigrant Children Who Are Gifted.* ERIC Document Reproduction Service No. ED 358676, 1993.

Heacox, D. *Differentiating Instruction in the Regular Classroom.* Minneapolis, MN: Free Spirit Publishing, 2012.

——. *Making Differentiation a Habit: How to Ensure Success in Academically Diverse Classrooms.* Minneapolis, MN: Free Spirit Publishing, 2009.

Heller, K., et al, eds. *International Handbook of Giftedness and Talent.* New York: Elsevier, 2000.

Hockett, J. *Using Lesson Study as a Differentiation Professional Development Tool.* Best Practices Institute, University of Virginia, March 5–7, 2009.

Hogan, D., and J. Tudge. "Implications of Vygotsky's Theory for Peer Learning." In *Cognitive Perspectives on Peer Learning,* edited by A. M. O'Donnell and A. King. Mahwah, NJ: Erlbaum, 1999.

Hughes, C., and W. Murawski. "Lessons from Another Field: Applying Co-Teaching Strategies to Gifted Education." *Gifted Child Quarterly, 45* (2001): 195–205.

Jacob K. Javits Gifted and Talented Students Education Act (2001). Retrieved from www.gpo. gov/fdsys/pkg/PLAW-107publ110/pdf/PLAW-107publ110.pdf

Johnson, D., and R. Johnson. *Circles of Learning: Cooperation in the Classroom.* Edina, MN: Interaction Book Company, 1986.

Johnson, S., and L. Sheffield. *Using the Common Core State Standards for Mathematics with Gifted and Advanced Learners.* Waco, TX: Prufrock Press, 2013.

Kanter, R. M. *Confidence: How Winning Streaks and Losing Streaks Begin and End.* New York: Crown Business, 2006.

Kaplan, S. "Concentric Circles of Knowledge." *Tempo (Texas Association for the Gifted and Talented newsletter), 22, no. 2* (2002).

——. *Differentiating Core Curriculum and Instruction to Provide Advanced Learning Opportunities.* Sacramento, CA: California Association for the Gifted, 1994.

Kendall, J. *Understanding the Common Core State Standards.* Alexandria, VA: ASCD, 2011.

Kenny, D., F. Archambault, and B. Hallmark. *The Effect of Group Composition on Gifted and Non-Gifted Elementary Students in Cooperative Learning Groups.* Storrs, CT: National Research Center on the Gifted and Talented, University of Connecticut, 1995.

Kise, J. *Differentiated Coaching.* Thousand Oaks, CA: Corwin, 2006.

Klein, S. S., and A. H. Harris. "A User's Guide to the Legacy Cycle." *Journal of Education and Human Development, 1(1)* (2007): 1–16.

Knight, J. "What Good Coaches Do." *Educational Leadership 69, no. 2* (2011): 18–22.

Kowal, J., and L. Steiner. "Instructional Coaching." *Issue Brief.* Center for Comprehensive School Reform and Improvement, September 2007.

——. "Principal as Instructional Leader." *Issue Brief.* Center for Comprehensive School Reform and Improvement, September 2007.

Landrum, M. *Consultation in Gifted Education.* Mansfield Center, CT: Creative Learning Press, 2002.

Landrum, M. S., C. M. Callahan, and B. D. Shaklee, eds. *Aiming for Excellence: Gifted Program Standards.* Waco, TX: Prufrock Press, 2001.

Lehman, Elyse Brauch, and Carol J. Erdwins. "The Social and Emotional Adjustment of Young, Intellectually Gifted Children." *Social/Emotional Issues, Underachievement, and Counseling of Gifted and Talented Students (Vol. 8)* (2004): 1–8.

Lewis, C. *Lesson Study: A Handbook of Teacher-Led Instructional Improvement.* Philadelphia, PA: Research for Better Schools, 2002.

Lewis, J., *Language Isn't Needed: Nonverbal Assessments and Gifted Learners.* San Diego, CA: Growing Partnerships for Rural Special Education Conference Proceedings, March 29–31, 2001.

Lyon, M. "Academic Self-Concept and Its Relationship to Achievement in a Sample of Junior High School Students." *Educational and Psychological Measurement, 52* (1993): 201–211.

Mandel, H., and S. Marcu. *The Psychology of Underachievement.* New York: Wiley, 1988.

Marland, S. P., Jr. *Education of the Gifted and Talented: Report to the Congress of the United States by the Commissioner of Education (Government Documents, Y4I. 11/2:G36).* Washington DC: US Government Printing Office, 1972.

Marzano, R. J. *Transforming Classroom Grading.* Alexandria, VA: ASCD, 2000.

Matthews, M. "Gifted Students Talk About Cooperative Learning." *Educational Leadership, 50, 5(2)* (1992): 48–50.

McCall, R., C. Evahn, and L. Kratzer. *High School Underachievers: What Do They Achieve as Adults?* Newbury Park, CA: Sage, 1992.

McCoach, D. B, and D. Siegle. "Factors that Differentiate Underachieving Gifted Students from High Achieving Gifted Students." *Gifted Child Quarterly, 47* (2003): 144–152.

McKnight, K. S., and M. Scruggs. *The Second City Guide to Improv in the Classroom: Using Improvisation to Teach Skills and Boost Learning.* New York: Wiley, 2008.

Moon, S. M., ed. *Social/Emotional Issues, Underachievement, and Counseling of Gifted and Talented Students.* Thousand Oaks, CA: Corwin Press, 2004.

Murawski, W., and L. Dieker. "Tips and Strategies for Co-Teaching at the Secondary Level." *Teaching Exceptional Children, 36(5)* (2004): 53–58.

National Research Council. *Minority Students in Special and Gifted Education.* Washington, DC: National Academy Press, 2002.

Neihart, M., et al. *The Social and Emotional Development of Gifted Children: What Do We Know?* Waco, TX: Prufrock Press, 2002.

Newmann, F. M., and Associates. *Authentic Achievement: Restructuring Schools for Intellectual Quality.* San Francisco, CA: Jossey-Bass, 1996.

Newmann, F. M., W. G. Secada, and G. A. Wehlage. *A Guide to Authentic Instruction and Assessment: Vision, Standards, and Scoring.* Madison, WI: Wisconsin Center for Education Research, 1995.

Nielsen, E. M., et al. *Characteristics of Intellectually Gifted Students and Gifted Students with Learning Difficulties.* In an unpublished manuscript. Albuquerque Public Schools, 2000.

Nieto, S. *Language, Culture, and Teaching: Critical Perspectives.* Philadelphia, PA: Taylor & Francis, 2009.

O'Donnell, A., and J. O'Kelly. "Learning from Peers: Beyond the Rhetoric of Positive Results." *Educational Psychology Review, 6* (1994): 321–349.

Olszewski-Kubilius, P., L. Limburg-Weber, and S. Pfeiffer, eds. *Early Gifts: Recognizing and Nurturing Children's Talents.* Waco, TX: Prufrock Press, 2003.

Patrick, H., et al. "Reconsidering the Issue of Cooperative Learning with Gifted Students." *Journal for the Education of the Gifted, 29 (1)* (2005): 90–108.

Perleth, C., T. Schatz, and F. J. Monks. "Early Identification of High Ability." In *Designing Services and Program for High-Ability Learners: A Guidebook for Gifted Education,* edited by J. H. Purcell and R. D. Eckert. Thousand Oaks, CA: Corwin, 2006.

Peters, W., H. Granger-Loidl, and P. Supplee. "Underachievement in Gifted and Talented Students: Theory and Practice." In *International Handbook of Giftedness and Talent,* edited by K. Heller, et al. Amsterdam: Elsevier, 2000.

Piechowski, M. "Emotional Giftedness: The Measure of Interpersonal Intelligence." In *Handbook of Gifted Education,* edited by N. Colangelo and G. Davis. Boston, MA: Allyn & Bacon: 1997.

Pintrich, P., and E. DeGoot. "Motivational and Self-Regulated Learning Components of Classroom Academic Performance." *Journal of Educational Psychology, 82* (1990): 33–40.

Purcell, J. H., and R. D. Eckert, eds. *Designing Services and Programs for High-Ability Learners: A Guidebook for Gifted Education.* Thousand Oaks, CA: Corwin, 2006.

Putnam, R. T., and H. Borko. "What Do New Views of Knowledge and Thinking Have to Say About Research on Teacher Learning?" *Educational Researcher, 29(1)* (2000): 4–15.

Reis, S., and D. B. McCoach. "The Underachievement of Gifted Students: What Do We Know and Where Do We Go?" *Gifted Child Quarterly, 44* (2000): 158–170.

Reis, S. M., et al. "Why Not Let High Ability Students Start School in January?" *The Curriculum Compacting Study (Research Monograph 93106).* Storrs, CT: University of Connecticut, The National Research Center on the Gifted and Talented, 1993.

Renzulli, J. S., and S. M. Reis. *Enriching Curriculum for All Students.* Thousand Oaks, CA: Corwin, 2008.

——. "The Schoolwide Enrichment Model: A Focus on Student Strengths and Interests." In *Systems and Models for Developing Programs for Gifted and Talented,* edited by J. S. Renzulli, et al. Mansfield Center, CT: Creative Learning Press, 2009.

Rimm, S. *Why Bright Kids Get Poor Grades and What You Can Do About It.* New York: Crown, 1995.

Rimm, S., and B. Lowe. "Family Environments of Underachieving Gifted Students." *Gifted Child Quarterly, 32(4)* (1988): 353–359.

Ritchhart, R., M. Church, and K. Morrison. *Making Thinking Visible: How to Promote Engagement, Understanding, and Independence for All Learners.* New York: Wiley, 2011.

Robinson, A. "Cooperative Learning and High Ability Students." In *Handbook of Gifted Education,* edited by N. Colangelo and G. Davis. Boston, MA: Allyn and Bacon, 2003.

Rogers, K. "Grouping the Gifted and Talented: Questions and Answers." *Roeper Review,* September 1993.

——. *The Relationship of Grouping Practices to the Education of the Gifted and Talented Learner: Research-Based Decision Making Series.* Storrs, CT: The National Research Center on the Gifted and Talented, The University of Connecticut, 2001.

Rogers, K., et al. *A Menu of Options for Grouping Gifted Students.* Waco, TX: Prufrock Press, 2006.

Rosenholtz, S. J. *Teachers' Workplace: The Organization of Schools.* New York: Teachers College Press, 1989.

Schunk, D. "Modeling and Attributional Factors Effects on Children's Achievement Behavior: A Self-Efficacy Analysis." *Journal of Educational Psychology, 73* (1981): 93–105.

——. "Self-Efficacy Perspective on Achievement Behavior." *Educational Psychologist, 19* (1984): 48–58.

——. "Sequential Attributional Feedback and Children's Achievement Behaviors." *Journal of Educational Psychology, 76(6)* (1984): 1159.

Schunk, Dale H., and Barry J. Zimmerman, eds. *Motivation and Self-Regulated Learning: Theory,* *Research, and Applications.* New York: Routledge, 2012.

Seigle, D., and D. McCoach. "Issues Related to the Underachievement of Gifted Students." In *Fundamentals of Gifted Education,* edited by Callahan, C., et al. New York: Routledge, 2012.

Slavin, R. "Cooperative Learning." *Review of Educational Research, 50* (1980): 315–342.

Smutny, J. F., ed. *Designing and Developing Programs for Gifted Students.* Thousand Oaks, CA: Corwin, 2003.

Sousa, D. A. *How the Brain Learns.* Newbury Park, CA: Sage, 2011.

Sternberg, R. "Cultural Conceptions of Giftedness." *Roeper Review, 29 (3)* (2007): 160–164.

Sternberg, R. J., and L. F. Zhang. "What Do We Mean by Giftedness: A Pentagonal Implicit Theory." *Gifted Child Quarterly 39* (1995): 88–94.

Stiggins, R. "From Formative Assessment to Assessment for Learning: A Path to Success in Standards-Based Schools." *The Phi Delta Kappan, 87(4)* (2005): 324–328.

Stiggins, R., J. Chappius, and S. Chappius. *Classroom Assessment for Learning: Doing It Right, Using It Well.* Upper Saddle River, NJ: Pearson, 2011.

Tomlinson, C., K. Brimijoin, and L. Narvaez. *The Differentiated School.* Arlington, VA: ASCD, 2008.

Tomlinson, C., and M. Imbeau. *Leading and Managing a Differentiated Classroom.* Arlington, VA: ASCD, 2010.

Tomlinson, C. A., and J. McTighe. *Integrating Differentiated Instruction and Understanding by Design.* Alexandria, VA: ASCD, 2006.

Tomlinson, C., and D. A. Sousa, *Differentiation and the Brain.* Bloomington, IN: Solution Tree, 2011.

Treffinger, D. J., et al. *Enhancing and Expanding Gifted Programs: The Levels of Service Approach.* Waco, TX: Prufrock Press, 2004.

Tschannen-Moran, B., and M. Tschannen. "The Coach and the Evaluator." *Educational Leadership 69 (2),* 10–16.

U.S. Department of Education. *National Educational Longitudinal Study. 88. Final Report: Gifted Education Programs for Eighth Grade Public School Students.* Washington, DC: Office of Planning, Budget, and Evaluation: United States Department of Education, 1991.

———. *National Excellence: A Case for Developing America's Talent.* Washington, DC: Office of Educational Research and Improvement, 1993.

Van Merriënboer, J., and P. Kirschner. *Ten Steps to Complex Learning.* New York: Routledge, 2012.

Van Tassel-Baska, J. "Characteristics and Needs of Talented Learners." In *Content-Based Curriculum for High Ability Learners,* edited by J. VanTassel-Baska and C. Little. Waco, TX: Prufrock Press, 1998.

———. *Excellence in Educating Gifted and Talented Learners.* Denver, CO: Love Publishing Company, 1998.

———. *Using the Common Core State Standards for English Language Arts with Gifted and Advanced Learners.* Waco, Texas: Prufrock Press, 2013.

Webb, J., et al. *Misdiagnosis and Dual Diagnoses of Gifted Children and Adults.* Tucson, AZ: Great Potential Press, 2005.

Webb, N., and A. Palincsar. "Group Processes in the Classroom." In *Handbook of Educational Psychology,* edited by D. C. Berliner and R. C. Calfree. New York: Simon & Schuster, 1996.

Wiliam, D., et al. "Teachers Developing Assessment for Learning: Impact on Student Achievement." *Assessment in Education, 11(1)* (2004): 49–65.

Winebrenner, S., and D. Brulles. *The Cluster Grouping Handbook.* Minneapolis, MN: Free Spirit Publishing, 2008.

Wormeli, R. *Fair Isn't Always Equal: Assessing and Grading in the Differentiated Classroom.* Portland, ME: Stenhouse, 2006.

Zimmerman, B. "Dimensions of Academic Self-Regulation: A Conceptual Framework for Education." In *Self-Regulation of Learning and Performance: Issues and Educational Applications,* edited by D. H. Schunk and B.J. Zimmerman. Mahwah, NJ: Erlbaum, 1994.

Index

Page references in *italics* refer to figures; those in **boldface** refer to reproducible forms.